Growth Globalization and Agriculture in India

Growth Globalization and Agriculture in India

S.S. Somra
Kuldeep Singh

BOOKWELL
New Delhi

ISBN: 978-81-89640-99-6

First Published in 2010 by:

BOOKWELL

Head Office:

3/79, Nirankari Colony, Delhi 110009, India
Ph: 91-11-27601283 Fax: 91-11-23281315
E-mail: bkwell@nde.vsnl.net.in
Website: www.bookwellindia.com

Sales Office

24/4800, Ansari Road, Darya Ganj,
New Delhi-110002, India
Ph: 91-11-23268786, 23257264
bookwell@vsnl.net

Typeset by:
A R Computers, Delhi

Pinted and bound in India by:
D.K. Fine Art Press (P) Ltd.

To
Our Families and Friends

Preface

This book is our attempt to understand the changing scenario of development process and growth and its impact on agriculture development in India. As we know, the economic development is the primary objective of the majority of the world's developing nation. In recent years it has emerged as a major area of debate and analysis both in terms of theoretical and empirical research. India's economic growth has received potential attention in recent years. It is also evident that the India's growth has accelerated over the past two decades. India has a strong, vibrant and fast-growing economy which is rapidly integrating with the global economy. The strategy of rapid growth or more recent term in our country the strategy of 'inclusive growth' combines empowerment with entitlement and investment. Education empowers, improved health care empowers, employment guarantee entitles, fulfilling quota obligations entitles. Through a combination of offering entitlement, ensuring empowerment and stepping up public investment the growth process can be made more inclusive. In the short run these essential services impact directly on welfare, in the long run they determine economic opportunities for the future.

Although the focus of attention in this book is empirical analysis of data and their interpretation but in the first chapter there is detail try to explain the recent trends of growth and globalization in India as well as World. The second chapter devoted to earlier studies to prepare a base of present compendium. In next chapter described the detail explanation of national scenario of agricultural trends in recent time and the last chapter for results and suggestions.

Now the policy challenge for India is not to raise growth from 8 to 10 percent. Rather the primary challenge is to sustain rapid growth while extending rapid growth and its benefits to more regions, sectors and people. Rapid growth is not a 'natural' state for an economy keeping rapid growth requires continuous effort. In recent years the empirical literature on economic growth and convergence has devoted increasing attention to inter-regional analysis. The established results on inter-regional convergence appeared to be quite robust for different countries, with most reporting a trend of convergence although at different degrees of significance. Thus, the issues should be in front line to face the forthcoming challenges of development process and rapid growth. In recent debate on agricultural development, efforts from every part of economy have been made to improve the agricultural performance through the instruments of technological innovation and institutional innovation. One of the major challenges in the 11th Five Year Plan is to reverse the deceleration in agricultural growth. The two major sources of growth in agriculture, viz., area expansion and productivity growth, which served well in the past, are now plagued with some limitations. It is argued that any significant technological breakthrough cannot be expected in the near future and hence, one has to depend on the exploitation of the potential of the existing technology. Therefore, another alternative which may prove to be very useful in this context, at least in the short run, is to move towards diversification into high value crops. Thus, the several issues there need to resolve in the appropriate manner for smooth run of the economy on the path of rapid development or growth process.

We are thankful to the Department of Economics, University of Rajasthan, Jaipur, for giving an opportunity to study the subject. We hope this will be helpful to know the subject at a glance.

Last, but not least, our thanks to Shri S.S. Khurana of Bookwell Publications of New Delhi, for the excellent publication of the book.

October 2009

S.S.Somra
Kuldeep Singh

Contents

1

Introduction

As we know it is a well known fact that agriculture plays an important role in development, such as provision of food to the nation, enlarging exports, transfer of manpower to non-agricultural sectors, contribution to capital formation, and securing markets for industrialization (Johnston and Mellor, 1961). Economic welfare of a nation or region depends upon its level of economic development. In material term economic development means availability of more and better goods and service. But in reality, this definition may not to be appropriate because the efforts and sacrifice that go into obtaining such goods and services must also be taken into account. Economic development means more leisure, better health, more time to read, even more time to contemplate the good life (Henry, 1963). The generation and sustenance of economic growth, especially in the early stages of most developing countries, are to a large extent, determined by the performance of agricultural sector (Rennis and Fei, 1961). In India, an agricultural sector unresponsive to stimuli or unstable in nature may substantially impede steady growth of the economy. No doubt, the present government is very much cautious about to provide strengthens to agricultural sector and presently there made several provisions in the eleventh plan for this purpose but their performances is now awaited.

India's economic growth has received potential attention in recent years. It is also evident that the India's growth has accelerated over the past two decades. Sweeping economic reforms that commenced in 1991 have included the delicensing of most industries, deregulation of industries earlier monopolized by the public sector, liberalization of foreign trade through a steady reduction in tariffs and freeing up of the foreign investment limits in nearly all industries. These measures have had far reaching consequences and today, India has a strong, vibrant and fast-growing economy which is rapidly integrating with the global economy (Ernst & Young, 2006). India is forecast to become the third largest economy in the world, after China and the US, by the year 2050 overtaking all other developed economies (Wilson and Purushothaman, 2003).

Now the policy challenge for India is not to raise growth from 8 to 10 percent. Rather the primary challenge is to sustain rapid growth while extending rapid growth and its benefits to more regions, sectors and people. Rapid growth is not a 'natural' state for an economy keeping rapid growth requires continuous effort.

In recent years the empirical literature on economic growth and convergence has devoted increasing attention to inter-regional analysis. The established results on inter-regional convergence appeared to be quite robust for different countries, with most reporting a trend of convergence although at different degrees of significance. The neoclassical growth theory as proposed by Solow-Swan and the 'catching-up' theory maintain that there will be convergence in levels of per capital income across countries.

Convergence refers to the process by which poorer countries or regions grow faster than their rich counterparts. In other words, the economic distance between them is eroded such that most of it is eventually disappeared. The 'convergence theory' is based on whether economies or regions, which are poorer, tend to grow faster than rich ones or there are automatic forces that lead to 'convergence' over time in the levels of national income or product. The question of 'convergence' often centers on the connection between growth of neighboring region and ones own region.

Inclusive Growth

Basically, the term includes all segments/sections of society should actively participate/engage in the process of a nation's development. Last thirty years has seen considerable developments in thinking on development policies. The standard policy reforms included in the Washington Consensus (The concept and name were first presented in 1989–1990 by John Williamson, an economist from the Institute for International Economics, Washington DC. The Washington Consensus contained a set of 10 recommendations that synthesized the policies considered necessary for the recovery of Latin American economies from the financial crises of the 1980s and cycles of high inflation and low growth) have the potential to be growth promoting. Many countries have adopted the Washington consensus, i.e., the enforcement of property rights, maintenance of macroeconomic stability and integration with the world economy and creation of a sound business environment. However, experiences of last 15 years have shown that impact of these reforms is heavily dependent on circumstances. Growth strategies are likely to differ according to domestic opportunities and constraints. The disappointments with the Washington Consensus led to the Barcelona consensus (Sixteen leading economists, gathered in Barcelona in September 2004 to discuss effects of economic reforms, lessons for future policy making, and performance of international economic systems, and issued a consensus on growth and development of 2004). The key recommendation of the Barcelona consensus is that the growth strategies require a sense of priorities. This has led to the development framework for growth diagnostics (Hausmann,, Rodrik and Velasco, 2005). i.e., a strategy for figuring out the policy priorities.

Growth diagnostics require in depth knowledge of the economy that is being analyzed (Leipziger, and Zagha, 2006). The strategy is aimed at identifying the most binding constraints on economic growth such as limitations in mobilizing sufficient domestic or foreign finance, low levels of human capital and technological capabilities, weaknesses in governance structures and the poor functioning of institutions that regulate markets or provide public goods and social services. The importance and relevance of these constraints tend to vary from country to country.

A striking feature of India's growth performance over the past decade has been the strength of the services sector. Average services grew more slowly than industry between 1951 and 1990. Growth of services picked up in the 1980s, and accelerated in the 1990s when it averaged 7.5 per cent per annum, thus providing a valuable prop into industry and agriculture which grew on average by 5.8 percent and 3.1 percent respectively. The growth of GDP during 2002-06 is 7.2 percent. Here the growth of the agriculture sector is 1.7 percent, growth of industry sector is 8.3 per cent and growth of services is 9.0 percent, these figures slightly change in later phase 2006-09.

The strategy of 'inclusive growth' combines empowerment with entitlement and investment. Education empowers, improved health care empowers, employment guarantee entitles, fulfilling quota obligations entitles. Through a combination of offering entitlement, ensuring empowerment and stepping up public investment the growth process can be made more inclusive. Inclusive growth also means empowering the disadvantaged. The strategy for inclusive growth is to provide access to basic facilities such as health, education, clean drinking water, etc. to the common people. In the short run these essential services impact directly on welfare, in the long run they determine economic opportunities for the future.

Inclusive growth in India dates back to the study by World Bank (2006) on India Development Policy Review: Inclusive Growth and Service Delivery: Building on India's Success. The study outlined two most pressing challenges for public action in India are Institutional reform to enhance the capacity of public sector institutions to ensure the effective delivery of core services and sustaining rapid growth and making the process of economic growth more inclusive – across sectors, across regions, and bringing the benefits of higher income and living standards to more people.

Theoretical Developments of Convergence

The most striking aspect of the per capita income distribution of the economies is very large and has persistent disparities There have been "growth disasters" economies in which per capital income have fallen and "growth miracles" economies which have risen rapidly up the world income distribution. One of the first questions we might ask is whether there is a systematic tendency for poor countries to grow faster than rich ones, which would allow them to catch up.

Convergence theory dates back to the standard neo-classical growth model with exogenous technological process and a closed economy. Neo-classical growth models for closed economies are given by Solow (1956), Cass (1965) and Koopmans (1965). Their model states that the per capita growth rate tends to be inversely related to the starting level of output or income per person in the economy. In particular, if economies are similar in respect to preferences and technologies then poor economies grow faster than rich ones.

The seminal theoretical contributions of Romer (1986) and Lucas (1988) on endogenous growth mechanisms have generated a lively empirical literature. This literature has primarily focused on the so called 'convergence hypothesis'. The hypothesis asserts that differences in contemporaneous per capita income between any pair of economies will be transitory so long as the two economies possess identical technologies, preferences and population growth rates Bernard and Darlauf, (1996). By implication the effects of initial stocks of human and physical capital on per capita output differences will be transitory so long as these other factors are accounted for.

In recent years, since the appearance of the pioneering studies Baumol (1986) Barro (1991) and Mankiew et al. (1992)

considerable effort have been devoted to identifying changes over time in the cross sectional distribution of per capita income between economies. These studies have observed that economies with low initial income tend to grow faster than economies with high initial incomes with controlled savings rate and population growth. This finding has been treated as an evidence of convergence. There are many studies Baumol (1986), De Long (1988), Dowrick and Nguyen (1989) and Barro and Sala-i-Martin (1995) of the international processes of growth and convergence across countries among others and regional growth patterns within any given country.

A summary statistics is used to measure convergence directly employing coefficient of variation (C.V.) by Baumol and Wolff (1988), Metha, Crihfield and Gietz (1992), Izraeli and Murphy (1997) and Roberts (1997). Izraeli and Murphy (1997) have also used Bourguignon's L-statistics to measure convergence directly.

Empirical models which estimate a relationship of the form $y_{it} = f(y_{io})$, where 'y_{it}' measures the size of some economic unit 'i' at time 't', have a long tradition in the economics literature. It is known that cross sectional estimation is hazardous in the case where 'y_{it}' tends to converge towards steady state values, which differ across 'i'; or in other words, when there are heterogeneous individual effects. Islam (1995) for example, has pointed out that, since the omitted individual effects are correlated with the explanatory variable 'y_{io}', the estimated coefficient on the latter is upward biased. Recent studies like Funke and Strulik (1999) and Goddard and Wilson (2001) have used panel estimation of convergence.

Evidence of Convergence and Divergence in India

There are a number of studies on the convergence literature across Indian states. Cashin and Sahay (1996) Marjit and Mitra (1996), Ghose, Marjit and Neogi (1998), Rao, Shand and Kalirajan (1999) and Dasgupta, Maiti, Mukherjee, Sarkar, Chakrabarti (2000) have addressed the issues relating to convergence in India. Cashin and Sahay (1996) examined the growth experience of 20 states of India during 1961-91 using Solow-Swan neoclassical growth model in a cross-sectional framework and found evidence of absolute convergence. They also verified that central grants speed up the convergence process. Marjit and Mitra (1996) have stated that the states of India are diverging in terms of their per capita income. They used scattered plots between base period per capita net state domestic product and the annual average growth rates of the states to identify 'divergence'. Ghose, Marjit and Neogi (1998) obtained a relationship between per capita net state domestic product and its growth rate across the states over 35 years to conclude 'divergence'. Rao, Shand and Kalirajan (1999) have shown divergence in the per capita income across states during 1960-61 to 1994-95. They have observed that inter-state disparities are accentuating over the years. Dasgupta et al. (2000) offer analytical description of the economic performance of Indian states using per capita (net) state domestic product over the year 1960-61 to 1995-96. Their analysis draws the conclusion that Indian states tend to diverge in per capita SDP but converge in shares of different sectors in the SDP. However, all of the studies probably have taken per capita (net) state domestic product as the source of convergence or divergence using cross-sectional data.

The process of economic development depends on the pace of development in the important sectors (Primary, Secondary and Tertiary) constituting an economy. Agriculture is not only an important sector of an economy rather it also feed other sector of the economy. As such, the degree of agricultural development determines greatly the rate of growth of an economy (Schultz, 1964). In developing economy the extent of agricultural development becomes even more important because of the dominance of the agricultural sector in such economies. As we know, with agricultural development, activities in the secondary and tertiary sector get accelerated which in turn induce agricultural development and there is cumulative process of development leading to higher rate of growth in the economy. In this regard for Indian economy (Pangaria2009), the government through giving the subsidies to the people is increasing the deficit more .Instead, it should push more reforms, especially for industries. The agriculture, service and other sectors have not been affected, but it is industries that have faced the brunt of economic meltdown. Meanwhile, Indian Government in 11th plan is more concentrate on agriculture and rural development.

In recent debate on agricultural development, efforts from every part of economy have been made to improve the agricultural performance through the instruments of technological innovation and institutional innovation. One of the major challenges in the 11th Five Year Plan is to reverse the deceleration in agricultural growth. The two major sources of growth in agriculture, viz., area expansion and productivity growth, which served well in the past, are now plagued with some limitations. It is argued that any significant technological breakthrough cannot be expected in the near future and hence, one has to depend on the exploitation of the potential of the existing technology. Therefore, another alternative which may prove to be very useful in this context, at least in the short run, is to move towards diversification into high value crops (Government of India, 2006).

Literatures on modern agriculture technology adoption studies reveal that several subjective and objective factors are responsible for the incomplete adoption of High Yielding Varieties (HYV). In a study by (Goyari, 2007), it was observed that majority of sample farmers were found adopting new paddy seeds because of above mentioned advantages of new seeds. Along with such advantages, HYV seeds have been found to exhibit higher fluctuations in yields and profits across plots and across farm households than traditional seeds. So, to avoid risk, a rational farmer may like to allocate his available land between two technologies (between new and local varieties) rather than completely switching to the former. This argument, as pointed out by (Saha, 2001), is based on two things; one, farmers are risk averse and two, the HYV cultivation involves greater risk compared to traditional paddy cultivation. Farmers' considerations of higher risk associated with HYV paddy cultivation has been considered as an important factor among many socio-economic factors acting on the incomplete adoption of HYV (Feder etc.,1985).

Growth, Globalization and the World

The general scenario of world development during last three-four decades remained very changing from different aspects of multidimensional process of development point of view. Simply, the higher economic growth increases human development which will then declines poverty. If income distribution is normal, then disparities decrease. On the other hand, positive association between openness and growth does not confirm the decline of poverty and disparities at all times. Several studies showed different views. However, there is a causal relationship among growth, globalisation and disparities. (Stiglitz, 1998, Hurroll and Woods, 2000) argued that globalisation leads to increase in disparities as trade openness increases differentials in returns to education and skills. Globalisation marginalizes certain groups of people or geographic reasons and opening up lags behind development of adequate institutions and governance. (Agenor, 2003) found U shaped relationship between globalisation and poverty indicating that globalisation at low (high) levels tends to increase (decrease) poverty. He used trade and financial openness to compute a simple globalisation index based on principal component analysis using data of 62 countries during 1995-2001 and computed regression equation between Gini coefficient and globalisation index and found negative relation. Over the last 100 years, global disparities by most measures have been increasing. The ratio of average income of the richest to the poorest country in the world increased from 9:1 at the end of the 19th century to about 30: 1 in 1960 to more than 60: 1 today. (Birdsall, 2002) remarked that asymmetric globalisation widens the disparities. Moreover, (Pritchett, 1995) found that the ratio of GDP per capita of the richest to the poorest country rose from 8.7 in 1870 to 38.1 in 1960 and 51.6 in 1985. The standard deviation of log per capita income which was between 0.513 and 0.636 in 1970, it rose from 0.867 in 1960 to 1.025 in 1985.

The neo-classical growth theory predicts convergence whereas endogenous theory predicts less convergence or divergence. The empirical evidence showed that during the first wave of globalisation, convergence in per capita income and real wage took place within the Atlantic economy due to an increase in international trade and massive international migration. The deglobalisation period is characterized as widening disparities between richest and poorest regions and among Atlantic economy. The golden age period was a 25 years period of rapid growth, relative stability and declining disparities. There was a considerable convergence among Western Europe and OECD and a decline in the GDP gap in per capita income between the poorest and the richest regions. Similarly, (Lindert and Williamson, 2001) found that a significant globalisation disparities relationship does not exist. On the contrary, the Human Development Report (2005) showed that the decomposition of disparities using Gini and Theil index proved that world disparity enhanced up to 1990s, then declines. The disparities in OECD and Latin American Countries were gradually stipulated but reverse was seen in South Asian countries. Disparities in the Africans, East and Central European countries rose till 2000, and then declined till 2015. The report also observed that out of 73 countries, 53 have seen disparities rise and political influence were found in those researches which do not support in conclusion that "globalisation is good for the poor" or that anti inflationary policies are "pro-poor". In every region, during 1960-80 and 1980-1998, except East Asia and South Asia, the later period showed remarkably slower growth. Their regression did not show the relationship between openness of the economy and the income of the poor.

The World Bank - a sparing critic of growth, arrived at the following conclusion in one of the recent world development report (1990), "Many developing countries have not merely failed to keep pace with the industiral countries; they have seen their incomes fall in absolute terms." Equally emphatically, declares the world resources (1992-93) report-over the past twenty years, "clearly, there has been no narrowing of the gap between rich and poor countries. Economically the gap is widening.' After same four decades of energetic growth efforts, more people than ever before, 1.1 billion, now live in poverty. There has been a gradual decline or marginalisation of third world countries in the world economy. Between 1950 and 1973, the Third-World share in world exports dropped from 31.1 per cent to just 18.4 per cent. Again, between 1980 and 1989' the average per capita income in Africa declined by 2.2 per cent. "Development options" are rarely even considered in regard to Africa any longer-an entire continent seems to be slipping into the "role of an international welfare case." A majority of the "role of an international welfare case". A majority of the "hopeful looking" countries of the 70s, the newly industrialising countries, also became bogged down in crisis and poverty. Where there has been some economic progress, mounting empirical evidence shows that it has been largely to the benefit of the already better off social groups. "For many of world's poor, the 1980s was a 'lost decade' -a disaster indeed." (WDR, 1990, p. 7) Only a few export oriented NICs from the Asian region (the four tigers- South Korea, Taiwan, Singapore and Hong Kong, as well as Malaysia and Thailand) have improved their position in the world economy. (Marmora and Massner, 1989) thus, then, economic growth viewed growth viewed globally, has certainly not trickled down. And whatever economic growth that has happened in the third world, it has been "growth without development," (regardless of how development is defined). (Braun, 1990, p. 56)

About the regional disparities, Friedman and Alonse (1967) have urged that in transitional societies, the regional problem thrusts itself on policy makers during the period of early industrialisation when, for a variety of reasons, activities come to be concentrated in one or few centres. These centres do not only grow so rapidly as to creates problems of an entirely new order, but also act as suction pumps, pulling in the more dynamic elements for the more static regions regional policy becomes crucial. The transition from a rural to an industrial economy requires fundamental changes in spatial organisation and concentration of industrial developments in growth centres usually results from the attempt to define full benefits of external economics. This is what has been termed as the dualistic structure of developing economies : a centre of rapid intense of growth and periphery whose economy is either stagnant or defining. Examples are to found in many countries including Brazil, India, Pakistan, Mexico, Columbia and Venezuela.

Growth, Globalization and the India

In India the aforesaid topic became the matter of discussion recently, Pangaria (2009) ask in a interview, I think the late prime minister Narasimha Rao was the real mind behind the policy of liberalization. At that times as finanace minister Manmohan singh was a bit critical of Rao's idea of bring up liberalized industrial policy. But later he carried forward the idea. In this reference I want to mention the views of late Prof.B.S.Minhas in 1999, at Amritsar in Indian Economic Association conference inaugural session. Prof. Minhas in his speech says, at that time around in 1977 when I was advocacy these reforms these peoples (he indicates toward persons sited on stage including present Prime Minister Manmohan singh) were called me an American Agent and at that time what happened with me every one knows (late Indira Gandhi out him from planning commission), but, I am happy later on this package is launched by Manmohan Singh. I (Somra S.S.) was also there in that conference. But whereas, I think the liberalization process in child age started by late Indira Gandhi, in Mild age late Rajeev Gandhi and in broad age or intensive phase late Narsimha Rao's, but at that time it was became a compulsion of Indian Government for survival in the rest of the world. Regarding the globalization in India probably more or less the similar views described by Prof. Jagdish N. Bhagwati (2009) in his lecture on 'Indian Reforms : Past Achievements and Future Challenges' at Jaipur in memorial lecture of Prof. Raj Krishna. But, no doubt the successes of the globalization process in favour of our nation absolutely depend on the right path of directions or a mature policy package of policies designed by policy makers and leadership of nation, because the international platforms (W.T.O, I.M.F., W.B. etc.) policies or international economic relations only we can explore in our favour if we have a high degree of international maturity or understanding, otherwise the backwash effects will overwhelmed the benefits of spread effects. India is a young country of world (around 40% population of country between the age group of 15-40 that is most productive age group) with good human resources. Now after this brief story again we concentrate on the review of some recent studies on Indian, growth and globalization. In a research (Jha, 2000) found that change of Gini coefficient was -4.73 in rural area and -0.6 in urban area during 1957-63, but the change of head count ratio was -6.63 in rural area and -2.92 in urban area having the average growth rate of 3.94 per cent. On the other hand, change of Gini were -0.73 in rural area and -0.95 in urban area and the change of rural and urban head count ratios were - 14.23 and - 11.43 respectively during 1963-64 to 1989-90 with the GDP growth rate of 4.03 per cent. But, during the period of 1990-91 to 1996-1997 the change of Gini coefficients were 2. 40 in rural area and 2.17 in urban area but the change of head count ratios were - 2.21 in rural area and - 4.18 in urban area with the growth rate of 5.63 per cent. Therefore, globalization increase growth rate, decreased poverty ratio but increased disparities in India. Suljit S. Bhalla, (2003), calculated shape of distribution elasticity for India as 0.8 and change in Gini was -1.6 and Head Count Ratio was 48.2 and 29.4 in 1999 and the elasticity of poverty growth was - 2.4 and hence net impact of growth on poverty reduction is 1.92 i.e. growth diminished poverty and disparities during 1983-1999. It is too low in Bihar and too high in Kerala and West Bengal. Bhowmik D. (2000), calculated regression equation between Gini coefficient and growth rate of GDP during 1956-57 to 1990-91 and found that one percent increase in growth rate diminished Gini by 0.01598 per cent per year although the test is insignificant. Similarly the regression equation between the two during 1991-92 to 1999-2000 showed that one per cent rise in growth rate stipulated the Gini coefficient by 0.05368 per cent per year. But the estimate is insignificant. It means that growth enlarged disparities in the reform period. Moreover, the disparities widens among the Indian states since Gini of the State Domestic Product during 1980-81to 1990-91 increased at the rate of 0.149 per cent per year but it increased at the rate of 0.412 per cent per year during 1991-92 to 2001-2002 which asserted that the degree of disparities rose or accelerated in the reform period among the States or it can be said that the disparity widens among the Indian states. This can also be verified by the poverty Disparity index which showed that the index in rural area was 23.19 per cent in 1973-74 that enhanced to 40.96 per cent in 1987-88 and further to 67.93 per cent in 1999-00. In urban area the index was 27.75 per cent in 1973-74 which stepped up to 67.75 per cent in 1999-2000. This means that disparity widens in rural and urban area. That is, rich states became richer and the poor became poorer (Pal, 2003). Even, the coefficient of variation of average growth rates among the states jumped from 0.14 in the 1980s to 0.29 in the 1990s which showed the uneven development where southern states performed better than the eastern and central states. Again, the growth, inflation and trade off do not exist in the development of states. (Bhattacharjya and Sakthivel, 2005).

Therefore, globalisation fosters growth in India and reduces poverty but increased disparities in the reform period. In addition to that the globalisation produces jobless growth or reduces the employment growth rate. As per NSS (National Sample Survey) data, found that the growth rate of employment came down from 2.7 per cent per annum during 1983-94 to 1.07 per cent during 1993-2000 when GDP growth rate went up from 5.2 per cent to 6 per cent and the employment rate further accelerated to 2.8 per cent during 2000-2005, on the other hand, unemployment rate also increased from 7.3 per cent in 1999-2000 to 8.3 per cent in 2004-05. Even, the employment elasticity has fallen from 0.41 to 0.15 during the period from 1983-84 to 1993-94 and 1993--94 to 1999-2000 which showed that the employment growth decelerated while GDP growth rate accelerated. More convincing evidence is that 50th and 60th round NSS data asserted that the male unemployment increased from 5.6 per cent to 9 per cent in rural areas and from 6.7 per cent to 8.1 per cent in urban areas during 1993-94 - 2004. Again, the female unemployment increased from 5.6 per cent in 1993-94 to 9.3 per cent in 2004 in rural areas and from 10.5 per cent to 11.7 per cent in urban areas (ET, 2006). The sectoral GDP growth rates are asymmetric where tertiary sector growth rate is accelerating but primary and secondary sectors are stagnant in the 90s including the deceleration of employment growth rate. Hence, there is a weak linkage between sectors in the growth process (Bathla, 2005).

Agriculture and Economic Development

Agricultural development is an integral part of overall economic development. The Indian economy comprises of several important sectors, which contribute to total national product. But by far, agriculture is the main stay of Indian economy and prosperity of agriculture can significantly contribute to the general prosperity of the nation. With around a 24.2 per cent contribution to gross domestic product, agriculture still provides livelihood support to about two-thirds of country's population. The sector provides employment to 56.7 percent of country's workforce and it is the single largest private sector occupation. Agriculture accounts for about 14.7 per cent of total export earning and provides raw material to several industries. Agriculture forms the backbone of Indian economy and despite large industrialization in last 60 years; agriculture still occupies a place of pride. Various studies revealed that manufacturing sector in the past, has been receiving more resources than would have been under a free trade scenario. This was done by high protection to the manufacturing sector. On the other hand, agriculture received less resources compared to what it would have, under free trade environment. Measured on the basis of normal protection, Indian agriculture was heavily discriminated against the manufacturing sector (Gulati, 1994). This clearly reveals that, on a locative efficiency grounds, more resources ought to flow to the agricultural sector which would help in attaining higher levels of efficiency in resource allocation and in turn welfare.

Agriculture contributes to economic development in a number of ways. The important areas of contribution of agricultural sector relate to; increased food supply; Platform of agricultural exports; increased transfer of labour resource; Additional capital formation, and Additional purchasing power as a result of an increasing level of income. (Jonhson and Mellor, 1961)

It provides workers to industry, furnishes demand for industrial output, provides saving for use in industry, yields revenue to Government, earn foreign exchange through export to pay for important capital equipments and raw materials needed in other sectors and supplies food for consumption by worker in industry (Laberger, 1968). The agricultural contribution can be classified into following heads: Agriculture makes a product contribution by increasing the supply of food and fiber products; Agriculture makes the market contribution through its trade contacts with other sectors, and Agriculture makes a factor contribution by releasing labour force for non-farm occupations (Kuznets, 1961).

The role of agriculture is sometimes misunderstood. Assuming that agriculture contributes little to economic development the process of economy development is presented as one of transformation of a predominantly agriculture economy into a predominantly industrial economy. Industrialization has been regarded as the sine qua non of economic development. It is said that a take off into industrialization fails to occur mainly because the comparative advantage of exploiting productive land and other natural resources delays the time when self-reinforcing industrial growth profitably gets under way (North, 1973). There is another line of argument undermining the role of agriculture in economic development. Assuming that economic development occurs in specific location matrix, these location matrixes primarily industrial urban in composition and the exiting economic organization works best at or hear the centre of a particular matrix it is believed that industrial development is the prime mover in economic growth and that agriculture is a dependent variable in the overall pattern of industrial-urban growth.

The sustainable agricultural development is also a part of the overall strategies of economic development. Though traditionally said to be in harmony with nature, yet in practice we observe that till recently the constitution of India and the overall legal system were blind to such considerations. While steps are being taken in this new area of ecological economies yet they are few and far between and the authorities also are not very serious to implement them vigorously. In the context of widespread and acute poverty, it is very difficult to educate the public about the importance of environment protection and to transform the development process into a sustainable one. Moreover, the absence of any single indication to measure the progress towards sustainable agriculture makes the monitoring of sustainability further difficult.

Among Asian countries, the South Asian nations: India (1997), Nepal (1997), Pakistan (1997) and Sri Lanka (1997) have provided national information on sustainable agriculture to the Commission on Sustainable Development. The following nations within the region have not provided information to the Commission; Bangladesh, Bhutan and Maldives. and South-East Asian countries; Indonesia (1997), Malaysia (1997), Myanmar (2000), Philippines (1997), Singapore (1997 and 2000), Thailand (1997) and Viet Nam (1997) have submitted information to the Commission on Sustainable Development. Those have not provided information to the Commission include; Brunei Darussalam, Cambodia and the Lao People's Democratic Republic.

Disparities in economic and social development across the regions and intra-regional disparities among different segments of the society have been the major planks for adopting planning process in India since independence. Apart from massive investments in backward regions, various public policies directed at encouraging private investments in such regions have been pursued during the first three decades of planned development. While efforts to reduce regional disparities were not lacking, achievements were not often commensurate with these efforts. Considerable level of regional disparities remained at the end of the Seventies. The accelerated economic growth since the early Eighties appears to have aggravated regional disparities. The on-going economic reforms since 1991 with stabilisation and deregulation policies as their central pieces seem to have further widened the regional disparities (Bhattacharya, 2004, Hanumantha Rao, 2007). The seriousness of the emerging acute regional imbalances has not yet received the public attention it deserves.

As we known, India used the planning strategy for long term sustainable growth in agriculture and it has so far passed through four major transitional phases for agrarian point of view. (1) The phase of community development during the fifties. (2) The phase of "green revolution" focused on growth since the mid-sixties. (3) The poverty eradication phase beginning the seventies. (4) The phase of liberalization during nineties. These phases shows the evidence of some notable achievement in Indian economy but the overall thrust of the process is still too weak and insignificant to promote development of backward areas with chronic poverty and stagnant backward rural economy.

Agriculture sector in India underwent drastic policy reforms during the almost last two decades on account of liberalization and WTO agreement on agriculture (AoA). These reforms have had mixed effect on the agriculture sector in India and this effect vary from state to state , region to region and crops to crops. An analysis of the impact of reforms on the nature and extent of integration between the world and domestic commodity markets over the years has shown the empirical evidence to suggest that the extent of integration between commodity markets in Haryana with that of world market increases during in post reform period. More specifically, the short-run elasticity estimates using error-correction model have shown a turnaround during liberalization indicating faster transmission of world prices to the domestic market than that they did prior to liberalization period which in turn has significant effect on the trend and variation of domestic commodity prices (Brigit 2003).

The economy of Haryana is also dominated by the agricultural sector which attributes more than 50% of state's domestic product and nearly 70% of the total population earns its livelihood from agriculture directly or indirectly. Hence, it is evident that agriculture is the base of state economy. It is the need of the present time that we may analyse the various programmes and policies being executed by state and central government for agriculture development. State economy is based on the growth of various agricultural activities such as increase in productivity of crops, increase in irrigation facilities, availability of fertilizers and seeds, technology etc. No doubt, Haryana is an important state of India so far as its contribution to the agricultural development is concerned. Notwithstanding, it is a clinch, it is true that agriculture is the backbone of Haryana as well as Indian economy. In India two-third of the labour force engaged in agriculture and related activities. Agriculture has always been in the forefront of policy discussions in India even in the 11th plan also. The Green Revolution (GR) approach that was started in the late 1960s, has transformed the Indian economy from a food-deficit to a self-sufficient one. But unfortunately, its benefits were spread disproportionately in favour of the wealthier farmers, especially of agriculturally developed regions, avoiding the small and marginal farmers, in particular and agriculturally underdeveloped regions in general. Therefore, its benefits have largely been reaped by the large farmers of developed regions as they have better access to resources. There have, now, been ample evidences that inter-region and inter-farm disparities in the agricultural development has widened in the post-GR period (Singh, 2005). Keeping this in backdrop, in the present work there tried to examine the inter-district disparities in the agricultural development in Haryana and also tried to identify the major factors in explaining the disparities and suggests policy interventions to alleviate it. Though, India and as well as Haryana achieved a significant progress in various field of agricultural activities, yet there remains some backward areas which cannot achieve the development process if necessary steps are not taken to improve them.

The Problem and Unforeseen Effect of Regional Development

After Second World War a phenomenon and dramatic rise emerged in the regional conscious leading to conferences on regionalization setting up of permanent bodies for regionalization and volume of literature in the forms of books, articles, bulleting etc. This has also lead to application of more and more sophisticated techniques in regionalization.

Disparity in regional development, particularly in agriculture development is a universal phenomenon, while some regions have witnessed faster growth and prospering, others remain stagnant and back ward. These backward regions are found in developed as well as in developing countries. India is not exception to this problem.

There will try in present work to examine this aspect of regional disparities in Haryana in light of some theories about origin and enhancement of regional disparities. Regional balances imply uniform distribution of the planned investment among different regions of the country. From another point of view, regional balance requires a distribution of investment in such a manner that the regional rate of growth be equal, thus eliminating regional disparities of growth rates that have prevailed so far. Neither of these interpretations is consistent with the accepted social objective of reduction of prevailing disparities on the contrary, they would lead to a situation of increasing regional disparities. To diminish regional disparities, it is necessary that the backward regions should plan to have a higher rate of growth than the developed areas.

A perfect regional balance is not possible partly because of regional factors like resources, endowment, and partly due to the tendency of new investment areas with infrastructural development facilities. The favoured regions attract both private and public investment and develop into areas with infrastructural development of facilities. Attraction of both private and public investment by such regions results in accentuation of regional imbalance in the process of development.

The location factors such as the availability of cheap power, modern means of transport and communication, banking, insurance and such other services because the concentration of industries in a few urban regions as these factors tend to cluster mainly in urban areas (Myrdal, 1964).

In recent year, balanced regional development has become the main objective of economic policies pursued in many countries. The record of social development of nations reveals marked regional differentiations, which claims to embrace both time and space in economic theories and policies. Neglect of spatial factors in growth theories had been one of the major limitations in economic literature from the day of Adam Smith till recently. The assumption of perfect mobility of factors between regions and the neglect of distance, agglomeration economies and locational preferences constituted the foundation of the traditional economics of efficient utilization of resources and overall economic growth.

The existence of regional disparities is almost a common and global phenomenon. Both developed and underdeveloped countries are gripped with the problem of regional disparities and imbalance. Even the richest country of the world, the U.S.A., has the problem of unbalance regional development. Small and rich countries like England, France, Italy etc., are also confronted with this problem. The countries like Russia, China are also not free from the problem of regional disparities (Richardson, 1973). Since the different regions grow at very unequal rates, causing inter-regional and intra-regional imbalances, these give birth to various types of socio-economic problems. Many developed countries of today, emphasized regional development in fifties, though regional development began to receive attention in the western countries in the 1930's due to welfare considerations (Koropeckys, 1972).

The important thing is not that every type of industry or agricultural operation should be developed in every region but "the more fundamental target is that inter-personal disparities are reduced (Dutta, 1972). Thus balanced regional development means the maximum utilization of the potentialities of an area in order to give its inhabitants the full benefit of possible economic progress in relation to overall economic growth.

Regional imbalances usually result in under utilization or even non utilization of natural and human resources. The result is that the gap between the lagging region and developed region goes on widening and this generates tensions, which may inhibit the very process of development.

Even if the initial start is accidental, powerful forces make for a spatial concentration of economic growth-around the initial starting points. The distribution of natural resources is not uniform in any country. The pace of development, therefore, varies between regions. Regions, which are favourably placed, advance at greater rate and thus arises the problem of inter-regional disparities. Regions having high concentration of resources attract more industries. Industry naturally tends to get concentrated in regions where there is already an infrastructure, a skilled labour force, a market and specialization of function. Thus industrialization often focuses on certain regions, ignoring other regions.

Thus the gap between rich and poor regions gets continually widened. The dictum "nothing succeeds like success" holds true for developed regions, then dictum "nothing fails like failure" seems to be true for the poor regions.

Many development and growth theories have proved that regional disparities and imbalances are in heart in the progress of development and their degree goes on changing with the stages of economic development. However, there are differences of opinion disparities during the process of economic development.

Unforeseen Effect

Regional disparities in economic activity have both favourable and unfavourable effect. According to Myrdal have stated two types of effects (Myrdal, 1957); (1) Spread effects (2) Backwash effect we shall discuss, in brief here these two effects one by one.

Spread Effects

The main cause of regional disparities is the weak spread effect and strong Backwash effect. Spread effect are considered to be favourable effects when the growth process starts in the advanced regions, it will benefit the less developed region in many ways, when growth poles expend, it will provide more employment opportunities to the people of the less developed or developing areas, and, therefore, the living standard and the marginal productivity of the people will tend to rise and there will be decline in the disguised unemployment. On the other hand the developed regions may depend on the backward regions for food and raw material and may, thus, stimulate the development of agriculture there. The whole region around the growth poles will be benefited in increasing agricultural output by exporting its output to the growth poles. So this process may create new 'growth point' and can lead towards regional balance. Such developments are bound to occur if the economies of the two types of regions are at all complementary.

Backwash Effects

These are unfavourable effects. In the early stages of growth, rapid growth in the effects on the less developed regions, which are called (Backwash effects). Backwash effects have adverse effects on the following variables and investment policies.

Labour Migration

Skilled labourer migration is likely to extend from the less developed region to relatively more developed regions due to higher productivity and better standard of living. Labour migration, therefore, will further aggregate interregional the inequality.

Capital Migration

Inter regional movement of capital are also likely to accentuate disparities. Capital migration takes place through banking and other financial facilities from the poor region to the developed regions, because of the underdeveloped market, lack of enterprises and lack of enterprises and lack of external economics in the less developed regions. International migration of capital is attracted from backward regions by the higher profits in the advanced regions are an account of better infrastructural facilities etc.

Government Policy

If the object of the Government is to maximize growth of national product than Government may follow certain polices in regard to regional allocation of public investment in social overheads, which may accentuate regional disparities.

International Linkages

In the early stages of growth international linkages are relatively weak so that the spread effect of technological and social changes and income multipliers in the growth centers will fail to have much impact on the less developed areas. Through adverse terms of trade, they may begin to develop their primary resources or shift to imports, and thus the spread effects may not trickle down to the backward areas which would be further left behind (Mahajan, 1982). Regional disparities diverge initially and converge later on because of market forces or deliberate policy measure in response to pressure from the less developed regions (Williamson, 1965). Hughes argued "..... a free market system of organization, by nature, causes advance regions (whatever the original cause for advance) to grow, at least in part, at the expense of other region (Hughes, 1961). Consequently, once income differences emerge they tend to become self-perpetuating, unless some exogenous influence, e.g., government or chance, to act to offset market forces ... income differentials are still relatively large doses not argue for leaving the problem of equality to be solved by' spread effects...". The hypothesis of 'self perpetuation' was found valid in the empirical study by (Booth, 1964) in United Sates.

To quote Singh, "Economic inequalities between the northern and southern part of Italy are too well known. Several regions of the United Kingdom, Scotland and Wales for example, are suffering from stagnation and unemployment due to shifts in the industrial location. France is worried for a long time about the over concentration of population and industry in the Paris regions" (Singh, 2005).

But the extent of the problem is more acute and widening from plan to plan in all the developing countries. Myrdal rightly observes, "There is a tendency inherent in the free play of market forces to create regional inequalities and that this tendency becomes the more dominant, the poorer country is".

The Concept and Criteria of Indicators

The term indicator has quite often been used in statistical references, but has never been defined in a precise manner. Even the standard dictionaries define indicator as one which shows, indicates or points out. But the term has, as one which shows, indicates or points out. But the term has, as a matter of fact, a wider connotation than its dictionary meaning. The term indicator is generally conceived as synonymous with variable as well as index number. However, the minute observation helps to bring out a sharp distinction between them. The statistical handbooks generally provide raw data regarding the variables which may or may not indicate the relevant phenomenon. An indicator viewed as a combination of matters of facts (data) and matters of relation (theory) can be constructed only through a correct sequence between factual and logical order (Bell, 1947). It is, therefore, through an appropriate transformation of the variables (which eliminates the effects of non-essential factors) within a theoretical format than an indicator can be obtained (Kundu, 1980).

On the other hand, the term indicator also differs from the index number which is defined as a quantity that shows by its variations the changes over time or space of magnitude which is not susceptible of direct measurement in itself or direct observation in practice (Kendall and Buckland, 1983). While the index number generally conforms to a set form (or to certain alternative forms), the indicator has apparently no such formulation, although it too often measures indirectly the magnitudes which are not susceptible of direct measurement and usually reflects more than what it represents.

The term indicator can better be understood by observing the relationship between basic statistics and derived series. The basic statistics is described as primary data available in Censuses, Sample Surveys and administrative records, whereas the derived series are those calculated from the primary statistics and are usually in the form of averages, percentages, ratios etc. The indicators are generally derived series designed to portray the state, and trends in social conditions which are, or likely to become, the subject of public action or concern. They have to focus on main facets of the well-being of the population, effectiveness and efficiency of the social services and distribution of well-being and the use of and benefits from the social services over the population.

Thus, the indicators should essentially be of current significance, indicate current trends and be useable for current analysis, measurement of progress and determination of policies. Daniel Bell has rightly tried to conceive the indicators as statistics that articulate the occurrence of a given phenomenon. They are derived from the analytical frame in which the term denoting the phenomenon has meaning and relevance. Einstein's statement in this regard is that indicators must be sought not through the abstract logic of mathematics but the underlying theory, essentially conceptualising the social and economic reality.

As stated above, indicators have to serve certain basic purposes, which, in turn, also play a deceiver role in making their broad classification. The classification of indicators is done in many ways. The descriptive indicators, which constitute one type of category, are generally being used for analysing the trends of overall and sectoral development, making predictions and monitoring the progress. A second category of indicators relates to policy objectives or programme outputs. At the programme level, these indicators are being used for establishing horizontal linkages between the programmes. The other indicators required for interpretation and explanation, constitute the third category called analytic indicators. This category is constituted by the indicators, which basically help in establishing casual relationships between dependent and independent variables. This kind of classification is essentially required for building interpretative or analytical models.

Another way of classifying indicators may be as follows: some are macro-indicators, whereas some others are micro-indicators. Some are designated as policy indicators while the rest are called performance indicators. Some are output indicators and some other are input indicators. Some are more direct indicators of current situation while some others are less direct or indirect of services or facilities. Some are designated as flow indicators and some others are called stock indicators. Most of the indicators measure what exist while a few express tendencies. But all the indicators are, without exception, in the form of averages, proportions, ratios, rates of certain more synthetic function of the basic data have no technical relevance.

Criteria of Indicators

As to selection of indicators, we find that three basic criteria have generally been stressed in the recent literature. The first and foremost criterion is that indicators should reflect goals of development policy. In other words, they should be indicators of performance in terms of output, employment, etc. rather than those of resources alone. Second, they should occupy at least some place or position in an integrated system or model, whether explanatory or predictive. A third and more ambitious criterion is that indicators should closely be associated with theories of development. An inference, which can be drawn with the help of these criteria, is that selection of indicators should directly be concerned with their uses in the planning process.

It has not been possible so far to evolve any scientific formula through which one can determine the appropriate size of indicators sector. It is, however, customary among the development planners to usually prefer a conservative list of indicators which could provide at least a correct skeleton of socio-economic development. It is generally remarked that too many indicators, which cannot be combined into a composite index of development, fail to provide even a summary view of development. It would, therefore, be desirable to follow the principle of compromisation and represent the progress achieved by picking up at least one key indicator and three-four supplementary indicators against each of the policy goals/objectives. In the present case, since the main objective is to analyse changes in the district-wise pattern of agricultural development during 2004-05 over the year 1984-85, preference has been given to only those indicators which could reflect development of agriculture, and also help in analysing the development situations.

Agricultural Development Indicators

The most of the studies conducted in the field of agricultural development the focus is generally centered on the analysis of input-output relations. But in the present study to depart from this traditional way of analysing the situation, efforts have, therefore, been made here to represent agricultural development by considering not only output and input indicators but also those relating to modernisation and technological break-through in agriculture as would be evident from the following;

A_1 Productivity of food grain; A_2 Production of food grain; A_3 Percentage of gross irrigated area to total cropped area; A_4 Cropping intensity; A_5 Area under High Yield Variety (HYV); A_6 Number of tractors; A_7 Use of fertilizer; A_8 Number of pump sets; A_9 Use of pesticides and A_{10} Agricultural labour.

The above mentioned indicators can broadly be classified into three groups. The first group consisting of A_1, A_2 and A_4 indicators relates to the overall performance of agriculture, the indicators A_3, A_5 and A_6 falling in the second group are those directly associated with the first group and those (A_7, A_8, A_9, A_{10}) belonging to the third group and known as casual factors contribute favourably to the indicators of both the first and the second groups. In other words, the use of fertilizer, irrigation (third group) helps in augmenting the cropping intensity and the area under both the high yielding varieties and number of tractor (second group), which, in turn, have a direct bearing on the performance of agriculture in terms of higher yield rates (first group).

The indicators A_1, A_2 and A_3 have been selected to exhibit the overall performance of agriculture in terms of agricultural productivity, production labour productivity and availability of agricultural produce for consumption of the population, besides showing the effects of all technological inputs on land. The intensity of cropping A_4, which is measured through the ratio of gross to net cropped area, indicates the rate of utilisation of net area under cultivation in different districts and throws light on the scope of bringing additional area under multiple cropping. It is deemed to be a composite-expression of area, yield and cropping pattern. Moreover, the proportion of area under high yielding A_5, which is an outcome of utilisation of several inputs like improved seeds, fertilizer and irrigation, shows the extent of modernisation in agriculture.

The indicators of consumption of fertilizer A_7 and consumption of pesticides A_9, number of pump sets A_8 and agricultural labour A_{10} have been selected as complementary inputs.

The Concept of Region

The concept of region has a special significance in economic planning as the latter aims not only at the continuing increase of the aggregate production of the economy as a whole but also at an all-round progress of the different regions with in economy (Mahalanobis, 1960). Regional studies of resources and possibilities give direction and balance to economic planning and help avoid costly mistake and anticipate future contingencies wisely and constructively (Pitamber, 1962). The concept of region developed by the geographers like Demergeon Ratzal, Hetterner Roxby, Morran Herberston, Blache and Brunches, etc. during the latter part of the 19th Century proved the most important turning point in the history of geography. Perhaps no term in the geographical literature has received more attention than region (Ginsburg, 1971). It is simply and generally known. Still uncertainties remain to its meaning and significance. It is fairly vague (Ahmad and Singh, 1980) for it has different people or group of people and even to the same people or group in different circumstances (Teripa and Koyada,1968). The ambiguity surrounding the term 'region' is so much that there is no unique definition of the concept of region and regional delineation is often arbitrary.

A region is a geographical and socio-economic entity delimited as an administrative unit or a combination of such unit when the context is clear. It is viewed not as isolated fragments but as part of a complete economy-wise pattern comprising a number of organized units. It is an area homogeneous in respect of particular set of conditions determined by the purpose for which it is delineated. Uncertainties surrounded the term 'region' have given rise to very numerous definitions of a region. Following (West, 1966 and Fisher, 1969) these definitions may be classified broadly into (1) Subjective definition, and (2) Objective definition. Subjectively, region is taken as an idea by accepting the nation as a one point economy and arbitrarily dividing it into as many sub-division as the need be, independent of the consideration of space (Chand and Puri, 1983). An objective definition tries to identify a region in its separate entity independent of the individuals that comprise it. An objective definition is done in term of collectivities viewed from various angles; political, geographical, economic, potential and development.

Region is often interchangeably used with 'area'. The two terms are, however, not the same. An 'area' is always associated with at least four properties; scale, location, content and boundary. It may or may not possess homogeneity or uniformity as to content and organization. It is the presence of any one or both of these additional properties which makes 'area' a 'region'. Area is thus more general term and regions are special kinds of areas. A region must have some limits otherwise it can not have its identity as an area (Myrdal, 1969).

Region is also to be distinguished from 'space' Contrary to a region. Space is unbounded. Space by definition involves a three dimensional boundless void. It is only a setting with in which object can be located. Obviously then, it is difficult to define the character and content of a region with in a particular set of words. A region can be perceived in different ways by different individual depending on their bias. This opportunistic ignorance (Ahmad and Singh, 1980) has resulted in considerable vagueness surrounding the meaning of a region. Many hundreds or thousands of words have been written on this topic without coming to fully satisfactory answer. The only safe statements are there is no unique definition (Richardson, 1973).

Agricultural Region

Homogeneity is not a matter of accident but it results of several geographical facts, e.g., location, geology structure and mineral resources geomorphology, climate, drainage, soils, vegetation and agriculture, industry, population culture and politics (Ahmad & Singh, 1980) . An area homogeneous in respect of a particular set of conditions is formal region and includes soil region, climate region, economic region, socio-cultural region and like. We got natural or physio-geogaphical region when physical homogeneity, i.e., uniformity in topography or climate is stressed. A natural region may be mountainous region or agricultural region or certain industrial basin or climate region.

Obviously, agricultural region and natural region are closely interlinked as many agricultural indicators have common property with natural factors. Even though socio-economic factor play their part, the crop structure depends largely upon topography, soil and climate. As such, definition of agricultural region is to be preceded by physical regionalisation of territory (Gupta, 1961). In definition of agricultural region factors like rainfall, irrigation, land formations holding size, pressure of agricultural population types and composition of soils etc. should be taken into account.

Agricultural Regionalisation

This section summerises the process of regionalisation first in India and then in Haryana with specific reference to agricultural regionalisation. The first attempt to classify regions and sub-regions based on the homogeneity of hypsography structure and climate was made in India by (Stamp, 1927) classified India into 3 major regions and 22 sub-regions. A similar scheme of natural regions was presented by J.N.L. Baker in 1928. Except these few works, regionalisation had largely been neglected in India during the pre-independence era.

The first major post-independence attempt was made in 1951 Census of India. During fifties (Rao & Nath, 1949) etc. attempted regionalisation based on homogeneity of physical and demographic condition. Agricultural regionalisation was also attempted by (Seng, 1948, Thornev, 1959, Sharma, 1973) and others. The national Atlas of India (1957), The Council of Applied Economic Research, The Indian Council of

Agricultural Research and like government and semi-governmental organizations also stressed agricultural regionalisation.

Thorner delineated India into 16 agricultural regions using seven indicators. Two momental works by (Mitra, 1964) and the planning commission made the year 1964 a landmark in the history of regionalisation. Mitra with the help of 63 variables divided India into 7 region, 31 sub regions and 89 divisions following ranking approach. The planning commission divided into 15 resources developments regions and 61divisons on the basis of physical condition, topography, soil geological formation, rainfall, cropping pattern and development of irrigation and mineral resources.

So far Haryana is concerned, very few attempts have been made to have agricultural regionalisation of the economy of Haryana. Haryana is sharply divided into four zones mentioned below on the basis of agro-climate conditions in the state, rather than economic or natural regions (Gupta, 1984). Further attempts made by government time to time.

1. Karnal - Kurukshetra - Ambala - Panchkula - Yamunanagar
2. Rohtak - Jhajjar – Sonipat – Jind – Panipat - Khairthal
3. Hissar – Sirsa – Bhiwani - Fathebad
4. Gurgaon – Faridabad – Mohindergarh - Rewari

Region – 1 is the more prosperous region while region – IV is the most backward region in the state. Other regions lie in between two. Since the entire state is predominantly an agricultural one regions with well developed irrigation facilities are better off as compared to those regions where irrigation facilities are scares.

Objectives of the Study

The present study is an attempt to analyse regional variations in agricultural development and its varied factors, and assess the relationship between them. This would help determine the direction in which further investment in agriculture can be made or whether the existing surplus of any particular factor in the region can be for a better or further utilisation. The determination of variation in agricultural productivity and their probable causes would, thus, make it possible to demarcate the region according to its physic socio-economic conditions. Besides, the same would generate possibilities to minimize the disparity and provide a congenial structure and balanced growth of agriculture development in Haryana.

Although Haryana is relatively a small state, it shows a lot of spatial disparities. Agriculture is not exception to it. Since the level of development and favourable natural endowments are bound to affect the performance of agriculture, therefore, a different behaviour of costs and returns may be expected over different regions in the state. Under such situation, it seems important to analyse the regional imbalances in area, production, productivity and use of inputs and irrigation facilities in an agriculturally advanced state like Haryana. This would help us to identify the factors responsible for it. The present study is an addition in this direction. The broad objectives of the study are; to examine the disparities in area, production and productivity over regions in the state; to examine the disparities in the uses of various inputs and to spell out the factors affecting regional disparities, to reflect the district - wise pattern of agricultural development in Haryana since 1985 and onward, focusing on inter-district variations in level and pattern of agricultural development. With in the frame work of this broad objective, the specific objectives set out for the study are as follows;

1. To study and analyse the concept and criteria of indicators and regions and select suitable for assessing and analyzing the district-wise level and pattern of agricultural development;
2. To examine, in brief, the various methods for construction of composite index of agricultural development and make choice of the suitable for the present analysis;

3. To measure the levels and pattern of agricultural development of different districts since 1985 and onward in the state and try to examine the situation of country also.
4. To study and evaluate the district wise pattern of agricultural development in the selected time period for showing upward and downward movements of different districts in level of agricultural development; and
5. To suggest measures they could help in improving the fate of less developed districts/states and achieving the objectives of balanced regional agricultural development.

Methodology of the Study

The data from various sources have examined through some statistical techniques such as, co-efficient variance, factor analysis and growth rates estimations etc. to identify the level and pattern of agricultural development in Haryana. No doubt earlier these methods frequently used by several scholars as per the literature at international level , A.K.Sen, Atkinson, in India M.N. Pal, Hemlata Rao, Dholakia and Dholakia, A. Kundu and S.S.Somra etc.

Development is a multi-dimensional phenomenon. The scholars of different discipline define it in different ways with varying stress on its aspects. But generally they share with the view that it is an outcome of the progress made in the different sectors economic activities. The economic activities relating to primary sector reflect their association with rural living. The process of agricultural development involves both of economic and structural changes not only at macro-level but also concurrent changes in the economic activities over different regions including districts as micro level units. The pooling of selected indicators representing various agricultural activities is not very much needed in case of single variable analysis. However, in a situation like the present one where multi variable analysis is under consideration, working out composite index of development is felt imperative for the purpose of convenient analysis and unless indicators pertaining to those activities, are combined together, it would probably be an insurmountable task carry out a comparative analysis of level and pattern of agricultural development for the different districts and thereby have conclusive and meaningful results. Hence, crucial stage in a multivariate analysis like the present one is that of constructing a large number of agricultural development indicators into the group indices.

The coefficient of variance measured by the formula as;

$$C.V. = \frac{\sigma}{\overline{X}} \times 100$$

Where, C.V. = Coefficient of variance; σ = Standard deviation and $\overline{X}$ = mean.

The co-efficient of variation is used to compare the variability of two or more series. The series (or group) for which the C.V. is greater is said to have more variation or conversely less consistent, less form, less stable or less homogeneous. On the other hand, the series for which C.V. is less is said to have smaller variation or more consistent, more uniform, more stable or more homogeneous.

To assess the growth pattern of districts at different points of time, there has been used compound growth rate method as;

$$\text{Growth Rate} = \text{Antilog } [(\log P_1 - \log P_0)/t - 1] \times 100$$
$$\text{Growth Rate} = [(P_1/P_0)^t - 1] \times 100$$

Where, P_1 = Value of current year; P_0 = Value of Base year and t = Time Period.

The Principal Component Analysis (Factor Analysis) produces Components (Factors) in descending order of their importance and factor loadings which explain the relative importance of different variables in explaining variance in the phenomenon. Most of the studies using 'Factor Analysis' adopted 'First Principal Component' as guiding principle for determining individual indicator weights. In the present study, all the 'Principal Components' (Factor derived) are taken into account to determine relative weights of selected variables so as to reflect maximum possible variation in the agricultural development. The selected variables are standardised by equalising their variance and calculated as under;

$$Z_{ij} = \frac{X_{ij} - \overline{X}_i}{\sigma_i}$$

Where, Z_{ij} = Standardised value of ith variable for jth district; X_{ij} = Original value of ith variable for jth district; $\overline{X}_i$ = mean value of ith variable σ_i = Standard deviation of ith variable.

The weights for the variable determined by applying above mentioned techniques are in accordance with the contribution made by the variable in inter-districts variations. Higher weights are assigned to those variables which contribute more towards inter-state variations and vice versa.

Composite Index for Agricultural Development is calculated as;

$$I_{jt} = \sum_{i=1}^{n} \left(\frac{Xij - \overline{X}i}{\sigma i} \right) a_{ij}$$

$\overline{X}i$ = Mean value of i_{th} variable

or

$$I_{jt} = \sum_{i=1}^{n} Z_{ij}\, a_{ij}$$

Where, I_{jt} = Composite Index of jth district for t period of time; Z_{ij} = Standardised value of ith variable for jth distirct and A_{ij} = Factor loading of ith variable for jth district.

Source of Data, Choice of Years and the Limitations of the Study

This study is based on the analysis of district-wise data pertaining to 19 districts of the state namely; Ambala,

Panchkula, Yamuna Nagar, Kurukshetra, Khairtal, Karnal, Panipat, Sonipat, Rohtak, Jhajjar, Faridabad, Gurgaon, Bhiwari, Mahendragarh, Bhiwani, Jing, Hisar, Fatehabad, Sirsa.

The database of the study is primarily the statistical Abstract of Haryana published by Directorate of Economic and statistics (D.E.S.) Haryana (Chandigarh). Besides this, the relevant data has been collected from various official sources such as other publication of the Director Economic and statistics, Director of land Records, Director of Agriculture and Department of Forest of the Government of Haryana. Frequent there has also been use of various economic journals, reports and others publication in the course of the study.

To study the district-wise pattern of agricultural development in Haryana, there used the Triennium Ending 1986-87 (i.e. 1984-85 through 1986-87) and Triennium Ending 1989-90 (i.e., 1987-88 through 1989-90) have been computed the data for 12 district, and the Triennium Ending 1992-93, 1995-96 and 1998-99 (i.e. 1990-01 through 1992-93, 1993-94 through 1995-96 and 1996-97 through 1998-99) have been computed the data for 16 District, and the Triennium Ending 2001-02 and 2004-05 (i.e. 1999-2000 through 2001-2002 and 2002-03 through 2004-2005) have been compared the data for 19 districts. Composite index of development have been calculated for major 16 districts of Haryana on three points of time, TE 1992-93, TE 1998-99 and TE 2004-05 for agricultural sectors of the economy. Composite indexes have been calculated not only to measure the level of development but also to divide the districts objectively into four categories; High, Medium high, Medium low and low.

There are some problems with district wise data sequence of the time duration of study period 1985 to 2005. In the state the data sequence of state records are available in very much heterogeneous ways like from 1985 to 90 there were only 12 districts, from 1990 to 99 there were 16 districts in the state, and from 1999 to 2005, there are 19 districts as per state records. Hence, there tried to analyse the state agriculture pattern during probably these 20 years, the data sequence for C. V. and growth rates etc. up to 1990 we have taken 12 districts and from 1990 to 1999 we have taken 16 districts and 1999 and onward we have taken 19 districts. To shows the basic scenarios of agricultural development pattern from 1990 to 2005 through composite index of the districts we have arrange the data sequence of the 16 districts. To general comparison as per necessary we have also compare the date sequence of 12 districts from 1984 to 1990. In year 1995-96 and 1996-97, there merge the district Panch Kula into Ambala and in year 97-98 and 98-99, there merge the districts Panchkula, Jhajjar and Fatehabad into Ambala, Rohtak and Hissar respectively. Thus, this kind of things is the part of limitations of the study.

Hypothesis of the Study

The efforts have been made in the present study to examine the following hypothesis;

1. The objective indicators are expected to explain the district-wise level and pattern of agricultural development and help in assessing inter-district and inter-state disparities;
2. The changes in strategies of agricultural development around nineties have had a desired impact on reducing regional disparities;
3. The degree of regional disparities varied from one area to another area with in the state or country;
4. The degree of regional disparities changed with the change of aggregation unit;
5. The diversified structure of economy leads to a higher level of agricultural development; and
6. The low level of agricultural development is related to low productivity, less use of modern technology, inadequacy of infrastructure and low degree of modernization etc.

Framework of the study

The book framed into five chapters. The pluralistic planning efforts of previous decades in Haryana for agricultural development, the historical perspective, problems, objectives, hypothesis, methodology, period of time, source of data concept, classification criteria for selection, selection of indicator, organization of study and limitation of the study noted in the introductory chapter. The second chapter devoted to the literature reviewed and historical prospective of Haryana and study of background of study. Whereas the third chapter describes, in detail, the strategy for agricultural policy, regional aspects, factors affecting the regional agricultural development and comparison with the other states of India and impact of liberalization on agriculture development in Haryana. With the help of composite indices, C.V. etc. attempts have been made in the fourth chapter, to analyse inter-district level and pattern of agricultural development and spatial diversification of agricultural development in Haryana at selected three points of time by grouping the districts into high, medium high, medium low and low categories according to the similarities in levels of their development. The final chapter endeavours to derive certain significant conclusions and suggestions which could provide at least some guidelines for transformation of economy with a view of ameliorating the fate of less developed districts.

2

Earlier Studies and a Profile of the Study

It has been acknowledged that there is no alternative to eliminate poverty except rapid development. The important question about, nation, state or region development is not 'whether to develop' but, how to develop? The problem of regional disparities in development is taken in consistent with the concept of development. It is endemic to the development process, as manifestation of spatial injustice and should be reduced for attaining the goal of justice and egalitarian society. But, in reality the regional disparities in development are more acute and quite persistent at global, national and state level. Therefore, it would be quite fruitful exercise to explore the theoretical expositions and actual position with regard to regional disparities at the various scales of spatial units in agriculture development process.

Various empirical studies have been conducted by many scholars' agencies to estimate the extent and nature of regional disparities in economic development in India and abroad. Some important and recent empirical studies have been reviewed here. The review of these studies provide broad spectrum about inter-regional and intra-regional disparities in economic development and agricultural development in particular. Thus, these studies will provide a supportive base to design an appropriate hypothesis and methodology of present study to examine the actual picture of pattern of agriculture development in the state with the help of some statistical and econometric tools.

Review of Literature

The interest in the different views on the pattern of regional inequalities developed in the 1950's. Early thoughts on spatial economic phenomena were limited to location theories (Thunen 1826, Weber 1909 and Losch, 1940). In explaining inter-regional trade, Ohin, 1933, predicted regional equality of income through the conception of equalization of factor prices. Theoretical generalizations about the pattern of spatial development over time and the process of transmission of growth of one region to another had been provided by (Myrdal, 1957) and (Hirschman, 1958) by explaining the concept of "spread" or "trickling-down" effects, and "backwash" or "polarization" effects.

While studying the difference among the state per capita incomes of the 48 States of the United States during the period 1919 to 1954, (Hannna, 1959) observed a pronounced narrowing of inter-state differentials. Hanna formulated the hypothesis that as the national level of income increases, the regional disparities decreases, which is known as convergence hypothesis. (Perloff et al., 1960), studying regional economic growth of U.S. economy during the period 1870-1950 observed the tendency of convergence of per capita income differentials among the States. In another study on the U.S. economy during the period 1880-1949-51, (Kuznets and Easterlin, 1960) found, "The growth in per capita income in various parts of the country was accompanied by a marked narrowing of relative interstate differences".

The hypothesis that regional disparity increases initially and decreases later as the economy develops had been supported by (Alonso, 1968) theoretically. This hypothesis had also been found empirically valid by (Williamson, 1965) by studying the economies of large number of developed and developing countries, including India, taking per capita income as the indicator of development. He observed, "rising regional income disparities and increasing North-South problems is typical of the more mature stages of national growth and development. Koropeckyj (1972), examined empirically the record of Socialist countries of East Central Europe and (erstwhile) USSR in regard to the disparity of regional development by taking industrial employment as representative of the regional level of industrialization and of economic development, and found the validity of Williamson's hypothesis "which can also be represented by an inverted 'U'. Richardson (1973) argued that "the trouble with Myrdal's views is that they are difficult to translate into a formal model", while Kaldor's suggestion is an improvement in this respect he suggested a variant of the Cumulative Causation theory, emphasizing the operation of increasing returns to scale in the industrially advanced areas of a country which is benefited due to increasing returns to scale when trade opens up between the developed and backward regions (Kaldor, 1970). No doubt the increasing gap between rich and poor is not good for societies there are several kind of results propounded by (Sen, 1973) and (Atkinsan, 1983), to measurement of inequalities in their different - different works at different time.

It is acknowledged that the agricultural development should be assessed not only by the trends in the agricultural production and productivity which reflects the essence of various agricultural developmental measures but also on the basis of various physical inputs like labour (human and animal), irrigation, fertilizers, improved seeds, extent of cultivated area, etc. "Assessment of the level of development of each of these physical inputs can reflect broadly the potential level of agricultural development which may or may not be deflected in the average productivity levels" (Sharma, 1973). More precisely, agricultural productivity is a function of a variety of factors including physical, social, economic and technological, each acquiring its specificities as component in an interacting system over time. The combined effects of these factors manifest itself in per hectare productivity in a given area (Bhatia, 1968). Agricultural production function relationship can be explained by specifying a particular production (output per hectare) to traditional inputs such as labour, animal power and water, and to modern inputs such as fertilizers, high yielding varieties of sees, pesticides, etc., (Shafi, 1984). The regional differences in output per hectare are attributed to differences in the quantum of the availability of the inputs. Several empirical studies have proved that environmental factors provide a base and determine the agricultural productivity (Krishan Lal and Kohli, 1964; Ram Dayal, 1965; Tambad, 1965; and Sharma, 1966). In order to overcome environmental productivity, a package of technological measures like irrigation, fertilizers, HYV seeds and mechanisation has been adopted. The institutions and social factors like caste, social values, education, training, etc., are also important determinants of agricultural productivity. Rao and Brahma estimated the regional disparities in India, selecting six indicators of the three sectors of the economy and adopting the method used by Richard Stone in building up regional economic distances for U.K. by this method each region can be represented by point and the distances between any two points represents the distance in development. They classified the major states into three categories: (a) 'Most Developed' group having distances range up to 1.5 points, three states viz. West Bengal, Maharashtra, Gujarat came in this category, (b) 'Not so Developed' group having distance range 1.5 to 3.0 points; Tamil Nadu, Karnataka and Punjab came in this category, (c) 'Least Developed' group having distance range of 3.0 to 4.5; the rest of the 14 states came in this category. The study proved that development during the first 15 years of planning in India did not lead to reduction in regional disparities and states experienced no significant change in their status of development as group continued to contain broadly the same states (Rao and Brahma, 1973). Verma and Das made an attempt to estimate the regional development level in Bangladesh by applying component analysis, developed by Pearson and Hotelling, selecting 17 indicators covering all aspects of the economy. They classified all the districts of Bangladesh into four levels of development.

They found that the districts of Bangladesh were characterized by wide disparities with the maximum value of Index 15.45 and the minimum value 3.81 while the average Index value was 7.03 (Verma & Das, 1974). Hemlata Rao prepared Composite Index of Development using Factor Analysis and Rotated Matrix analysis and identified the backward states of India. She selected 24 variables from specific sectors like Agriculture, Industry, Education and Banking 1955-56 to 1965-66. The Composite Index of Development (CID) figures showed that none of the states was developed in all sectors. National average of CID registered an upward trend over time, i.e. from 13.37 in 1956 to 15.96 in 1965. The coefficient of variation of overall CID of states declined from 19.70% to 13.75% indicating general decline is absolute differentials between the states. This decline in degree of disparities was not shared by all sectors, while industrial and banking sectors moved in favorable directions, agriculture and education sectors moved in opposite direction (Rao, 1977). Mohapatra taking per capita incomes of 17 major States of India found that inter-regional disparities were increasing at a much faster rate during the post 1966-67 period although divergence of per capita incomes was continuing during 1960-61 to 1973-74 (Mohapatra, 1978). Das and Dalvi used the share and shift technique for projecting regional and sectoral growth rates. The study analysed the data of State Domestic Product (SDP) at constant prices (1960-61) which were collected for 13 broad sectors and 14 major state of India for the period 1960-61 to 1974-75. The estimated growth rate for different sectors and the selected states for the period 1960-75 reveals that 14 states together attained on average growth rate of 3.56 percent per annum. Haryana had the highest growth rate (5.34 percent) and was followed by Punjab (4.85 percent), Karnataka (4.79 percent) and Jammu & Kashmir (4.46 percent) whereas the Uttar Pradesh had the lowest growth rates of 1.92 percent. On the basis of growth rates, 14 states could be classified into two broad groups; States having growth rate above the national average–Assam, Haryana, Jammu & Kashmir,

Karnataka, Kerala and Punjab; Sates having growth rates below the national average–Andhra Pradesh, Maharashtra, Gujarat, Madhya Pradesh, Rajasthan and Tamil Nadu (Das and Dalvi, 1981). Somra applied the Factor Analysis to assess the level and pattern of economic development of Rajasthan during 1985 to 1995 with the help of fifteen indicators (Somra, 1999). Chhipa and Sagar studied the regional differentials with respect to banking development by applying the Factor Analysis, for the year 1977, selecting 11 banking development indicators. On the basis of Factor Analysis result, they classified states as Highly Developed, Moderate Developed, Low Developed and Very Low Developed. Index value of highly developed group comprising Kerala, Punjab, Maharashtra and West Bengal varied from 5.436 to 6.421. While the very low developed group comprising Rajasthan, Assam, Madhya Pradesh and Orrisa and Index value was varying from 1.697 to 2.076. they also applied the technique of Regression Analysis to measure the influence of non-banking variable like per capita state domestic product, literacy rate, infrastructure development, urbanization etc. they observed that the literacy rate has emerged as the most dominant variable influencing the level of banking development in all the states in India (Chhipa and Sagar, 1981). Bharadwaj analysed and compared the regional disparities in economic growth during British rule period (1891-1946) and independent India (1947 to 1978-79). Her study revealed import-export led growth pattern during British rule period and proved that only a few regions having import-export based industries viz. Madras, Bengal (Calcutta) and Bombay were more developed, Punjab is exception having agriculture-based growth pattern. Some cantonment townships like Meerut were also developed and rest of India was underdeveloped. Since independence, over the plan period, the strategy of industrialization varied, especially in Second Plan, of course, some new interior centers emerged, but the dominance of British favoured regions was not effectively reduced. During the period 1950-51 and 1960-61, there were some tendencies towards narrowing of disparities, but thereafter the gulf between the developed and underdeveloped regions went on widening year by year. Uneven impact of Green Revolution on states was main cause of increasing disparities (Bharadwaj, 1982). Nair attempted to test the "concentration cycle hypothesis" which states that inter-regional disparities increase initially but narrow down in later stages of development. Thus inter-regional inequalities trace out an inverted U-shaped curve over the period. The analysis of inter-state income differentials was carried out for 17 major states of Indian Union during the period 1970-80 with the help of weighted and unweighted coefficients of variation, State Relatives and rank correlation. The states were ranked in terms of per capita net domestic product. Punjab occupied the first rank during the whole decade while Bihar remained at the bottom. States such as Punjab, Haryana, Maharashtra and Gujarat were at the top four positions while Bihar, Uttar Pradesh, Madhya Pradesh and Orissa occupied bottom places. There were hardly any noticeable changes in the ranking order over the period 1971-81 (Nair, 1983). Singh examined the trends in inter-state disparities amongst 17 major states during 1951-81 on the basis of net state domestic product at constant prices. The study revealed that all the selected states registered steady increase in total state domestic product but the increase in per capita terms was generally low except in a few states like Punjab, Haryana and Maharashtra. The coefficient of variation in per capita declined from 28.29 per cent in 1950-51 to 23.79 per cent in 1955-74 and remained stable between 1961-63. A clear divergent trend in regional disparities was observed during post-green revolution period. On the basis of annual growth rates the 17 states have been grouped into four categories: (a) Very High Growth: Punjab, Haryana and Maharashtra, (b) High Growth: Jammu & Kashmir, Assam, Karnataka, Gujarat and Kerala, (c) Low Growth : Orissa, Andhra Pradesh, Rajasthan, Tamil Nadu, and (d) Very low Growth : Uttar Pradesh, Bihar, West Bengal and Madhya Pradesh. The study showed a positive association in the level of per capita income and growth rates, as a result of which inter-state income disparities have tended to widen during the period 1961-81 (Singh, 1984). Gupta attempted to examine the industrial disparities amongst 17 major states in India during 1961-81 on the basis of four core indicators of industrial development relating to manufacturing sector-value output, value-added, person employed and total productive capital employed. Hirschman Herfindalh (H.H.) Index and Theil's Index were computed to measure the regional concentration. The values of both the indices declined from 16.22 to 9.64 per cent and 14.40 to 11.30 per cent respectively over the period leading to the conclusion that backward states were catching up with the developed ones in industrial development. Williamson's unweighted and weighted coefficients of variation were used to measure the disparities among the states. The coefficients of variation of all the four indicators both in terms of states' percentage to All-India total and per capita had also fallen over the period 1961-81, indicating that there has been a decline in industrial disparities amongst the selected states. In order to examine the locational patterns of industries among the states over the period Magnitude Rating showed that in relative terms Maharashtra, West Bengal, Tamil Nadu and Gujarat were more developed than others but were experiencing a declining trend while other states were showing improvement slowly and gradually in industrial sector. In brief, the results of all the measures selected to examine the industrial disparities revealed that there had been decline in inter-state industrial disparities over the period 1961-81 though the process was slow (Gupta, 1985). Desai analysed the process of industrial diversification of 23 Indian states over two points of time, 1964 and 1980-81, by calculating coefficients of specialisation whose value varied between zero and one. The study revealed that the states like Andhra Pradesh, Orissa, Himachal Pradesh, tripura and Goa, Daman & Diu reported decrease in the value of coefficient of specialisation over time. This implied that these five states showed the tendency of industrial diversification. Three states, namely, Bihar, Kerala and Andaman & Nicobar reported no significant change in their respective value of coefficient of specialisation over time while other 15 states out of 23 states showed the tendency towards specialisation of industries, indicating lack of diversification of industries. Rank correlation worked out between value of coefficients of specialisation for the year 1964 and 1980-81 for the regions under consideration was 0.87 which proved significant at 1 per cent level of significance, indicating that over the period Indian states have not shown any significant change in terms of relative spatial diversification. This result revealed that the efforts at regional balance, though strengthened the process of industrialisation in the backward states, but not much dent has been made in the relative spatial structure (Desai, 1986). Kannan has attempted to estimate the inter-regional disparities in banking development amongst the major 17 states in India for the period 1969-84. Index of banking development was constructed with the help of Factor Analysis technique for the selected 17 states. The study revealed that there was no significant variation in the ranking pattern of sates. However, during 1975-84 substantial reduction in the regional disparities in banking development was noticed. The coefficient of variation of banking development index reduced from 56% in 1975 to 35% in 1984. The view was further supported in 'Distance Analysis'. The states were grouped into five clusters. The economic distance between least developed states and most developed states reduced from 7.97 to 6.48 over the period 1975-84. The distribution of credit among the different states indicated a greater degree of concentration than that noticed in deposits. Rural inter-state disparities considerably decreased during 1975-84. The credit-deposit ratio of rural branches improved by 11 per cent during the period, this could be responsible for the decline in the variations of inter-state banking development index during this period (Kannan, 1987). Joshi made an attempt to examine the relationship between economic development and the level of infra-structure at the district level in Uttar Pradesh with the help of regression analysis for the period 1980-81. Ten core infra-structural indicators pertaining to agriculture, industry and overall development were taken as independent variables for the analysis along with three dependent variables; Net Domestic Output Per Capita, Gross Value of Output per hectare of Net Sown Area and Value Added Per Industrial Worker. The study revealed positive correlation between the development indicators (dependent variables) and infra-structural indicators (independent variable). However, in many cases, the association proved non-significant in most of the cases, though the sign of the coefficients were generally in the expected direction. One of the reasons for weak statistical association between the dependent and independent variables was that development of infra-structure did not cross the minimum threshold in most of the districts most of the facilities were development could be felt only after some time. The study found that irrigation in case of agriculture and banking in case of industry turned out to be the most important factors affecting the level of development (Joshi, 1987). Reddy attempted to examine the regional disparities in the development of small scale industries (SSI) sector in Andhra Pradesh. The study examined the inter and intra-regional disparities for the period 1971-85 in the development of industrial sector by computing Composite Index of Industrial Development on the basis of performance indicators viz. number of units, employment potential and investment levels. The state was divided into three regions; Andhra, Rayalseema and Telangana. The compounded growth for selected indicators for the period 1971-80 and 1980-85, indicating that growth of SSI in Andhra and Rayalseema regions, was almost same, while Telengana region had higher growth rates during both the periods. The industrial development of 23 districts of Andhra Pradesh was also examined which were ranked on the basis of the composite index. The study revealed that the development of small scale industries depended on resource potential, entrepreneurial abilities, financial capabilities and other infrastructural facilities. Infrastructure proved key factor in industrial development. The study found that the districts having good infrastructural facilities recorded better performance (Reddy, 1988). Rao attempted to study the trends income inequalities and poverty in four newly industrialised countries (NICs) (HongKong, South Korea, Singapore and Taiwan) and four middle income countries (MICs) (Indonesia, Malaysia, Philippines and Thailand) of middle Asia during the period 1965-84. The study shows that the average annual growth rate of GNP per capita in the four NICs was higher (6 to 8 per cent) than that of three of the four NICs-Indonesia, Malaysia and Thailand (4 to 5 per cent). Almost all the selected 8 countries experienced a significant increase in the share of industry in GNP. All the countries enjoyed a relatively higher export-GDP ratio in 1984 as compared to 1965. The four NICs did extremely well in alleviating poverty. High erates of expansion reduced poverty significantly in the NICs (Rao, 1989). Sharma examined the inter-state disparities in terms of the nutritional level in all states and union territories in India with particular reference to Assam. An attempt was also made to examine the problem from both the quantitative and qualitative aspects considering seven core indicators related to consumer expenditure, data about which were taken from 38th Round of National Sample Survey. The Component index of Nutrition was constructed for all states by using equal weights. The study revealed that the state like Haryana, Sikkim, Himachal Pradesh, Punjab and Andaman & Nicobar Islands were the nutritionally richest regions while Orissa, Goa, Daman & Diu, Kerala, Pondicherry were among the poorest. The Component Index based on taxonomy also placed Haryana at the top position, followed by Himachal Pradesh, Punjab, Rajasthan and Sikkim while Orissa was placed at the bottom of the taxonomic scale. Other states with a poor nutritional level of living were Manipur, Meghalaya, Goa, Daman & Diu and West Bengal. The study showed that even the states with highest nutritional level were far from the ideal value. In brief, India is still at a nutritionally poor level and wide inter-state disparities in the level of nutrition (Sharma, 1992). Kantawala and Rao analysed the inter-state disparities in sectoral development in India during 1970-71 to 1985-86, selecting eight agricultural indicators of services sector. They used composite index tool to estimate the sectoral development and rank correlation analysis to show the change in positions or the states in their ranks. Examining the relative position of states with respect to all sectors, they concluded that in the case of industrial and service sectors the disparities among states declined marginally, while the inter-state disparities in the case of agricultural sector increased over time. The development was lagging in all sectors of the economy of the states like Assam, Bihar, Madhya Pradesh, Orissa and Rajasthan. Moreover, the developed states have been growing at faster rate as compared to the backward regions. The study also proved that the relative position of states have not changed significantly considering the overall development (Kantawala and Rao, 1992). Rangacharyulu examined the rural development of major 17 states in India by selecting five core indicators pertaining to rural development. Composite Development Index of rural areas were developed for three points of time, 1971, 1981 and 1987. The methodology adopted for this exercise included Principal Component Analysis and the factor weight matrix rotated by Varmax method. The states were ranked on the basis of factor scores. In order to trace the changes in the position of the states based on the rank across the three points of time the 17 states were classified into three broad groups. 'High group' which included Punjab, Haryana, Kerala, Gujarat and West Bengal (ranks between 1 and 5); 'moderate group' which included Assam, Rajasthan, Karanataka, Himachal Pradesh, Orissa, Tamil Nadu and Jammu & Kashmir (ranks between 6 and 12); while Uttar Pradesh, Maharashtra, Andhra Pradesh, Madhya Pradesh and Bihar constituted the 'low group'. There were no significant changes in the positions of majority of the states over period 1971-87 so far as rural development was concerned. However,

Gujarat, which was in high group both in 1971 and 1981, fell to the moderate category in 1987, while West Bengal slipped from high group (1971) to moderate (1981 and 1987). Punjab occupied the first position in respect of all the three points while the second and third positions were shared by Kerala and Haryana. On the lower side, the states of Madhya Pradesh and Bihar had most backward rural sector. Out of 17 states, ten states have been progressing and six had fluctuating trend while the alone state of Rajasthan exhibited a declining trend consistently from its base position in 1971 (Rangacharyulu, 1993). Mazumdar made an attempt to analyse the interstate disparities in per capita state domestic product (PCSDP) for the period 1960-86 to check whether regional disparities were divergent or convergent during this period. The study also introduced price differentials in the per capita state domestic products series of fourteen major states of India. With the help of coefficients of variation of per capita state domestic product of 14 selected states, the study revealed that interstate income variations were on the increase with fluctuating trend during the period. Furthermore, the study revealed that the divergence was more with the introduction of inter-state price differential in PCSDP series of the selected states as the trend rates of the coefficients of variation were higher than the trend rates of the coefficients of variation at all India constant prices (1970-71=100) as well as current prices (Mazumdar, 1993). Verma and Das attempted to analyse the performance of agriculture in a regional frame based on land revenue system prevailing in India during pre-independence period. The divided Indian agriculture sector into four zones (regions); (A) Zamindari Region (Bihar, West Bengal, Orissa, Uttar Pradesh and Assam; (B) Rayotwari Region (Tamilnadu, Karnataka, Kerala, Andhra Pradesh, Maharashtra and Gujarat; (C) Mahalwari Region (Punjab and Haryana); (D) Jagirdari Region (Madhya Pradesh and Rajasthan). The study period 1891-1976 was divided into four intervals; 1891 to 1947 (pre-independence period), 1946-47 to 1955-56, 1956-57 to 1965-66 and 1966-67 to 1975-76. The composite Index of Agricultural

Efficiency showed that Mahalwari region remained at the top, followed by Rayotwari region in both pre- and post-independence period, Zamindari and Jagirdari regions remained at the bottom though interchanged their rank positions in the post-Independence period and Zamindari region dropped to bottom during post-Independence period. The study showed that planned efforts have not been able to alter the basic agrarian structure to control these socio-economic cross-currents and institutional forces which kept the goal of growth with equity unfulfilled and the goal of regional balance unachieved. The real experience of green revolution in India also confirmed that technological development was possible only when a parallel institutional change also took place which paved the way for wider adoption of technology (Verma and Das, 1995). Jayadevan try to analysed inter-state variations in the rates of growth of employment in organised industry as a whole and in 17 selected organised manufacturing industries in India and 15 major states during the period 1976-77 to 1987-88. The annual compound rates of growth of employment and output were calculated by fitting an exponential function. The study showed that all India level, the value-added in organised industry grew at 6 per cent per annum over the period 1966-67 to 1987-88. The state like Madhya Pradesh, Uttar Pradesh, Andhra Pradesh, Punjab, Haryana, Rajasthan, Tamil Nadu, Gujarat and Karnataka had growth rates of value-added which exceeded the all India average. On the other hand, rates of growth of value-added in organised industry as a whole and in individual organised industries were caused by the variations in the rates of growth of output rather than the variations in the levels of per worker real wages (Jayadevan, 1995). Anuradha and Rao collectively analysed inter-state disparities in the level of industrial development over the period 1970-71 to 1985-86. They applied Williamson's unweighted and weighted coefficient of variation and Hirschmman Herfindalh (H.H.) Index and Theil index to examine the disparities amongst 15 major states. Both weighted and unweighted coefficients of variation for selected indicators (except per capita productive capital in state disparities in industrial sector declined over time. Hirschman Herfindalh (H.H.) Index and Theil Index also supported the results. All the index values except Theil Index for productive capital declined over time. To examine the locational pattern of industries among the states two measures; Magnitude Rating (MR) and increasing Rating (IR) were computed. The result of Magnitude Rating revealed different trend in the selected states on different criteria. Only Karnataka showed declining Marginal Rating on all criteria. The results of Increasing Rating showed that developed states like Maharashtra, Gujarat had highest Increasing Rating (more than unity) while the states like Andhra Pradesh, Assam, Bihar, Karnataka, Kerala, Orissa, Madhya Pradesh (except in productive capital), Uttar Pradesh and West Bengal had Increasing Rating value less than unity, indicating higher level industrial activities in the developed states like Maharashtra and Gujarat during the period. It was concluded that regional disparities in industrial development definitely converged over time regardless of the variable and index taken into consideration. Magnitude of inter-state disparities tended to decline significantly though in relative terms but in absolute terms the process of industrialisation was characterised by an inequality in its spatial distribution (Anuradha and Rao1995). Subramanian examined the inter-state differences in the level of family health in all the states (except Tripura) according to health Survey 1992-93. A taxonomic approach was applied and Composite Index of family health for each state was constructed on the basis of ten important indicators pertaining to family health. The states were ranked on the basis of Composite Index of family health, 23 states were classified into three categories; 'high ranked' states (Kerala, West Bengal and Tamil Nadu); 'low ranked' states (Nagaland, Rajasthan, Madhya Pradesh, Bihar) and other states were included in the category of 'medium rank' (Subramanian, 1995). Das and Barua examined the regional inequalities amongst 23 states in India during 1970-92. Net State Domestic Product (NSDP) and its various components; agriculture, primary products, manufacturing, infrastructure and services of selected states were examined by applying Theil Index of inequalities, correlation analysis, Ordinary Least Square (OLS) method. The results of inequality indices indicated that except in primary products, regional disparities increased over the period 1970-92 in all the sectors of the Indian economy. The annual average rate of growth of inequalities was highest in agriculture (4.26 per cent) followed by NSDP (3.55 per cent) and these were highly significant. The increase of inequality in manufacturing (1.5 per cent), infrastructure (1.85 per cent) and services (0.50 per cent) was found to be positive but not significant while for the primary products (comprising only forestry and logging, fishing and mining & quarrying) regional inequalities were significantly decreasing at the rate of 2.8 per cent during the period. The relationship between economic growth and inter-regional inequalities was also studied to know what happened to regional disparities in India over the period as economy moved from a very highly restrictive trade regime to gradually liberalised trade. Negative correlation coefficients between the inequality indices and exponential annual growth rate in almost all the cases revealed that Indian economy has been developing but overall regional disparities widened during the period 1970-92. However, Negative correlation coefficients were found non-significant except in infrastructure and agriculture. Regression analysis results also proved that agriculture, services and unregistered manufacturing sectors were significant contributors of inter-regional income inequalities in India during 1970-92 (Das and Barua, 1996). Rana try to analysed the inter-state disparities on the basis of large number of social, economic, and infrastructural factors during the period 1971-95. Coefficient of variation figures worked out for selected indicators revealed that inter-state disparities widened in terms of economic indicators and the disparities reduced in social and infrastructural sector over time. The study found that the pattern of development of Indian economy was not uniform with respect to all the indicators rather it was of mixed nature Some of the Indian states were found economically advanced and some were socially more developed. However the states of Orissa, Bihar, Madhya Pradesh and Jammu & Kashmir were backward with respect to all indicators. The study proved that economic development does not necessarily lead to social development and vice versa. The state of Punjab as revealed from the values of Physical Quality of Life Index (Rana, 1997).

Dholakia and Dholakia, (1993) estimated the sources of growth of Indian agriculture for three sub-periods during 1950-51 to 1988-89. They also estimated the contribution of adverse weather conditions and intensity of resource use to total factor productivity growth (TFPG). It was found that TFPG has contributed significantly to the accelerations of agricultural growth facilitating release of scarce resources from agriculture to other sectors in the economy. Thus, TFPG in agriculture had been the prime driving force behind the acceleration of overall growth in the Indian economy achieved during the eighties. The main determinant of TFPG had been found to be the use of modern inputs like fertilizer, HYV seeds, and irrigation.

Except to these all there are several other studies were undertaken to explain the development and regional disparities in the states. the pattern of regional disparities in agriculture can be analysed in terms of uneven changes characterised by production organisational shifts, and new crops-wise, class-wise and region-wise differences is of course corroborated by a number of studies (Krishnaji, 1975; Bhalla and Alagh, 1979;. Dev, 1985; Sawant, 1987, etc.). By implication, these studies suggest that the regions could be broadly grouped into three, depending on the pattern and pace change. (1) Regions showing signs of dynamic and, more or less, sustained changes (as in Punjab, Western Uttar Pradesh, Haryana, etc). (2) Regions in slow transition and showing the signs of distinctly uneven changes. (3) Regions showing virtual stagnation.

The outcome of the green revolution on the yield of certain crops (wheat, and to a lesser extent maize, etc.) in the initial period of green revolution was noticeable increasing the regional disparity both in the yields and nature of crops. (Krishnaji, 1975) Moreover, agrarian strategy, at least during this period, also aimed at maximising yields per unit land in developed areas through a connected application of all inputs. Paradoxically, however regional disparities in yield of all crops taken together, measured by the coefficient of variation, did not increase significantly at the district, region or state level during the 1960s or still later periods (Bhalla and Alagh, 1979; Dev, 1985; Sawant, 1987).

These results appear to hold because of three main reasons. Firstly, several regions (like Gujarat, Rajasthan etc.) experienced fairly rapid growth rates in the area under high valued cereals. (Krishanji, 1975; Sawant, 1987; Reserve Bank of India, 1984). Secondly, compensating price movements in the case of slower growing non-foodgrain crops also tended to mitigate value differences in yield per acre. (Misra, 1985; Sawant, 1987) The net outcome of these factors was such that between the early 1960s and the late 1970s, the relative ranking of different states in the value of crop production per hectare remained more or less invariant, with West Bengal and Tamil Nadu occupying the first three places. (Misra, 1985) Thirdly, several regions with initial low and medium productivity levels experienced rapid growth rates in overall yields, whereas many of the regions the fertile alluvial or coastal or delta plains experienced low growth rates in land productivity. {The regions which experienced growth rates in yield exceeding 2.5% between 1962-65 and 1975-78 are Gujarat (Dry Areas), Gujarat (Sourashtra), Haryana(Eastand West), Punjab (North and South), Jammu and Kashmir(Mountainous and outer Hills), Karnataka (Inland Northern), Maharashtra (Eastern), Rajasthan (Western and Eastern), Uttar Pradesh (Western),Tamil Nadu (Coastal Northern)—only the Tamil Nadu (Coastal Northern) region had an initial productivity level greater than Rs. 1300 per hectare} (Mahendra Dev,1985). On the other hand, several regions, with high initial levels of land productivity, showed low growth rates in productivity up to the late 1970s { These regions comprised virtually the whole of the Eastern part of the country, Andhra Pradesh (Inland Northern and Southern), Gujarat (Eastern and Southern) and Tamil Nadu (Coastal Inland) } (Mahendra Dev, 1985).

During 1962-65 and 1970-73, districts experiencing high growth rates for all crops were concentrated in Punjab, Haryana, Uttar Pradesh and Rajasthan with these states accounting for 36 of the 50 high growth districts. Gujarat, Karnataka and Tamil Nadu accounted for another 10 of the high growth districts. Only one out of 60 high growth districts was located in the central or eastern regions At the other end, 133 out of the 289 districts studied experienced growth rates below 1.5 per cent per annum. Most of these were located in Andhra, Bihar, Karnataka, Gujarat, Madhya Pradesh, Orissa and Uttar Pradesh. (Bhalla and Alagh, 1979). Between 1969-72 and 1981-84, state level results sustained high growth rates (over 3 %) in Punjab and Haryana and an acceleration to high growth rates in a few states in the North, West and South (e.g. Maharastra, Gujarat Uttar Pradesh, Andhra Pradesh). Growth rates in Karnataka and Rajasthan show some declaration compared to the 1960s, but remained above average. For a similar period (1970-73 to 1980-83), Bhalla and Tyagi (1989) show that while in the decade ending in the triennial 1968-69 to 1970-71 only 71 districts (out of 284), accounting for 25 per cent of gross cropped area, experienced agricultural output growth rates above 3.5 per cent, by the end of the decade, the number had increased to 95 districts, covering nearly 40 per cent of the area.

It has been noted among the significant features of the growth pattern that emerged during this period was the continuation of very high growth rates in most of the original green resolution areas, the appearance of a large new set of the high growth districts in the major states (e.g.,Uttar Pradesh, Andhra Pradesh, Gujarat and Maharastra) Tamil

Nadu and West Bengal and the downward shift of some districts in Rajasthan and Madhya Pradesh (Bhalla, 1988).

The growth results have to be interpreted with some caution, since growth rates are notoriously unstable in certain regions due to severe output fluctuations. Instability is particularly high (and, moreover, has grown in the recent period) in Gujarat, Karnataka, Maharashtra; Rajasthan, Orissa. (C.H.H.Rao et al., 1988). The growth rates have been high income of the 'lagging' states (particularly Karnataka and Maharashtra, whereas Kerala and Tamil Nadu continue to register negative growth rates). As a result, the declining share of the Eastern region in total foodgrains production has been reversed, whereas the North-Western region continues to amount for a growing share of foodgrain production, (Patnaik,) explored in greater detail below.

For the decade of the 1960s (1960-63 to 1970-73), except for a few regions in the North and North-West, South, South-East and Bengal, all other regions (a total of 27 regions out of 49 regions)experienced negative growth in labour productivity. (Kundu and Raza, 1982) This picture is also confirmed by a more disaggregated analysis by Bhalla and Alagh. Further, between 1962-65 and 1975-78, a number of regions with low initial levels of labour productivity, low or medium rates in this variable { Jammu and Kashmir (Jhelum) Uttar Pradesh (Eastern) Andhra Pradesh (Inland Northern) Bihar (Northern and Southern) Rajasthan (Southern) Maharastra (Inland Eastern) Madhya Pradesh (Inland Eastern) }, or otherwise experienced declining labour productivities { Gujarat (Northern plains) West Bengal (Himalyain) West Bengal (Eastern plains) Gujarat (Southern plains) Madhya Pradesh (Eastern) Orissa (Southern) Mdhya Pradesh (Inland western) } (Mahendra Dev, 1986). Thus, several regions, chiefly in the eastern, central and western parts appear to be caught in the productivity low growth trap.

The growing disparity in labour productivity also implies that regions, which have experienced faster growth, have experienced increases in yield with smaller changes in the net sown area per worker, whereas in low growth regions yield increases and changes in the net sown area per worker have largely offset each other. (Kundu and Raza, 1982; Mahendra Dev, 1986). Thus, the underlying employment elasticities and the pattern of labour are generated by the disparities growth processes are different across region.

Analysing the pattern of labour use in agriculture, Bhalla and Allagh (1979) find an increase in the labour absorption per sown hectare (which they refer to as the 'suction mechanism'), in areas experiencing rapid growth. Their conclusions are not corroborated by two the studies with overlapping periods of investigations. (Kundu, and Raza, 1982 and Mahendra Dev, 1985) In any case, in the more recent period, the rapidly growing regions have experienced a drop in labour adsorption per gross sown hectare. (Vaidanathan, 1986; Bhalla, 1988) Bhalla finds a 'berak' in this respect around the mid 1970s. On the other hand, the stagnant regions, where perhaps there in a greater compulsion to subsist through farming, the high level of labour adsorption per sown hectare continues to grow.

Bhalla (1988) has focused on this and argued that differences in employment elasticities are associated with differences in growth processes as well as associated changes in land-lease and labour markets, and have distinct outcomes for the regional differences in poverty and wages. Bhalla argues for a broad regionalisation of agrarian zones based on the above data. She divided the high agricultural and productivity growth states in the 1970s (Punjab, Haryana, Uttar Pradesh) or labour absorbing (Andhra Pradesh, Gujarat Maharashtra) character of their growth. The medium low growth states of Karnataka, Rajasthan, Madhya Pradesh, exhibit mixed characteristics in terms of employment characteristics of the labour saving-labour using character of their growth. Finally, she considers the law growth states of Orissa, Tamil Nadu, West Bengal, and Bihar as 'agriculturally involutes' since they exhibit extremely low growth, with extremely high growth rates in labour absorption per hectare.

The nature of 'associated' changes such as changes in land, lease and labour markets-symptomatic of an uneven penetration of capitalism in agriculture, is the subject matter of a number of detailed investigations, and is not pursued here. (See, for instance, Bharadwaj and Das, 1975;Bardhan and Rudra, 1978; Byres, 1981; Khasnabis and Chakaravarty, 1982; Harris, 1982; Chatopadhyay and Bhattacharya, 1984) But Bhalla's conclusion, mirrors Byres's analysis above on a more macro plane. While the broad regionalisation suggested by Bhalla may be open to question in view of the intra-regional differences their analysis again emphasis the acceleration of certain trends implying drastic changes in the production organisation of agriculture in certain regions : one notes; especially, the unevenness of such changes and their implications for the rural poor. The more limited subject matter of this section viz. the persistence of low levels of labour productivity, growing disparities in it, and negative growth rates, is itself to great concern, given the links between labour productivity and poverty (Mahendra Dev, 1986; Parthasarthy, 1987; Rao and Deshpende, 1987; Vadyanathan, 1988), as well as with wage rates. (Bhalla, 1988)

The level of agriculture yield is known to be significant correlated with the key demographic variable. But the strength of this relationship declines with time {During 1962-65, the correlation between yield per area and net sown area per worker, per capita land availability and population density, at the National Sample Survey (NSS) redion level are -0.58, -0.78 and +0.60. All correlations are significant at one percent level (Ladejinsky) }. The level of yield is also related to the level of rainfall and negatively related to the proportion of rainfall during June-September. (Bardhan, 1983) Furtrher, the environmental demographic variables are also related to a number of structural variables. Such as concentration of land and assets, average size of holding, proportion of agricultural labours, incidence of tenancy, as the state level in the early 1960s. (Vaidyanathan, 1988) But many of these relationships break down or assume more complex forms in 1970s or later.

Thus in the early 1970s, the land concentration ratio is significantly correlated with fertilizer use per hectare and the number of irrigation pumps per 10,000 hectares, pinpointing some of the new processes at work. Further, the correlation of these variables in explaining changes yield. This is directly confirmed by regression analysis (Ranade, 1980), which also indicates a high degree of complementarities between irrigation and the use of other modern inputs(Bhalla, 1987).

Further, the level of labour productivity in the 1960s and 1970s is related to per worker cultivable land and yield raising variables (fertilizer use per hectare, capital expenditure per hectare and proportion of land irrigated). A significant proportion of variation in labour productivity in the high growth districts is explained by the use of capital inputs on the one hand, and by output augmenting biological inputs on the other. (Bhalla and Alagh, 1979) Output augmenting factors like per worker land availability, use of fertilizer etc. explain fairly large properties of inter-district variations in labour productivity. This confirms the increasing importance of capital in Indian agriculture. But the relationship gets watered down for medium and law growth districts. (Bhalla, 1987)

Recently, the disparity in the impact of the growth factors under different ecological settings, and over different growth phases, has received some attention. The impact of technical inputs, particularly irrigation (regarded as a 'leading input' and complementary to the other inputs is a case in point. According (Vaidyanathan, 1988) the pattern of growth is not explicable in terms of the level, or growth, or irrigation. National Sample Survey regions have been reclassified, by level and growth rate of irrigation, as also by level of rainfall. Understandably, the irrigation growth rate has a greater impact on areas with low rainfall. But there are areas where the pattern of growth is not explicable in terms of the variables such as the concentration of land and assets average size of holdings, proportion of agricultural labourer,s incidence of tenancy, as the state level in the early 1960s. He cites the low growth rate of Tamil Nadu, a state with a high level of irrigation, and concludes that " The point that is being explained is the conjunction of irrigation development with major progress in plant breeding that made for much faster progress than growth." This still does not explain the case of dry regions with relatively low levels of rainfall and irrigation, which have experienced fairly high growth rates in agricultural production and productivity over phases (such as Gujarat and Karnataka). These regions have shown rapid increase in fertilizer application under rainfall condition, which also partly accounts for greater output instability. (C.H.H.Rao et al., 1988) Even so, in the absence of significant breakthrough in dry land rain-fed agriculture, the source of productivity growth remains perplexing to most analysts. (Rao and Deshpande, 1987; Vaidhyanathan, 1988). These results point to some of the explanations which have gained currently in explanations of agrarian development. The various policies in different plans have been launched by the government for meeting the gap of agrarian development among regions.

In the recent period, a number of studies (Ahluwalia 2000 and 2002; Nagraj, Varoudakis and Beganzous 1998; Rao, Shand and Kalirajan 1999; Shand and Bhide 2000) have observed that the regional disparities in India have widened, especially during the 1990s. However, these studies have used pre revised state domestic product (SDP) data. Further their analyses do not cover adequately the post-reform period, especially the late 1990s when the growth rate slackened at the aggregate as well as the regional levels.

Bhatttacharya and Sakthivel (2004), carried an inter-state study on the basis of State Domestic Product, they find the growth performance and structural changes in the domestic product of Indian states in the last two decades reveals that the development process has been uneven across states. While advanced industrial states have tended to leapfrog in the reforms years, other states have lagged behind. The regional disparities in growth rates become sharper in terms of per capita income.

It is now well established that the interstate disparities in the gross state domestic product (GSDP) have increased in the post-economic reform period beginning from the early nineties when compared to the eighties. In general, the richer states have grown faster than the poorer states (Ahluwalia, 2000; Dev and Ravi, 2003; Bhattacharya and Sakthivel, 2004; Hanumantha Rao, 2006). The regional disparities in per capita GSDP growth are even greater because the poorer states in general have experienced a faster growth in population.

An overall view of the above studies indicates a lot of studies regarding the disparities at national or international level. The above studies indicate that regional disparities in world and particularly in India have been widening, since early sixties. Presently, the Indian economy has moved from a very highly restrictive trade regime to liberalised trade and has been experiencing structural changes, encouraging privatisation and liberalisation and also contracting the scope of public sector. Therefore, there is urgent need of studying regional disparities at sectoral level as well as in overall economic development by applying suitable techniques and on the basis of large number of indicators of development, so that implications of New Economic Policy in this context should be examined.

A Profile and Background of the Study

Haryana became a state of India on November 1, 1966. The State comprises of 4 Divisions, 20 Districts, 67 Tehsils, 46 Sub-Tehsils, 119 Blocks, 106 Towns and 6995 Villages (as on 12.1.07). Bhiwani is the largest district according to area while the smallest is Panchkula. Population is the maximum in Faridabad and least in Panchkula. The total area of Haryana state is 44,212 sq. km and total population is 21144564 in 2001. The capital of Haryana is Chandigarh.

The present day Haryana is the region where, along the banks of the river Saraswati, the Vedic Civilisation began and matured. It was here that the Vedas were written, as the

Aryans chanted their sacred Mantras. Replete with myths and legends; Haryana's 5000 years old history is steeped in glory. It was here that 2nd battle of Panipat was fought and Krishna preached Bhagvad-Gita at the start of the battle of Mahabharat. It was the soil that saint Ved Vyas wrote Mahabharat in Sanskrit. It was the Mahabharat War, approximately in 900 BC, which gave to the region worldwide fame. Mahabharat knows Haryana as Bahudhanyaka, land of plentiful grains and Bahudhana, the land of immense riches. The word Haryana, occurs in a 1328 AD Sanskrit inscription kept in the Delhi museums which refers to the Haryana region as the heaven on earth.

The region has been the scene of many wars because of it being "The Gate way of North India." As years rolled by, successive streams of the Huns, the Turks and the Afghans invaded India and decisive battles were fought on this land. After the downfall of the Gupta empire in the middle of the 6th century AD, North India was again split into several independent kingdoms. The Huns established their supremacy over the Punjab. It was after this period that one of the greatest king of ancient India, Harshvardhan began his rule. He became the king of Thanesar (Kurukshetra) in 606 AD, and later went on to become the ruler of most of present day North India. In the 14th Century, the Tomar kings led an army through this region to Delhi.

Later the Mughal, Babur, defeated the Lodhis in the first battle of Panipat in the year 1526. Another decisive war was fought in Panipat in 1556, establishing the regime of the Mughals for centuries to come. Taking advantages of Humayun's death, Hemu had marched to Agra and Delhi and occupied it without difficulty. In response Bairam Khan (Akbar's guardian) marched towards Delhi. Both the armies clashed in the second battle of Panipat. Hemu was in a winning position when a stray arrow struck him in the eye. He feels unconscious causing panic among his troops. The tide of the battle turned and the Mughals won the battle. Towards the middle of the 18th century, the Marathas took control over

Haryana. The intrusion of Ahmed Shah Abdali in India culminated in the third battle of Panipat in 1761. Marathas' defeat in this battle marked the end of their ascendancy and the decline of the Mughal Empire leading to the advent of the British rule. In 1857, the people of Haryana, Joined the Indian leaders in the 1857 Revolt against the British Government. By the end of June, 1857, most of the present Haryana region was liberated from the British. But the British managed to put down the rebellion in November, 1857 by bringing in additional forces from outside the area.

The Haryana economy is dominated by the agricultural sector which contributes more than 50% to the state domestic product and nearly 80% of the total population drives its livelihood from agriculture in one way or other. As a result of the technological break through and infrastructure facilities build up by the state government, additional incomes are being generated in this sector of the state economy. It has been generally accepted that the average income of the farm household has gone up many times and consequently incomes of the other rural household has also gone up. As agriculture is the pivot of the state economy, it is quite important to analyse the cropping pattern various crops in various regions. area under different crops, productivity per hectare intensity of irrigation which leads to higher productivity, high yielding varieties, fertilizers, consumption of electricity etc.

Agriculture as a complex operation has been carried on in Haryana for ages but with change in eighties and nineties and its power in the economic life of the rural community and its contribution to the national food reserves after the new agricultural strategy needs little emphasis. The success of economic planning in the state for over four decades has been closely linked with the changing fortunes of agricultural productivity per unit area, efficiency irrigation etc. particularly after the so - called Green Revolution. Needless to say, the various agricultural development programmes, such as; Improvement in irrigation facilities for intensive agricultural land resources use; Use of exotic high - yielding seeds; Use of optimum qualities of fertilizers; Application of post - control methods; Multiplicity in Cropping; Development of intra - structural agricultural services; Soil and water management and conservation measure, i.e., efficient harvest of water crop; Agricultural extension programmers for the training in the use and application of modern farm technology and Emphasis on agricultural research and its application, to name a few, have been aimed at transforming traditional agriculture into modern agriculture in this area.

Share of Agriculture in the State Income

The level of economic development attained by a country or region depends upon the content and uses of its natural resources. In the words of W.A. Lewis "natural resources determine the course of development and constitute the challenge which may not be accepted by the human mind". In the state out of total land resources 86.99% is total cultivable area. Out of this cultivable area 212 thousand hectares is fallow land, 66 thousand hectares is uncultivable land excluding fallow land and the net areas sown is 3528 thousand hectares. Out of this net sown area, the area sown more than once is 2897 thousand hectares. The total cropped area in Haryana is 6425 thousand hectares. The total area under forests is only 1 percent of the total land area. Out of total land area of 44,21 sq.km. the area under forests is just 1149 sq.km. of this total area 59 percent exists only in two districts of Panchkula and Yamuna Nagar. It must be mentioned here that value of major forests produce in Haryana has shown a remarkable increase. In 1966-67 the total value of timber and firewood production was Rs. 21.49 lakhs which rose to Rs. 25.12 crores in 1999-2000.

In the last 42 years of Haryana existence agriculture has been the main source of state income. In 1970-71, agriculture contribution was Rs. 559.79 crores to state income (64.42 percent) out of total contribution of Rs. 562.73 crores (64.76 percent) of primary sector in the state income. In the year

2005-06 the contribution of agriculture has increased to Rs. 18988.08 crores in absolute terms. It still continues to be the largest contributor to the state income. Thus, one finds that the per capita income of Haryana increased from Rs. 427 in 1966-67 to Rs. 35044 in the year 2005-06 at current price.

The state of Haryana is not a land of tiny holdings as 25 percent of holding are in the size group of 2 to 5 hectares and 30 percent in the size group of 5 to 10 hectares. The Green Revolution benefited bigger holding more than smaller holdings, as bigger holdings, showed an income increase of 96 percent as compared to 36 percent on smaller holdings. Farming in north-east part of Haryana differs very much from that of south-west. North eastern part is commercially oriented but in the southern part there is subsistence dry farming. The regional variations in the patterns of distribution of natural agricultural factors and developed water supply alone may reflect a number of agricultural formations.

The areas having better rainfall and controlled irrigational facilities differ from the areas where rainfall is low (deficient) and uncertain. In the later case seasonal irrigational facilities are generally available to small proportion of the total cropped area. The future development of the potential water resources depends upon economic and political factors. The agricultural development in the rain fed areas would take a much longer time to stabilize at a higher level of production. Hence, the regional disparities, encountered in agricultural patterns and the varying level of agricultural productivity and developments are needed to be reorganized. The magnitude of difference in spatial distribution, association and agricultural formation, use of new technology in different regions or districts suitable soils and climate for the crop is varying in different regions.

The present study is confined to the area under principal crops in various regions, region wise, district wise production of principal crops, irrigation facilities from different sources and use of modern technology such as high-yielding varieties of seeds, fertilizers and other equipments etc. The agriculture development of Haryana was largely due to the introduction of new technology. The area under high yielding wheat from 2 percent in 1966-67 to 97 percent in 2004-05 and the area under high yielding rice increased from 0.2 percent to 68 percent. Due to the introduction of high yielding wheat and rice, the average yield of wheat increased from 1275 Kgs per hectare in 1966-67 to 3937 Kgs per hectare in 2004-05. The cropping intensity in Haryana increased from 1.22 per cent to 1.51 percent. Consumption of fertilizer per hectare, number of tractors increased from 4803 to 239814 in 2004-05. These factors contributed to the increase in agriculture productivity.

Conclusion

In conclusion there has been tried to analyses a broad spectrum of various issues related to the present study. In introductory part a brief analysis of development and regional disparities inter-relationship designed and in the continuation there has been tried to analysis the review of literature under the theme a lot of studies since beginning the 19th century to now from global to regional level reviewed that provide a support to the analysis in present work. In next segment there has been try to put a brief picture of Haryana state as its historical perspective or background, in this part an introductory analysis of different districts and the economic and social development and other related indications portrays in broad aspect to show the picture of the state at a glance. Thus these things collectively support to pave the appropriate way of further movement of the present work.

3

Agricultural Policy and Development Pattern in India

As we know, in the most of developing countries and particularly in India, agriculture is a way of life, a tradition, which, has shaped the thought, the outlook, the culture and the economic life of the people of India. Agriculture, therefore, is and will continue to be central to all strategies for planned socio-economic development of the country. Rapid growth of agriculture is essential not only to achieve self-reliance at national level but also for household food security and to bring about equity in distribution of income and wealth resulting in rapid reduction in poverty levels.

Since Independence, agriculture made rapid strides in India. In taking the annual food grains production from 51 million tonnes of the early fifties to 206 million tonnes at the turn of the century and it is 212 million tones in 2003-04, it has contributed significantly in achieving self sufficiency in food and in avoiding food shortages in our country. The pattern of growth of agriculture has, however, brought in its wake, uneven development, across regions and crops as also across different sections of farming community and is characterized by low levels of productivity and degradation of natural resources in some areas. Capital inadequacy, lack of infrastructural support and demand constraints such as controls on movement, storage and sale of agricultural products etc., have continued to affect the economic viability of agriculture sector. Consequently, the growth of agriculture has also tended to slacken during the nineties.

Over 400 million Indian farmers and farm workers have been the backbone of India's agriculture. Despite having achieved national food security the well being of the farming community continues to be a matter of grave concern for the planners and policy makers in the country. The establishment of an agrarian economy which ensures food and nutrition to India's billion people, raw materials for its expanding industrial base and surpluses for exports, and a fair and equitable reward system for the farming community for the services they provide to the society, will be the mainstay of reforms in the agriculture sector.

The Strategy for National Agriculture Policy

The national policy on agriculture seeks to actualise the vast untapped growth potential of Indian agriculture, strengthen rural infrastructure to support faster agricultural development, promote value addition, accelerate the growth of agro-business, create employment in rural areas, secure a fair standard of living for the farmers and agricultural workers and their families, discourage migration to urban areas and face the challenges arising out of economic liberalization and globalisation. Over the next two decades, it aims to attain markets and maximises benefits from exports of agricultural products in the face of the challenges arising from economic liberalisation and globalization. Growth that is sustainable technologically, environmentally and economically.

Sustainable Agriculture

The policy will seek to promote technically sound, economically viable, environmentally non-degrading, and socially acceptable use of country's natural resources land, water and genetic endowment to promote sustainable development of agriculture. Measures should be taken to contain biotic pressures on land and to control indiscriminate diversion of agricultural lands for non-agricultural purposes. The unutilized wastelands will be put to use for agriculture and aforestation. Particular attention will be given for increasing cropping intensity through multiple-cropping and inter-cropping.

The Government accords abiding importance to improving the quality of the country's land and soil resources. Reclamation of degraded and fallow lands as well as problem of soils gives high priority to optimize their productive use. Special emphasis laid on conserving soils and enriching their fertility. Management of land resources on watershed basis receives special attention. Areas of shifting cultivation receive a particular attention for their sustainable development. Integrated and holistic development of rain fed areas promoted by conservation of rain water by vegetative measures on watershed basis and augmentation of biomass production through agro and farm forestry with the involvement of the watershed community. All spatial components of a watershed, *i.e.*, arable land, no arable and drainage lines treated as one geo-hydrological entity. Management of grazing land receives greater attention for augmenting availability of animal feed and fodder. A long-term perspective plan for sustainable rain fed agriculture through watershed approach will be vigorously pursued for development of two thirds of India's cropped area which is dependent on rains.

Rational utilization and conservation of the country's abundant water resources promoted. Conjunctive use of surface and ground water will receive highest priority. Special attention will be focused on water quality and the problem of receding ground-water levels in certain areas as a result of over-exploitation of water resources for the optimum use of irrigation potential promoted. Use of in situ moisture management techniques such as mulching and use of micro overhead pressured irrigation systems like drip and sprinkler and green house technology encouraged for greater water use efficiency and improving productivity, particularly of horticultural crops. Emphasis will be placed on promotion of water harvesting structures and suitable water conveyance systems in the hilly and high rainfall areas for rectification of regional imbalances. Participatory community irrigation management will be encouraged.

Agro forestry and social forestry are prime requisites for maintenance of ecological balance and augmentation of bio-mass production in the agricultural systems. Agro-forestry receives a major thrust for efficient nutrient cycling, nitrogen fixation, organic matter addition and for improving drainage. Farmers encouraged taking up farm/agro-forestry for higher income generation by evolving technology, extension and credit support packages and removing technology, extension and credit support packages and removing constraints to development of agro and farm forestry. Involvement of farmers and landless laboures will be sought in the development of pastures/forestry programmes on public wastelands by giving financial incentives and entitlements of the usufructs of trees and pastures.

The history and traditional knowledge of agriculture, particularly of tribal communities, relating to organic farming and preservation and processing of food for nutritional and medicinal purposes is one of the oldest in the world. Concerted efforts will be made to pool, distill and evaluate traditional practices, knowledge and wisdom and to harness them for sustainable agricultural growth.

Food and Nutritional Security

Special efforts made to raise the productivity and production of crops to meet the increasing demand for food generated by unabated demographic pressures and raw materials for expanding agro-based industries. A regionally differentiated strategy pursued, taking into account the agronomic, climatic and environmental conditions to realize the full growth potential of every region. Special attention given to development of new crop varieties, particularly of food crops, with higher nutritional value through adoption of bio-technology particularly, genetic modification, while addressing bio-safety concerns.

Generation and Transfer of Technology

A very high priority accorded to evolving new location-specific and economically viable improved varieties of agricultural and horticultural crops, livestock species and aquaculture as also conservation and judicious use of germ plasma and other biodiversity resources. The regionalization of agricultural research, based on identified agro-climatic zones, will be accorded high priority. Application of frontier sciences like bio-technology, remote sensing technologies, pre and post harvest technologies, energy saving technologies, technology for environmental protection through national research system as well as proprietary research encouraged. The endeavour will be to build a well organized, efficient and result-oriented agriculture research and education system to introduce technological change in Indian agriculture up gradation of agricultural education and its orientation towards uniformity in education standards, women empowerment, user -orientation, vocationalization and promotion of excellence will be the hallmark of the new policy.

The research and extension linkages strengthened to improve quality and effectiveness of research and extension system. The extension system broad based and revitalized. Innovative and decentralized institutional changes will be introduced to make the extension system farmer-responsible and farmer-accountable. Role of Krishi Vigyan Kendras (KVKs), Non-Governmental organizations (NGOs), Farmers Organizations, Co-operatives, corporate sector and para-technicians in agricultural extension encouraged for organizing demand driven production systems. Development of human resources through capacity building and skill up gradation of public extension functionaries and other extension functionaries accorded a high priority. The Government endeavour to move towards a regime of financial sustainability of extension services through affecting in a phased manner. A more realistic cost recovery of extension services and inputs may be simultaneously safeguarding the interests of the poor and the vulnerable groups.

Inputs Management

Adequate and timely supply of quality inputs such as seeds, fertilizers, plant protection chemicals, bio-pesticides, agricultural machinery and credit at reasonable rates to farmers the endeavour of the Government. Soil testing and quality testing of fertilisers and seeds ensured and supply of spurious inputs will be checked. Balanced and optimum use of fertilizers will be promoted together with use of organic manures and bio-fertilizers to optimize the efficiency of nutrient use.

Development, production and distribution of improved varieties of seeds and planting materials and strengthening and expansion of seed and plan certification system with private sector participation receive a high priority. A National Seed Grid established to ensure supply of seeds especially to areas affected by natural calamities. The National Seeds Corporation (NSC) and State Farms Corporation of India (SFCI) restructured for efficient utilization of investment and manpower.

Protection to plant varieties through a sue generic legislation, granted to encourage research and breeding of new varieties particularly in the private sector in line with India's obligations under Trade Related Intellectual Property Rights (TRIPS) agreement. The farmers will, however, allowed their traditional rights to save, use, exchange, share and sell their farm saved seeds except as branded seeds of protected varieties for commercial purpose. The interests of the researchers also are safeguarded in carrying out research on proprietary varieties to develop new varieties.

Integrated pest management and use of biotic agents in order to minimize the indiscriminate and injudicious use of chemical pesticides can be the cardinal principle covering plant protection. Selective and eco-friendly farm mechanization through appropriate technology promoted, with special reference to rain fed farming to reduce arduous work and to make agriculture efficient and competitive as also to increase crop productivity.

Incentives for Agriculture

The Government endeavour to create a favourable economic environment for increasing capital formation and farmer's own investments by removal of distortions in the incentive regime for agriculture, improving the terms of trade with manufacturing sectors and bringing about external and domestic market reforms, backed by rationalization of domestic tax structure. It seek to bestow on the agriculture sector in as many respects as possible benefits similar to those obtaining in the manufacturing sector, such as easy availability of credit and other inputs, and infrastructure facilities for development of agri-business industries and development of effective delivery systems and freeing movement of agro produce.

Consequent upon dismantling of Quantitative Restrictions on imports as per WTO Agreement on Agriculture, Commodity-wise strategies and arrangements for protecting the grower from adverse impact of undue price fluctuations in world markets and for promoting exports formulated. Apart from price competition, other aspects of marketing such as quality, choice, health and bio-safety promoted. Exports of horticultural produce and marine products receive particular emphasis. A two-fold long-term strategy of diversification of agricultural produce and value addition enabling the production system to respond to external environment and creating export demand for the commodities produced in the country evolved with a view to providing the farmers incremental income from export earnings. A favourable economic environment and supportive public management system created for promotion of agricultural exports. Quarantine, both of exports and imports, will be given particular attention so that Indian agriculture can protect from the ingress of exotic pests and diseases.

In order to protect the interest of farmers in context of removal of Quantitative Restrictions, continuous monitoring of international prices undertaken and appropriate tariffs protection will be provided. Import duties on commodities used in agriculture rationalized. The domestic agricultural market liberalised and all controls and regulations hindering increase in farmers' income reviewed and abolished to ensure that agriculturists receive prices commensurate with their efforts, investment. Restrictions on the movement of agricultural commodities throughout the country progressively dismantled.

The structure of taxes on food grains and other commercial crops reviewed and rationalized. Similarly, the excise duty on materials such as farm machinery and implements, fertilizers, etc., used as inputs in agricultural production, post-harvest storage and processing reviewed. Appropriate measures will be adopted to ensure that agriculturists by and large remain outside the regulatory and tax collection systems. Farmers will be exempted from payment of capital gains tax on compulsory acquisition of agricultural land.

Investments in Agriculture

The Agriculture sector has been starved of capital. There has been a decline in the public sector investment in the agriculture sector. Public investment for narrowing regional imbalances, accelerating development of supportive infrastructure for agriculture and rural development particularly rural connectivity stepped up. A time-bound strategy for rationalisation and transparent pricing of inputs will be formulated to encourage judicious input use and to generate resources for agriculture. Input subsidy reforms pursued as a combination of price and institutional reforms to cut down costs of these inputs for agriculture. Resource allocation regime reviewed with a view to rechannelizing the available resources from support measures towards asset formation in rural sector.

An encouraging climate created through a favourable price and trade regime to promote farmers' own investments as also investments by industries producing inputs for agriculture and agro based industries. Private sector investments in agriculture also encouraged more particularly in areas like agricultural research, human resource development, post-harvest management and marketing. Rural electrification gives a high priority as a prime mover for agricultural development. The quality and availability of electricity supply will be improved and the demand of the agriculture sector will be met adequately in a reliable and cost effective manner. The use of new and renewable sources of energy for irrigation and other agricultural purposes also encouraged.

Setting up of agro-processing units in the producing areas to reduce wastage, especially of horticultural produce, increased value addition and creation of off-farm employment in rural areas will be encouraged. Collaboration between the producer co-operatives and the corporate sector will be encouraged to promote agro-processing industry. An interactive coupling between technology, economy, environment and society will be promote for speedy development of food and agro-processing industries and build up of a substantial base for production of value added agro-products for domestic and export markets with a strong emphasis on food safety and quality. The Small Farmers Agro Business Consortium (SFAC) will be energized to cater to the needs of farmer entrepreneurs and promote public and private investments in agri-business.

Institutional Structure

Indian agriculture is characterized by pre-dominance of small and marginal farmers. Institutional reforms so pursued as to channelize their energies for achieving greater productivity and production. The approach to rural development and land reforms has focus on the following areas.

Consolidation of holdings all over the country on the pattern of North Western States; Redistribution of ceiling surplus lands and waster lands among the landless farmers, unemployed youth with initial start up capital; Tenancy reforms to recognize the rights of the tenants and share croppers; Development of lease markets for increasing the size of the holdings by making legal provisions for giving private lands on lease for cultivation and agro business; Updating and improvement of land records, computerization and issue of land pass-books to the farmers and Recognition of women's rights in land. he rural poor increasingly involved in the implementation of land reforms with the help of Panchayati Raj Institution, Voluntary Groups, Social Activists and Community Leaders. Private sector participation promoted through contract farming and land leasing arrangements to allow accelerated technology transfer, capital inflow and assured and horticultural crops.

Progressive institutionalization of rural and farm credit will be continued for providing timely and adequate credit to farmers. The rural credit institutions geared to promote savings, investments and risk management. Particular attention paid to removal of distortions in the priority sector lending by Commercial Banks for agriculture and rural sectors. Progressive institutionalization of rural and farm credit continued for providing timely and adequate credit to farmers. The rural credit institutions geared to promote savings, investments and risk management. Particular attention will be paid to removal of distortions in the priority sector lending by Commercial Banks for agriculture and rural sectors. Special measures take for revamping of co-operatives to remove the institutional and financial weaknesses and evolving simplified procedure for sanction and disbursement of agriculture credit. The endeavors ensure distribution equity in the disbursement of credit. Micro credit promoted as an effective tool for alleviating poverty. Self Help Group-Bank linkage system, suitable to Indian rural sector, developed as a supplementary mechanism for bringing the rural poor into the formal banking system, thereby improving banks outreach and the credit flows to the poor in an effective and sustainable manner.

The basic support to agriculture has been provided by the co-operative sector assiduously built over the years. The Government will provide active support for the promotion of co-operative form of enterprise and ensure greater autonomy and operational freedom to them to improve their functioning. There need to stress on structural reforms to promote greater efficiency and viability and free them from excessive, Creation of infrastructure and human resource development, Improvement in financial viability and organizational sustainability of co-operatives, Democratization of management and increased professionalism in their operations and creating a viable inter-face with other grass-root organizations.

The Legislative and regulatory framework should appropriately amended and strengthened to achieve these objectives.

Risk Management

Despite technological and economic advancements, the condition of farmers continues to be unstable due to natural calamities and price fluctuations. National Agriculture Insurance Scheme covering all farmers and all crops throughout the country with built-in provisions for insulating farmers from financial distress caused by natural disasters and making agriculture financially viable made more farmer-specific and effective. Endeavour will be made to provide a package insurance policy for the farmers, right from sowing of the crops to post-harvest operations, including market fluctuations in the prices of agricultural produce.

In order to reduce risk in agriculture and impart greater resilience to Indian agriculture against droughts and floods, efforts made for achieving greater flood proofing of flood prone agriculture and drought proofing of rain fed agriculture for protecting the farmers from vagaries of nature. For this purpose, contingency agriculture planning, development of drought and flood resistant crop varieties, watershed development programmes, drought prone areas and desert development programmes and rural infrastructure development produce through announcement of Minimum Support Prices Policy for major agricultural commodities. The food, nutrition and other domestic and exports requirements of the country kept in view while determining the support prices of different commodities. The price structure and trade mechanism continuously reviewed to ensure a favourable economic environment for the agriculture sector and to bring about an equitable balance between the rural and the urban incomes. The methodology used by the Commission on Agricultural Costs & Prices (CACP) in arriving at estimates of costs of production periodically reviewed. The price structure of both inputs and outputs monitored to ensure higher returns to the farmers and bring about cost effectiveness throughout the economy. Domestic market prices closely monitored to prevent distress sales by the farmers. Public and co-operative agencies undertaking marketing operations strengthened.

The Government enlarges the coverage of futures markets to minimize the wide fluctuations in commodity prices as also for hedging their risks. The endeavour should be to cover all important agricultural products under futures trading in course of time.

Management Reforms

Effective implementation of policy initiatives call for comprehensive reforms in the management of agriculture by the Central and the State Government. The Central Government supplement/complement the State Governments' efforts through regionally differentiated Work Plans, comprising crop/area/target group specific interventions, formulated in an inter-active mode and implemented in a spirit of partnership with the States. The Central Government move away from schematic approach to Macro-Management mode and assume a role of advocacy, articulation and facilitation to help the States in their efforts towards achieving accelerated agriculture development.

The Governmental focus on quality aspects at all stages of farm operations from sowing to primary processing. The quality of inputs and other support services to farmers and agro processors created. Grading and standardization of agricultural products promoted for export enhancement. Application of science and technology in agriculture promoted through a regular system of interface between science and technology institutions and the user/potential users, to make the sector globally competitive.

The database for the agriculture sector strengthened to ensure greater reliability of estimates and forecasting which can help in the process of planning and policy making. Efforts made to significantly improve harness latest remote sensing and information technology to capture data, collate it, add value and disseminate it to appropriate destinations for managing the risk and in accelerating the growth process. The objectives to engage in a meaningful continuous dialogue with the external environment in the changing scenario and to have on-line and real time system of Agriculture on line capacity to analyze the signals emanating from the farms and the markets for the benefit of the farmers.

The Government of India as well as states trust that this statement of National Agriculture Policy receive the fullest support of all sections of the people and lead to sustainable development of agriculture, create gainful employment on a self sustaining basis in rural areas, raise standards of living for the farming communities, preserve environment and serve as a vehicle for building a resurgent national economy or the states economies.

National Scenario of Agriculture Development

The agriculture performance in India during 1950-51to1964-65 was mostly, an account of the expansion in cultivated area and on account of regional specialization requiring little investment resources, The trend of rate of growth of output was high with fluctuations (Vaidyanathan and Minhas, 1988; Chakaravarty, 1986). The faster growth during the First Five Year Plan had led to relative de-emphasizing of agriculture in terms of public investment in the Second Five Year Plan. This suggests that the planners considered agriculture sector as the bargain sector with large unexploited potential and the one which could provide the requisite agricultural surplus with a relatively short time lag, after putting a certain minimum infrastructure in place (Chakaravarty, 1984). However, subsequently, there was a fall in the agricultural output level and also there was greater output instability. It was increasingly being felt at that time that agricultural sector's unsatisfactory performance is operating as the binding constraint on the smooth growth of the industrial sector as well as the rest of the economy. This led to adoption of the green revolution technology.

During the period 1967-68 to 2004-05 the green revolution strategy aimed at rapid technology modernization of Indian agriculture by deliberately concentrating investments in crops and regions where returns were expected to be relatively higher and certain. As the exclusive emphasis of this strategy was on rising yield per cropped hectare through the intensification of inputs, the focus of agricultural development inevitably shifted to the developed regions and to the resources of rich farmers (Rao 1994). The bulk of the increase in agricultural output as a result of application of new technology has been concentrated in a small geographic area of Punjab, Haryana, parts of Utter Pradesh, Maharashtra, Gujarat, West Bengal, and Karnataka. The spread of new technology consisting of water seed-fertilizer was to be achieved through a policy package. This was done with the dual objectives of maintaining farm prices at affordable levels while ensuring that producers did not suffer on account of volatility in output prices and/or high input prices. However, the growth of output (Table-3.1) was a result of mainly; the increase in yield per hectare; change in the composition of gross cropped area (GCA) in favour of commercial crops and the regional technologically dynamic changes in the eighties to the eastern and central regions of the country. The period 1967 - 68 to 1979 - 80 was characterized by a slow down in the growth rates of GDP primarily as a result of reduced public and private investment. During this period, GDP grew at only 3.45 per cent per annum and the per capita income growth 1.11 per cent as compared with growth rates 4.00 per cent and 1.69 per cent per annum respectively during 1950-51 to 1964-65. There was a slow down in the growth rates of all the major sectors of the economy.

Table-3.1
Annual Growth Rates of Indian Agriculture

Year	*Agriculture Output*
1951-56	3.12
1956-61	3.17
1961-66	0.18
1966-69	8.02
1969-74	0.50
1974-79	4.82
1979-80	-14.34
1980-85	4.21
1985-90	5.01
1990-91	4.05
1991-92	-2.65
1992-93	6.41
1993-94	3.70
1994-95	4.45
1995-96	4.45
1996-97	10.48
1997-98	-3.54
1998-99	5.61
1999-00	2.87
2000-01	-6.20
2001-02	8.23
2002-03	-17.85
2003-04	22.54
2004-05	-7.07

Source: Computed from Various issues of Economic Survey and the Economic Survey 2005-06.

Gross product from agriculture recorded a growth of only 2.1 per cent per annum and agricultural output grew at 2.73 per cent per annum. In agriculture, a major development was the introduction of new Bureau seed- fertilizer technology during the mid sixties. To begin with, the new technology was confined to only the north-western states of India and to wheat production. But in the early seventies new varieties of rice were also successfully introduced not only in Punjab and Haryana but also in the coastal areas in the south. Even then, the spread of new technology remained limited to only a few regions of India. Because of this and because of persistent droughts and slow growth rates in the rain fed central and eastern regions, agricultural output recorded a growth rate of nearly 2.7 per cent per annum during 1967-68 to 1979-80 compared with a growth rates of 3.2 per cent per annum achieved during the previous period. This period saw two severe droughts, which, triggered major crises in the Indian economy. One of the important developments during the mid-sixties was the technological breakthrough in agriculture in the northwestern region which resulted in significant increase in agricultural output and income. But, the regional spread of technological revolution was highly uneven and this led to significant increases in the inter-state variations in the level and growth of agricultural output over this period.

In the green revolution belt, along with increase in output, total employment in agriculture increased at a rapid rate despite the introduction of labor, saving machinery. Rapid agricultural growth also led to a more rapid growth of manufacturing in agro-processing and consumer goods industries and in services and other tertiary sector through input, output and consumption linkages. More important, rapid agricultural growth succeeded in increasing the income levels of a large number of agricultural workers and thereby made a big dent in rural poverty in the green revolution areas. Nevertheless, one of the perplexing questions which remained unanswered is as to why despite high agricultural led growth for about a decade, the north western states failed to take off and to transform their economic structure?

Again during 1980-85 to 1990-91 compared in the growth rates of 4.5 percent per annum and after 1991-92 to 1996-97 the annual growth was probably near to earlier situation. However, during 1997-98 to 2004-05 there emerged a critical situation of agriculture sector and the annual growth rates decline from earlier level or may be negative. This period is probably stagnant phase or there slight decline in agriculture sector is remains concern. No doubt in 11th plan document government special stress on agricultural sector development to maintain the earlier record of growth rates.

Area, Production and Productivity

The seed-fertiliser technology introduced during the mid-1960s was originally primarily confined to wheat and rice. Later on, the new tech-no- logy was also successfully applied to some other crops like coarse cereals, oilseeds, cotton and sugar-cane. As a consequence of differential increase in yield levels and changes in relative prices, different crops have grown at different rates in most states. Table 3.2 gives details about growth of area, yield and out-put' of major crops in India during 1949-50 to 2004-05. The table shows that over the period 1949-50 to 2004-05, the highest growth rate in yield and output was recorded by wheat followed by cotton, oilseeds, rice, coarse cereals and sugarcane. The lowest growth rate in yield and output was recorded by pulses.

Area allocation among various crops has shown a measure of struc-tural rigidity that reflects the traditional character of Indian agriculture wherein foodgrains remain the predominant crop. Although the intro-duction of new technology did make some dent in this pattern, the impact was not significant till the beginning of the 1980s. It is only during the period 1980-83 to 2004-05 that many important changes took place in the cropping pattern in India.

During 1964-65 to 1990-91, for India as a whole, gross cropped area increased from 157.7 million hectares in 1964-65 to 174.5 million hectares in 1990-91. Foodgrains, which

Table-3.2
All India Compound Growth Rates of Area Production and Productivity of Major Crops

Crop	*1949-50 to1964-65*			*1967-68 to1980-81*			*1980-81to 1990-91*			*1990-91to 1998-99*			*1998-99 to 2004-05*		
	A	*P*	*Y*	*A*	*P*	*Y*	*A*	*P*	*Y*	*A*	*P*	*Y*	*A*	*P*	*Y*
Rice	1.21	3.5	2.25	0.77	2.22	1.46	0.53	3.76	3.21	0.53	1.81	1.27	-0.80	-0.43	0.37
Wheat	2.69	3.96	1.27	2.94	5.65	2.62	0.51	3.68	3.15	1.70	3.30	1.58	-0.48	-0.39	5.24
Coarse Cereals	0.90	2.25	1.23	–	–	–	--	--	--	-2.12	0.18	2.09	0.12	1.19	1.06
T. Cereals	1.25	3.21	1.77	0.37	2.61	1.70	-0.21	3.02	3.25	0.05	2.00	1.51	-0.54	-0.20	0.34
T. Pulses	1.72	1.41	-0.18	0.44	-0.4	-0.67	0.23	1.87	1.63	-0.14	0.81	0.55	-0.58	-1.54	0.97
Food grain	1.35	2.82	1.36	0.38	2.15	1.33	-0.13	3.04	2.82	0.05	1.86	1.39	-0.55	-0.30	0.25
Sugarcane	3.28	4.26	0.95	1.78	2.6	0.8	1.87	3.27	1.37	1.37	2.87	1.23	-1.37	0.82	-1.46
Oilseeds	2.67	3.2	0.3	0.26	0.98	0.68	2.85	5.99	3.06	1.51	2.83	1.60	0.38	-0.44	-0.83
Cotton	2.47	4.55	2.04	0.07	2.61	2.54	-0.96	3.15	4.15	3.25	3.06	0.18	-0.71	3.95	4.71
All Crops	1.58	3.15	1.21	0.51	2.19	1.28	0.26	3.46	2.65	0.37	2.38	1.37	-0.42	-1.52	-1.10

A = Area ; P = Production ; Y = Productivity

Source: GOI, Area and production of principal crops in India, Various Issues, Agricultural Statistics at a glance, Ministry of Agriculture, 2005-06.

accounted for 77.85 per cent of cropped area in 1964-65, still claimed 76.63 per cent of area during 1990-91. Not only that, the share of foodgrains in the total value of crop output (at 1993-94 prices), which was 60.02 per cent during 1962-65, was nearly constant at 60.27 per cent during 1990-91. There was hardly any diversification away from foodgrains. The new technology intro-duced during the mid-1960s failed to diversify the cropping pattern since it was also primarily confined to wheat and rice. But there were important cropping pattern changes within foodgrains at the all-India level as well as at the state level. The most important change was that because of significant yield and relative price advantages, during 1962-65 to 1990-91, at the all-India level, the area under wheat registered a phenomenal increase and its share in total cropped area increased from 8.92 per cent to 13.68 per cent. In contrast, the share of coarse cereals and pulses recorded a notable decline. There was hardly much change in area under rice at the all-India level, which hovered around 24 per cent of cropped area. During the time period 1990-91 to 2004-05 the results of area, production and productivity has not shown a considerable improvement during this time period 1990-91 to 1998-99. There is overall decline in area, production and productivity during 1999-2000 to 2004-05 the growth rate result became negative. That's why, the agriculture development position, particularly in second generation reforms period became drastic and it is matter of serious concern and there is need to revise the policy on priority level by policy makers.

State-wise Agricultural Development

Table 3.3, which gives levels and growth of aggregate crop output at the state level during 1962-65 to 2004-05, brings out several interesting features of the regional pattern of agricultural development in India since the mid-1960s. The 1962-2005 period has been divided into four sub-periods, namely 1962-65 over 1970-73 (1st Period), 1970-73 over 1980-83 (IInd Period), 1983-83 over 1992-95 (IIIrd Period) and

1996-99 over 2003-05 (IV period). Levels and growth rates have been worked out by taking triennium aver-ages for 1962-65, 1970-73, 1980-83, 1990-93, 1996-99 and 2003-05.

The new agricultural technology introduced during the mid-1960s led to significant growth in agricultural output. Despite considerable inter-state variations, most states shared the gains of the new technology. Taking the entire period 1962-65 to 2003-05, total agricultural output in India at constant 1993-94 prices increased at a compound annual growth rate of 2.11 per cent. During this period, the highest output growth rate of 2.19 per cent per annum was recorded by the north-western region of India, followed by the central and southern regions. The lowest growth rate of 1.6 per cent was registered by the highly populated eastern region. There were important changes during the various sub-periods in the pattern of agricultural development. During the first phase of the Green Revolution, that is from 1962-65 to 1970-73, the new technology was confined to wheat and the main beneficiaries were the irrigated north-western states of India, in particular Punjab, Haryana and western Uttar Pradesh. Another state that benefited from the wheat revolution was West Bengal. The new technology had hardly any impact on rice. The main food grain crop (rice) growing eastern and southern states were not able to derive appreciable gains from the new technology.

The southern states of Karnataka, Kerala and Tamil Nadu also registered medium to high growth, but in their case the new technology made appre-ciable contributions only in limited areas. Crop output in the dry rainfed states in the central region was hardly influenced by new technology and agricultural production in that region was characterised by sharp weather induced year-to-year fluctuations. While Rajasthan recorded a very high growth rate of 4.29 per cent, Maharasthra recorded a negative growth rate of 3.64 per cent with Gujarat and Madhya Pradesh recording a positive but low growth rate of nearly 2 per cent per annum. Since only a few states were able to derive substantial gains from the new

Table-3.3
State Wise Growth Rates of Agricultural Output, 1962-65, 1970-73, 1980-83, 1990-93, 1998-99 and 2004-05

State	*1970-73 over 1962-65*	*1980-83 over 1970-73*	*1990-93 over 1980-83*	*1996-99 over 1990-93*	*2004-05 over 1996-99*
Haryana	4.65	3.02	5.04	1.98	1.32
Himachal Pradesh	3.33	0.96	2.74	-0.11	-0.21
Jammu&Kashmir	5.37	3.47	0.17	0.49	-0.53
Punjab	6.63	4.74	4.22	0.73	1.55
Uttar Pradesh	2.54	2.77	3.06	2.47	-0.12
North-West Region	3.60	3.21	3.55	1.91	0.53
Assam	1.85	2.80	2.42	1.31	1.13
Bihar	1.12	-0.41	2.12	3.33	-1.33
Orissa	0.99	2.65	2.92	-5.14	0.29
West Bengal	2.37	0.68	5.97	2.99	1.43
Eastern Region	1.57	1.09	3.63	1.25	0.37
Gujarat	1.78	3.12	0.86	6.83	-0.83
Madhya Pradesh	1.97	1.28	4.53	3.86	-0.60
Maharasthra	-3.64	6.57	2.12	3.29	-0.75
Rajasthan	4.27	1.26	6.06	4.90	-0.70
Central Region	0.73	3.13	3.33	4.50	-0.93
Andhra Pradesh	0.93	3.61	3.42	1.52	-0.12
Karnataka	2.64	2.32	3.68	3.62	-1.75
Kerala	4.09	-0.91	1.92	3.60	-1.94
Tamil Nadu	2.67	-0.57	4.00	3.25	-8.44
Southern Region	2.40	1.38	3.43	2.19	-1.81
All States	**2.08**	**2.38**	**3.44**	**2.83**	**-0.13**

Source: GOI, Area and Production of Principal Crops in India, Various Issues, Ministry of Agriculture and Statistical Abstract of India 2005-06.

technology, regional inequalities were accentuated during this period. During the IInd period 1970-73 over 1980-83 and IIIrd period 1980-83 over 1992-95 the agricultural development and output growth rate shown overall and improvement probably in all states as per table 3.3. In the IVth period from 1996-99 over 2003-05, the agriculture development situation and growth rates in different states in probably stagnant or slight decline. This is an unsatisfactory picture of agriculture development while the government has started the IInd phase of liberalization and globalization. Thus the new economy policy benefits not occur up to now in the pocket of agriculture sector. No doubt, in 11th plan government made special efforts to development of agriculture sector to achieve the target overall higher growth rate of Indian economy.

State wise Productivity and Growth of NSDP in Agriculture

There is a clear evidence of sharp deceleration in agricultural growth at the all-India level. However, due to very large inter state variations in the agricultural aspects of various states; it is pertinent to look at the state level growth scenario. The level of agriculture productivity, measured by value added in agricul-ture (crop and livestock) per hectare of net sown area, and, growth rate in net state domestic product (NSDP) agriculture during 1984-85 to 1995-96 (refereed as period I) and 1995-96 to 2004-05 (referred as period II) are presented in (Table 3.4). States are arranged in an ascending order of productivity during mid-1990s. Per hectare productivity during the mid-1980s was highest in Kerala closely followed by West Bengal. Jammu and Kashmir ranked third and Punjab ranked fourth. The lowest level of agricultural productivity was recorded in Rajasthan, followed by Madhya Pradesh. Maharashtra ranked third from bottom with per hectare productivity of Rs 2,863 which was just 58 per cent of all-India average.

Ranking of various states based on the productivity witnessed profound changes during next 10 years after 1984-85 because of variations in the growth rate of NSDP agriculture. It is in-teresting to note that the two states, namely, Rajasthan and Maharashtra, which were among the bottom three states in term of level of productivity in mid-1980s, topped in the growth rate of NSDP agriculture during 1984-85 to 1995-96. These states recorded 5.52 and 6.66 per cent annual growth rate in value added in agriculture during Period I. Another low productivity state which witnessed more than 5 per cent annual growth in output during the first period was Gujarat. All the states except Orissa which had productivity lower than the national average, witnessed a higher growth in productivity as compared to the national average during 1984-85 to 1995-96. This shows that the growth experience during the decade before 1995-96 favoured agriculturally underdeveloped states more than the other states.

Agriculturally developed states, in terms of productivity, namely Punjab and West Bengal, also witnessed a reasonably high growth in output during 1984-85 to 1995-96. However, the growth rate in Kerala was just close to the national average. Haryana wit-nessed a relatively high growth (4.60 per cent) in this period Agricultural output in Tamil Nadu also increased at a high rate between mid-1980s and mid-1990s. This decade turned out to be very adverse for Orissa and Bihar (including Jharkhand) both of which witnessed very high year to year fluctuations in agricultural output with a negative growth rate.

High growth rates in NSDP agriculture during 1984-85 to 1995-96 helped West Bengal and Punjab maintain their lead in agricultural productivity towards the mid-1990s. But Rajasthan, despite a high growth rate during the first period, remained at the bottom in agricultural productivity. On the other hand, Kerala maintained the top position despite a relatively moderate growth rate.

The growth experience of the decade after 1995-96 is very different than that of the previous decade. It turned adverse for most of the states. The most affected state was Kerala, where the NSDP in agriculture shows an annual decline of 3.54 percent. This relegated Kerala from top position to fifth position in productivity per unit of land. The other states to witnessed a declining trend in NSDP agriculture during 1995-96 -2004-05 were Tamil Nadu and Madhya Pradesh (both new Madhya Pradesh and Chhattisgarh).

After witnessing a growth rate of 6.66 per cent during 1984-85 to 1995-96, Maharashtra's NSDP in agriculture remained almost stagnant during the next 10 years. Similar

Table 3.4
Level of Aggregate Productivity and Growth in NSDP (Agriculture) in the States

State	*NSDP Ag/Ha NSA at Current Prices*			*Trend Growth Rate in NS DP Agri at 1993-94 Prices*	
	1984-85 and 1985-86	*1994-95 and 1995-96*	*2003-04 and 2004-05*	*1984-85 to 1995-96*	*1995-96 to 2004-05*
Rajasthan	2264	7912	13984	5.52	0.30
Chhattisgarh		8586	13013		-0.91
Madhya Pradesh (old)	2319	9406	16745	3.63	-0.23
Madhya Pradesh (new)		9667	17939		-0.05
Maharashtra	2863	12712	19375	6.66	0.10
Orissa	4168	13499	26115'	-1.18	0.11
Gujarat	3748	14175	26404	5.09	0.48
Kamataka	3496	14481	19842	3.92	0.03
All-India	4973	17763	34349	3.62	1.85
Bihar (new)		18622	28915		2.82
Bihar (old)	6654	18743	32654	-1.71	3.51
Jharkhand		19124	44727		5.39
Andhra Pradesh	4478	20204	40653	3.18	2.69
Uttar Pradesh (new)		20413	39811		1.91
Uttar Pradesh (old)	5863	20896	40426	2.82	1.87
Assam	6617	23283	40671	1.65	0.95
Tamil Nadu	5338	24228	36677	4.95	-1.36
Himachal Pradesh	6561	25270	71775	1.64	3.51
Haryana	6672	26604	48154	4.60	1.98
Jammu and Kashmir	8736	30554	69113	2.18	3.25
Uttranchal		31296	53743		1.36
West Bengal	9499	34863	72295	4.63	2.67
Punjab	8467	35417	66864	4.00	2.16
Kerala	9564	38370	56341	3.60	-3.54

Sources: (1) State Domestic Product (State Series), Central Statistical Organisation, GOI, New Delhi, various issues. (2) Agricultural Statistics at a Glance, 2005-06. Ministry of Agriculture, GOI, New Delhi.

was the expe-rience of Orissa, where agricultural output remained almost stag-nant even after witnessing a negative growth during 1984-85 to 1995-96. Except Bihar, Jammu and Kashmir and Himachal Pradesh, all other states showed a deceleration in growth of NSDP agriculture after 1995-96. Agriculturally developed states like West Bengal and Punjab had been able to maintain a growth rate higher than the national average during 1995-96 to 2004-05. However, agriculturally underdeveloped states like Rajasthan, Maharashtra, Karnataka, Gujarat, Orissa and Madhya Pradesh witnessed a less than 0.50 per cent growth rate after 1995-96, which was very low initself and as compared to national average of 1.85 per cent.

The growth experience of the two periods shows that before 1995-96 the growth rate of agriculture in most of low productivity states was much higher than the national average and after 1995-96 their growth rates not only declined, but also turned out to be much lower than the national average.

Factors Affecting to Agricultural Development

Area under irrigation and use of fertiliser and electric power show a moderate to high increase in various states during the first period (1985-86 to 1995-96). The only exception to this was the use of power in agriculture in Himachal Pradesh. Net sown area in all the states either showed an increase or a stagnation, except in Bihar and Himachal Pradesh, which showed a slight decline during 1985-86 to 1995-96. During the second period, i e, 1995-96 to 2003-04 input use in most of the states either declined or increased at a slower rate as compared to the first period, with a few exceptions (Table 3.5).

After 1995-96, net sown area showed a decline in all the states except Bihar, Jammu and Kashmir and Punjab. The decline was more than 2 per cent per annum in Tamil Nadu and more than half a per cent in Orissa, Andhra Pradesh, Madhya Pradesh, Karnataka and Kerala. Net sown area

Table 3.5
Growth Rate of Factors Affecting to Agricultural Development

State	*Period*	*Net sown area*	*Irrigated area (percent)*	*NPK (Fertilizer)*	*Power consumption inagriculture*	*Change in crop pattern (%)*
Andhra	1985-86 to 1995-96	0.11	1.85	7.01	15.52	16.4
Pradesh	1995-96 to 2003-04	-0.71	-1.70	0.03	4.18	9.9
Assam	1985-86 to 1995-96	0.22	0.00	10.36	16.99	5.3
	1995-96 to 2003-04	-0.03	0.00	'19.92	NAC	4.8
Bihar	1985-86 to 1995-96	-0.54	1.37	2.40	4.44	5.7
	1995-96 to 2003-04	0.26	0.58	0.79	-4.33	3.2
Gujarat	1985-86 to 1995-96	-0.01	3.62	6.84	17.92	14.3
	1995-96 to 2003-04	-0.19	0.63	-0.74	5.36	8.7
Haryana	1985-86to1995-96	0.06	2.30	7.18	11.41	15.9
	1995-96 to 2003-04	-0.37	1.67	3.37	4.26	9.4
Himachal	1985-86 to 1995-96	-0.26	0.23	1.76	-6.83	4.0
Pradesh	1995-96 to 2003-04	-0.31	0.51	5.31	8.75	3,0
Jammu and	1985-86 to 995-96	0.14	0.71	2.95	17.83	3.8
Kashmir	1995-96 to 2003-04	0.29	0.14	4.14	-16.68	5.2
Kamataka	1985-86 to 1995-96	0.13	3.51	4.89	18.00	15.0
	1995-96 to 2003-04	-0.68	0.28	3.22	1.74	11.0
Kerala	1985-86 to 1995-96	0.27	1.31	2.52	10,48	8.5
	1995-96 to 2003-04	-0.50	-0.57	-0.26	-8,16	8.0

Table 3.5 continued

Table 3.5 continued

State	*Period*	*Net sown area*	*Irrigated area (percent)*	*NPK (Fertilizer)*	*Power consump-tion inagriculture*	*Change in crop pattern (%)*
Madhya	1985-86 to 1995-96	0.30	7.46	6.93	28.49	13.1
Pradesh	1995-96 to 2003-04	-0.67	1.50	-4.66	-7.72	7.3
Maharashtra	1985-86 to 1995-96	-0.11	3.36	8.11	13.62	10.4
	1995-96 to 2003-04	-0.28	2.43	2.48	-5.73	11.1
Orissa	1985-86 to 1995-96	0.10	2.08	5.10	16.92	23.1
	1995-96 to 2003-04	-0.80	-1.06	2.84	-7.03	7.7
Punjab	1985-86 to 1995-96	-0.05	1.26	1.58	7.66	10.3
	1995-96 to 2003-04	0.30	0.65	1.82	-0.73	6.6
Rajasthan	1985-86 to 1995-96	1.68	4.92	12.29	11.56	10.7
	1995-96 to 2003-04	-0.23	-0.89	-2.35	-1.19	10.5
Tamil Nadu	1985-86 to 1995-96	0.02	1.64	2.04	9.63	12.5
	1995-96 to 2003-04	-2.09	-3.01	-0.41	4.92	18.0
Uttar Pradesh	1985-86 to 1995-96	0.08	3.16	3.45	9.09	8.1
	1995-96 to 2003-04	0.05	1.41	2.65	-10.06	7.7
West Bengal	1985-86 to 1995-96	0.11	2.93	4.99	27.35	9.5
	1995-96 to 2003-04	0.00	NAC	4.38	-7.05	4.7
All-India	**1985-86 to 1995-96**	**0.29**	**2.91**	**5.20**	**13.36**	**7.9**
	1995-96 to 2003-04	**-0.46**	**0.68**	**2.10**	**-0.46**	**5.1**

NAC: Not available or not comparable.

Sources:

(1) Land Use Statistics at a Glance, Directorate of Economics and Statistics, Department of Agriculture and Cooperation, Ministry of Agriculture, Government of India, New Delhi.

(2) Agricultural Statistics at a Glance, Ministry of Agriculture, Government of India, New Delhi.

remained stagnant in Uttar Pradesh and in West Bengal. Area under irrigation followed a sharp decline in Andhra Pradesh, Tamil Nadu, Orissa, Rajasthan and Kerala. The magnitude of decline varied between 0.57 and 3.01 per cent per annum.

Expansion of irrigation slowed down in all the states. Use of fertiliser declined at more than 4.6 per cent in Madhya Pradesh. Other states which recorded a decline in fertiliser use were Rajasthan, Tamil Nadu and Gujarat. Only four states, namely, Assam, Himachal Pradesh, Jammu and Kashmir and Punjab showed higher growth in fertiliser after 1995-96 as compared to the period between 1985-86 and 1995-96. All the remaining states show lower growth in fertiliser after 1995-96 as compared to the previous decade. Power supply to agriculture witnessed a setback after 1995-96 in all the states except Himachal Pradesh which showed close to 9 per cent growth rate in power supplied to agriculture. States like Bihar, Jammu and Kashmir, Kerala, Madhya Pradesh, Maharashtra, Orissa, Rajasthan, Uttar Pradesh and West Bengal experienced a decline in power supply to agriculture while the remaining states witnessed lower growth rate of power supply in the second period.

Pace of crop diversification slowed down in all the states except Tamil Nadu and Maharashtra. The pace of diversification remained high in Rajasthan and Andhra Pradesh though it was lower compared to 1985-86 to 1995-96. It is interesting to observe that even high level of diversification in Tamil Nadu, Maharashtra and Rajasthan did not help in maintaining the tempo of growth in these states. We tried to explore this further, and from the secondary data, it seems as if farmers in these states are shifting crop pattern away from cash crops to low value crops. The reason for this could be a stress on water resources and high level of market risk associated with high value crops. However, this needs further probing.

Options for Revival of Agricultural Development

Some of the important causes for slowdown and poor growth of agriculture are obvious from the results discussed above. Most of the states have witnessed either a slowdown in growth or a negative growth in the area under irrigation, application of fertiliser, use of electric power used in agriculture and cropping intensity. Even the net cultivated area is also showing a decline in some of the states. Agricultural diversification, which is generally considered as a shift in resources from low value crops to high value crops, also shows a slowdown after 1995-96. In some places diversification seems to be moving in a reverse direction - with crop pattern shifting to low value crops. In order to find pragmatic options to revive agricultural growth, it is pertinent to explore the possibilities of raising level of factors associated with growth from their current level, which is presented in Table 3.5.

Despite progress in irrigation, the level of crop intensity continues to be quiet low in most of the states. In Andhra Pradesh, Karnataka, Tamil Nadu, Madhya Pradesh, Maharashtra, Gujarat and Rajasthan more than one crop is taken on less than 30 per cent of area under cultivation. This shows there is con-siderable scope to raise output through an expansion of area under double cropping.

Fertiliser use in the recent years is as low as 28 kg per/ hectare in Assam and as High as 328 kg per/hectare of net sown area in Punjab. Similarly, fertiliser use is below 40 kg per hectare in Rajasthan and Madhya Pradesh, and55 kg in Orissa. Increasing fertiliser use is a significant option for raising agricultural output in most of the states. Elasticity of crop output with respect to fertiliser use is estimated to vary between 0.134 and 0.700 in various states. Consumption of electric power per hectare was just 9 kWh in Assam, 30 kwh in Orissa and only 34 kwh. in Himachal Pradesh. Electric power used in agriculture varies between 80 and 300 kwh. in Kerala, Jammu and Kashmir, Bihar, Madhya Pradesh, West

Bengal, UP and Rajasthan, whereas it exceeded 1,000 kwh. in Andhra Pradesh, Gujarat, Haryana, Punjab and Tamil Nadu. Increase in electric supply to agriculture is important for promoting irrigation and thus raising output.

The coverage of irrigation in various states varies from 14-97 per cent. As can be seen from Table 3.6, there is a large gap between the current level and the ultimate irrigation potential except in the case of Punjab, Haryana and Rajasthan which have already exceeded the potential irrigation level. Bihar has water resources to extend irrigation to entire gross cropped area, with a further scope to provide irrigation to expansion in gross cropped area through an increased cropping intensity. Similarly, Uttar Pradesh has the potential to raise the level of irrigation to 95 per cent from the present level of 68.4 per cent, In Orissa and Assam irrigation can be extended to more than two-thirds of cropped area, whereas at present this facility is available to less than 27 per cent area. Elasticity of crop output with respect to irrigation is estimated to vary between 0.303 and 1.004 in various states. Because of low use of inputs, level of productivity of most of the crops is quite low in most of the states. There are several reasons for this; poor network of input distribution; lack of resources and non-availability of adequate credit for purchase of modern inputs; decline or stagnation in public investments in irrigation and other infrastructure during the 8th and 9th and up to mid 10th Five-Year Plans in real terms.

Improved technology is most important for the growth of output. Available evidence shows that there is a big gap between the level of yield with improved farm practices in farmers' fields and the yield with practices followed by the farmers. Besides the need for extension to transfer improved technology to farmers, the critical factor in this is the availability of quality seed. Most of the farmers do not distinguish between "seed and grain" and use common grain as seed. Research institutes have very limited capacity for seed multiplication and they can supply only quality seeds in small quantity. So far production and supply of quality seed were mainly entrusted to public sector agencies, namely, the National Seeds Corporation and the state level seed corporations. Compared to the need for quality seed in the country, these corporations as such are serving a limited purpose. India needs to develop a competitive market for seeds by expanding the role of public sector and by encouraging private sector in seed business in a big way. This feels that transferring some of the subsidies from other inputs to seed would be more paying.

Table 3.6
Level of Cropping Intensity, Irrigation, Fertiliser and Power Used in Agriculture during 2001-02 and 2003-04

State	*Cropping intensity (per cent)*	*NPK Kg/ Hectare*	*Power Cons/ ha KWh*	*Irrigated Area Actual (Per cent)*	*Irrigation Potential as Per cent of Current GCA*
Andhra Pradesh	122	176	1240	41.1	75.6
Assam	146	28	9	14.3	66.8
Bihar	135	105	123	47.6	123.5
Gujarat	114	89	1577	35.9	44.6
Haryana	180	270	1415	83.2	71.7
Himachal Pradesh	173	80	34	19.3	35.0
Jammu and Kashmir	148	91	160	40.5	72.4
Karnataka	116	118	832	25.0	39.7
Kerala	135	87	85	14.9	70.8
Madhya Pradesh	127	38	274	26.1	44.7
Maharashtra	127	95	549	17.1	32.7
Orissa	150	55	30	26.6	69.9
Punjab	186	328	1374	96.6	82.5
Rajasthan	128	40	244	29.5	25.2
Tamil Nadu	117	171	1927	51.0	72.7
Uttar Pradesh	154	188	292	68.4	94.8
West Bengal	176	213	178	50.8	62.7
All-India	**135**	**121**	**598**	**39.9**	**60.7**

Source: Calculated from various issues of statistical abstract of India.

Agriculture Development Scenario in Haryana

Present Haryana was agriculturally a less developed part of the former Punjab before its formation in 1966. The net irrigated area was 35.54 percent and 58.48 percent was in Punjab. Probably out of four one village was connected with road. The compound annual growth rate of agriculture was 1.2 % as compare to Punjab. After its formation no doubt the state has emerged as one of the leading state in the field of Agriculture in India. A general picture of agricultural development in the state explained as follows:

Trends in Area under Crops

In Haryana with the span of time, there has been a substantial change in the cropping pattern. There has been expansion of irrigation facilities, a shift in area in favour of more remunerative and less risky crops like rice, wheat, cotton, rapeseed and mustard and due to this a decline in area under bajra, jawar, maize, barley and gram. The area under principal crops is shown in Table 3.7. There are two main crops season in the state, one is Kharif or the season of summer crops, and another is the Rabi or the season of winter crops. The crops selected for Khrif are-Rice, Jowar, Bajra, Maize, pulses are among and other pluses; and oilseed are - Groundnut sesame, and other Khrif oilseeds. The crops selected for Rabi cereals are- Wheat Barley and small millets; pulses are - gram and the Rabi pulses and oilseeds are - Rape and mustard, lineseed. The Figures show the dominance of cereals crops in gross area sown.

The area under cereals is continuously increasing since 1985-86. This area was only 3197.1 thousand hectares in 1985-86. It increased to 4041.3 thousand hectares in 2004-05. The area under pulses was 846.3 thousand hectares in 1985-86. It decreased to 176.2 thousand hectares in 2004-05. The area under total oilseeds crops has increased from 380.1 thousand hectares in 1985-86 to 488.5 thousand hectares in 1990-91 and further to 714.6 thousand hectares in 2004-05.

Table 3.7
Area under Major Crops (Kharif and Rabi)

(000 ha.)

Crops/year	*1985-86*	*1990-91*	*1995-96*	*2000-01*	*2004-05*
Cereals	3197.1	3337.3	3570.7	4186.5	4041.3
Pulses	846.3	742	449.8	157	176.2
Oilseeds	380.1	488.5	611	414	714.6
Sugarcane	104.2	147.8	143.7	143.0	133.0
Cotton	344.1	490.6	651.8	555.4	621.2

Source: Statistical Abstract, Haryana, 1986-87 to 2005-06.

Now, the area under principal crops in various districts of the state is shown in table 3.8. The result shows the dominance of wheat and Rice crops in most of the districts of the state. Wheat crop occupies the most significant place in cropping pattern of all districts in the sate. The concentration of wheat crop was highest in Sirsa followed by Hissar, Jind, Fatehabad, Kaithal, Karnal, Sonipat, Bhiwani, Gurgaon, Faridabad, Kurukshetra, Jhajjar, Rohtak, and Panipat respectively. The area under rice is maximum in District Karnal followed by Kaithal, Kurukshetra, Jind, Sonipat, Panipat, Ambala, Fatehabad, Amuna Nagar, Sirsa, Faridabad, Rohtak, Jajjar, Bhwani, Panchkula respectively. The area under Bajra, Maize, barley etc. is very less in whole of the state as compared to wheat and rice.

It is fact that there is limited scope for increasing the cultivable area in the state. The percentage of net area sown to total area of the state has been fluctuating 'between' 83 percent to 85 percent since 2004-05. Haryana seems to have reached a saturation point as far as net area sown is concerned. Therefore, agricultural production is being increased through enhanced cropping intensity, change in cropping pattern, improvement in seeds of HYV and availability of better post-harvest technology. The effective use of biofertilizers including vermin compost, phosphatic and recycling of farm biomass for restoration of soil health and soil productivity, tackling of phalaris minor and other weeds, zero tillage, raised bed palting, adoption of water management technologies, etc. may be disseminated amongst the farmers for higher production projections.

Table-3.8

Area under Kharif and Rabi crops in Various District of Haryana (2004-05)

(000 ha.)

District	*Rice*	*Bajra*	*Rabi oilseeds*	*Maize*	*Wheat*	*Barley*
Ambala	73.6	0.4	1.5	3	82.3	-
Panchkula	6.8	0.5	1.2	9.4	17.5	-
Y. Nagar	58.7	1.0	2.4	1.9	72.3	-
Karnal	167.4	1.0	0.8	0.2	170.7	-
Kaithal	152.6	10.8	0.9	0.1	174.3	-
Kurukstra	121.8	0.1	0.9	0.2	113.9	0.1
Panipat	72.3	0.7	0.9	00	83.8	0.1
Sonipat	65.9	6.9	5.5	0.5	132.7	0.6
Rohtak	15	13.9	26.9	0.1	87.4	1.1
Jhajjar	13.4	25.4	55.4	0.1	84.1	1.1
Faridabad	28.3	10.3	5.2	0.2	135.8	1.8
Gurgaon	6.3	51.8	63.7	-	115.5	1.9
Rewari	0.4	50.4	71.5	-	44.9	00
M. Garh	00	85.1	99.6	-	40.5	0.4
Bhiwani	11.4	181.6	182.9	-	126.6	4.3
Jind	90.4	45.8	12.5	-	206.9	0.8
Hisar	28.3	61.9	71.2	0.1	202.4	3.8
Fatehabad	65.4	11.9	16.6	-	177.2	2.5
Sirsa	45.7	5.8	80.6	-	247.9	3.9
Haryana	1024.2	565.3	699.8	15.8	2316.7	22.4

Source : Statistical Abstract, Haryana 2005-06.

Agriculture production

There is a remarkable increase in agriculture production since 1966-67 in the state. The trends in agricultural production are shown in table 3.9. The figures shows remarkable increase in production of total food grains since 1966-67. Production of total foodgrans increased from 25.92 lakh tonnes in 1966-67 to 132.50 lakh tonnes in 2001-02, and is 130.25 lakh tonnes in 2004-05 showing decrease. Wheat and rice played a major role in pushing up the agriculture production. The production of rice was only 2.23 lakh tonnes in 1966-67. It increased to 30.10 lakh tonnes in 2004-05. Similarly the production of wheat which was 10.59 lakh tonnes in 1966-67 increased to 90.43 lakh tonnes during 2004-05. The result shows remarkable increase in production of Sugarcane, Cotton and total Oilseeds since 1966-67. The production of cotton increased from 395 thousand bales in 1966-67 to 2075 thousand bales in 2004-05 and the production of sugarcane increased from 5.10 lakh tonnes in 1966-67 to 8.23 lakh tonnes in 2004-05. It will be interesting to analyse crop wise production of various crops in terms of various districts of the state. The data is shown in Table 3.10. The production of rice is highest in Karnal showing 18.83 percent of total production of state, followed by Kurukshetra, Kaithal, Jind, Abmala, Fatehabad, Panipat, Yamunagar, Scnipat, Sirsa, Faridabad, Hisar, Rohtak, bhiwani, gurgaon, Pachnkula, Rewari respectively. Mahindra garh shows no prodution of rice as there is lack of irrigation facilities in district.

It is a well known fact that the important crop of Haryana is wheat, in which the state occupies third place in India after U.P. and Punjab. This crop is cultivated in all districts. Sirsa occupies the first rank producing 970 thousand tonnes (10.72 % of total production) followed by Jind 859 thousand tonnes Hisar 841 thousand tonnes Fatehabad 727 thosuand tonnes. To analyse the growth of agriculture production in Haryana, it is necessary to analyse index of agriculture production in the state. The index is shown in Table 3.11. Table 3.11 shows that index of agricultural production (Base Triennium ending 1981-82 = 100) has increased from 106.37 in 1980-81 to 243.01 in 2004-05. The indexes of foodgrain and non-foodgrains have increased from 107.02 and 104.72 in 1980-81 to 212.84 and 319.53 in 2004-05. The index number show remarkable increase in agriculture production leading to almost double during the span of 20 years. However, the rate of increase has been higher in non-grains as compared to food-grains due to higher profitability in the former.

Table 3.9
Crop-wise Production of Various Crops in Haryana

(000 tonnes)

Crops/ year	*1966-67*	*1970-71*	*1975-76*	*1980-81*	*1985-86*	*1990-91*	*2000-01*	*2004-05*
Kharif								
Rice	223	460	625	1259	1633	1834	2684	3010
Jawar	49	57	35	48	28	65	23	26
Maize	86	130	171	81	64	49	37	39
Bazra	373	826	608	474	315	526	655	746
Kharif Pulses	16	27	28	30	40	57	14	6
Food grain	747	1500	1467	1842	2080	2531	3413	3827
Rabi								
Wheat	1059	2342	2428	3490	5260	6436	9652	9043
Gram	531	789	907	455	625	469	52	91
Barley	239	124	221	181	160	107	127	58
Pulses	16	16	17	18	20	16	6	6
Foodgrain	1845	3271	3573	4144	6065	7028	9837	9198
Total food grain	2592	4771	5040	5986	8145	9559	13250	13025
Sugarcane	5100	7070	6870	4600	5010	7800	8220	8230
Cotton	345	374	465	643	745	1155	1383	2075
Total oilseed	92	98	79.4	187	287.8	638	565	836

Source : Statistical Abstract of Haryana, 1966-67 to 2005-2006

Table 3.10
Crop-wise Production of Kharif and Rabi crops in Various District of Haryana (2004-05)

(000 tonnes)

District	*Rice*	*Bajra*	*Maize*	*Wheat*	*Gram*	*Barley*	*Rabi oil seeds*
Ambala	233	00	7	267	0	0	2
Panchkula	18	3	25	39	1	0	1
Y. Nagar	191	2	5	245	0	0	2
Kurukshtra	468	00	0	463	0	0	1
Kaithal	399	17	0	7.6	0	0	1
Karnal	567	2	0	7.5	0	0	1
Panipat	164	3	0	362	0	0	1
Sonipat	124	11	2	529	0	3	6
Rohtak	26	25	0	320	1	2	30
Jhajjar	16	36	0	302	1	3	73
Faridabad	68	12	0	526	0	5	6
Gurgaon	18	67	0	407	1	4	74
Rewari	3	78	0	186	1	0	100
Mahendragarh	00	102	0	154	5	0	119
Bhiwani	14	188	0	415	57	9	198
Jind	201	67	0	859	0	3	16
Hisar	63	102	0	841	14	11	81
Fatehabad	280	23	0	727	1	6	19
Sirsa	157	8	0	970	10	12	93
Haryana	3010	746	39	9043	91	58	824

Source : Statistical Abstract, Haryana 2005-06.

Haryana is one of the largest contributors to food pool because of the results of higher production of foograins. State government is also fully committed to provide remunerative prices and timely support to the farmer by purchasing wheat and paddy at minimum support price on a large scale though a network of 331 purchase centers presently functioning in the state. During 2001-02, the government agencies purchased 64.07 lakh tonnes of wheat and 15.77 lakh tonnes of paddy, which is an all time record.

Table 3.11
Index of Agriculture Production in Haryana
(Base: Triennium Ending 1981-82 = 100)

Year	*Total food grains*	*Total non-foodgrains*	*All commodities*
1980-81	107.02	104.72	106.37
1990-91	165.90	222.27	181.12
1991-92	172.22	249.60	179.12
1992-93	174.59	219.15	185.49
1993-94	186.54	232.11	190.86
1994-95	173.47	252.30	205.14
1995-96	190.91	249.63	195.01
1996-97	189.42	294.50	220.21
1997-98	203.71	185.50	188.23
1998-99	133.35	199.01	202.38
1999-00	214.13	233.76	219.68
2000-01	216.66	234.96	221.85
2001-02	217.93	225.73	220.71
2002-03	201.60	247.05	214.46
2004-05	212.84	319.53	243.01

Source : Statistical Abstract of Haryana, 2005-06

Yield Pattern of Principal Crops

As we know, yield rate of crops is an important indicator of agricultural development. The yield rate of important crops is shown in table 3.12.The table shows that a yield rate of principal crops is quite high. The average yield rate of rice is 2434 kgs. per hectare in the state while on National level the yield rate is 1984 kgs. per hectare.

The average yield rate for wheat is 3401 kg. per hectare while at national level it is 2602.The yield rate of principal crops in terms of various districts of the state is shown in table 3.13. The table shows that Sirsa, Bhiwani, Fatehabad, Gurgaon, Faridabad, Karnal, Kurushetra, Ambala, Panchkula Yamuna Nagar have above state average yield per hectare for rice, whereas the district of Hisar, Rohtak, Jhajjar, Sonipat, Panipat, Kaithal, Jind have yield below the state average. In terms of wheat, the districts Hisar, Fatehabad, Sirsa, Karnal, Panipat, Kurukshetra, Kaithal, Jind, Rewari have yield rate above the state average, while the districts of Bhiwani,

Rohtak, Jhajjar, Sonipat, Gurgaon, Faridabad, Ambala, Panchkula, Yamauna Nagar and Mahindragarh have yield rate below the state average.

Table 3.12
Crop-wise Average Yield of Various Crops in Haryana

(kgs/hectare)

Crops	*1966-67*	*1970-71*	*1980-81*	*1990-91*	*2000-01*	*2004-05*
(A) Khariff						
(i) Rice	1161	1697	2606	2775	2559	2939
(ii) Jawar	181	277	354	792	209	272
(iii) Maize	988	1142	1134	1414	2339	2600
(iv) Bazra	418	939	544	864	1077	1318
(v) Kh. Pulses	421	500	811	838	519	384
Khariff Food grains	**505**	**984**	**1184**	**1684**	**1887**	**2240**
(B) Rabi						
(i) Wheat	1425	2074	2360	3479	4109	3901
(ii) Gram	500	742	629	722	675	843
(iii) Barley	1313	1150	1451	2092	2646	2639
(Rabi pulses)	320	381	500	667	750	854
Rabi Food grains	**906**	**1396**	**1754**	**2630**	**3963**	**3748**
Total Food grains	**737**	**1234**	**1524**	**2345**	**3088**	**3095**
(c) Commercial						
(i) Cotton	283	327	346	401	424	568
(ii) Kh. Oil seeds	899	767	912	500	400	342
(iii) Rabi Oil seeds	405	978	597	1338	1371	1177
Total Oils seeds	**435**	**696**	**606**	**1324**	**1361**	**1169**

Source : Statistical abstract of Haryana, 2005-06.

When to compare the yield rate of principal crops in Haryana with India as a whole as shown in table 3.14. The result shows that although the yield rate of principal crops is quite high while comparing with that of National level in Haryana, but there is enough scope to increase the yield rates further so as to bring these at per with the best in the world. The power of bio-technology to improve crops yield is today being recognised the world over. Haryana can take lead in this field by ensuring that research in laboratories reaches the field through extensive services.

Table-3.13
District-Wise Yield of Various Crops in Haryana

(kgs/hectare)

District	*Rice*	*Bazra*	*Maize*	*Wheat*	*Gram*	*Barley*	*Rabi oilseeds*
Ambala	3154	-	2380	3254	-	-	1590
Panchkula	2538	3042	2747	2180	-	-	1186
Y. Nagar	3229	2165	2362	3396	-	-	1187
Kurukshatra	3835	-	-	4064	-	-	1186
Kaithal	2609	1513	-	4115	-	-	1305
Karnal	3397	1722	-	4183	-	-	1060
Panipat	2277	2687	-	4311	-	-	1458
Sonipat	1879	1553	2500	3979	-	2680	1183
Rohtak	1749	1812	-	3680	695	1818	1102
Jhajjar	1235	1457	-	3595	749	2705	1329
Faridabad	2429	1248	-	3864	-	2681	1179
Gurgaon	2941	1293	-	3506	834	2076	1156
Rewari	2941	1569	-	4129	843	-	1408
M.Garh	-	1197	-	3754	713	-	1190
Bhiwani	1290	1032	-	3268	841	2267	1082
Jind	2213	1465	-	4148	-	2356	1262
Hisar	2263	1638	-	4162	784	2757	1146
Fatehabad	4307	1946	-	4105	1121	3193	1143
Sirsa	3411	1413	-	3911	1022	3096	1142
Haryana	2939	1318	2600	3901	843	2636	1177

Source : Department of Agriculture, Haryana Agriculture Statistics at a Glance 2001, Statistical Abstract of Haryana 2005-06.

Table 3.14
Yield rates of Principal crops

(kg/ha.)

Year	*Haryana*		*India*	
	Wheat	*Rice*	*Wheat*	*Rice*
1990-91	3479	2775	2280	1740
1995-96	3697	2225	2483	1797
1996-97	3880	2967	2679	1882
2000-01	4109	2559	2742	1927
2004-05	3901	2939	2602	1984

Source : Ministry of Agriculture, Government of India, Statistical Abstract, India.1990-91 to 2005-06.

Land Utilization Pattern

The land use pattern in the state over the years has shown the significant trend of strengthened and intensified agriculture defying the disadvantages bestowed by adverse agro-climatic conditions. Table 3.15, shows the land utilization of state 2004-05. From the perusal of result becomes clear that the percentage of net area sown was 82.88 percent of land in 1985 - 86 and 80.7 percent in 2004 - 05. It shows that it decreased by 2.18 percent during the period. The land not available for cultivation was 10.36 percent in 1985-86, whereas it was 12 percent in 2004-05. It also increased 1.64 percent.

Table 3.15
Land Utilization Pattern

(000 ha.)

Land use classification	*1985-86*	*1990-91*	*1995-96*	*2000-01*	*2004-05*
Forest	57	169	110	115	44
	(1.30)	(3.86)	(2.5)	(2.6)	(1)
Land not available	455	417	494	470	525
for cultivation	(10.36)	(9.52)	(11.2)	(10.7)	(12)
Fallow land	168	169	156	232	2.2
	(3.83)	(3.86)	(3.5)	(5.3)	(4.8)
Net Area sown	3613	3575	3586	3526	3528
	(82.881)	(81.66)	(85.3)	(80.1)	(80.7)
Other uncultivated land exclusive land	98	48	51	59	66
	(2.23)	(1.10)	(1.2)	(1.3)	(1.5)
Total	**4391**	**4378**	**4398**	**4402**	**4374**

Source : Statistical Abstract, Haryana. 1984-85 to 2005-06.

Input Indicators of Agricultural Development

To develop the agriculture in progressive way the following things mainly consider from input indicators point of view at here. The progressive agriculture demand among other things (i.e. favourable institutional and organisation structure), improvement in methods of irrigation, better seeds, better manures and fertilizers, land reclamation and soil conservation, use of mechanization, etc. In this context, an attempt has been made to analyse some of the important inputs indicators, namely; High yield seeds varieties; Fertilizers; Pesticides; Irrigation; Mechanisation and use of Modern technology.

High Yielding Seeds Varieties

As we know, the improved quality of seeds is essential for increasing agricultural production. Unless the farmer has good seeds of suitable varieties, he cannot get the best out of other inputs, such as irrigation, fertilizers, insecticides and machinery. With HYV (High Yielding Variety) seeds, it becomes possible for him to take to intensive agriculture because of resultant high yield and good economic returns. The use of High Yielding variety (HYV) seeds of major crops has increased considerable in the state since its formation in 1966. The area under HYV, in the state and various districts is in the table 3.16. The table shows that the state has made remarkable progress as far use of HYV is concerned. In the year 1966-67 there was practically no use of HYV in any of the principal crops in the state, but in the year 2004-05, 72.3 per cent of total area in rice, per cent in maize, 85.4 per cent in bajra and 98.7 in wheat were covered by HYV. As far as various districts of the state are concerned, the ratio of HYV in wheat in almost all the districts was 95% or above. It was 100% in Sonipat and between 98 to nearly 100% in 10 districts. Similarly in case of rice the ratio of HYV in total area was in excess of 90% in the districts of Panchkula and Rewari while it was more than 70% in Ambala, Yamuna Nagar, Kurukshetra, Sirsa, etc. It leads to the conclusion that still there is great potentiality of increasing the production of rice by improving the rate of HYV. This use of HYV in case of bajra was quite high but it was moderate in maize.

Table 3.16
Area under HYV Foodgrain in Haryana 2004-05

(Percentages of Total Area)

District	*Rice*	*Maize*	*Bajra*	*Wheat*
Ambala	88.3	50	-	99.6
Panchkula	88.2	69.1	-	91.4
Y. Nagar	88.6	63.2	-	98.2
Kurukshtra	68.1	50	-	98.3
Kaithal	88.5	-	74.1	98.5
Karnal	61.5	-	-	99
Panipat	63.6	-	-	97.9
Sonipat	65.3	80	87	100
Rohtak	60.3	-	93.5	97.3
Jhajjar	59.7	-	86.6	98.7
Faridabad	67.1	-	77.7	99.4
Gurgaon	79.4	50	90.7	97.8
Rewari	00	-	91.3	98
M. Garh	00	-	95.2	96.3
Bhiwani	70.2	-	71	98.7
Jind	69.3	-	96.1	98.6
Hisar	49.5	100	98.5	99.3
Fatehbad	81.0	-	100	98.8
Sirsa	63.5	-	100	99.6
Haryana	72.3	63.3	85.4	98.7

Source : Statistical Abstract, Haryana 2005-06.

Fertilizers

It is a well known fact that the use of chemical fertilizers is widely accepted as one of the key elements in the strategy for accelerating the growth of agricultural output in every part of the world. In this context, it is worth-mentioning that fertilizer played a very significant role in enhancing the agricultural productivity and ushering in green revolution in the state. Since the introduction of high yielding varieties, the consumption of chemical fertilizers has been increasing steadily as shown in table 3.17.The figure shows that total consumption of NPK (Nutrients) which was only 13,347 tonnes in 1966-67 increased to 70,060 tonnes in 1970-71 and jumped to the level of 9,30,295 tonnes in 2001-01. The trend has been common in case of all types of chemical fertilizers.

Table 3.17
Fertilizer Consumption in Haryana

(000 hectares)

Year	*Nitrogenous*	*Phosphatic*	*Potassic*	*Total*
1966-67	12626	574	147	13347
1970-71	60972	6860	2228	70060
1980-81	187385	31340	12098	230823
1990-91	453245	138005	5042	586292
2000-01	714308	206319	9668	930295
2001-02	742049	232161	9750	983960
2002-03	720494	250806	12298	983598
2003-04	761770	230252	17086	1009108
2004-05	845529	262272	16987	1124688
2005-06	847427	252570	28674	1128671

Source: Statistical Abstract, Haryana 2006-07.

Pesticides

The continuously growing uses of pesticides became the problems not only in Haryana, but also in other part of the nation and the word. Because of this there occurred some losses in agriculture due to weeds, diseases, insects, storage pests, rodent, etc. These things are needs of evolving appropriate plant protection measures.. The use of pesticides in Haryana is shown in the table 3.18. Table shows that consumption of pesticides was 273 tonnes in 1966-67. It increased to 2150 tonnes in 1980-81 and jumped to 5025 tonnes in 1999-2000 and decreased to 4650 tonnes in 2005-06.

Irrigation and Flood Control

The Water is one of the essential inputs to promote the various sectors of state Economy such as agriculture, industries, animal husbandry, fisheries, fisheries, forestry, etc. besides catering for the essential requirement of domestic use. According to an estimate, the state of Haryana needing about 34 million acre foot (M.A.F.) of water to meet out the annual requirements of all the water consuming sectors by the year 2005 whereas the level of its availability is only 18.8 M.A.F.

Therefore, the need of the hour is to create new resources of water as well as its utilization through an efficient network of canals. the decision of Hon'ble Supreme Court of dated 15th January 2002 for directing the time bound construction of Satluz Yamuna link (S.Y.L.) Canal has come as ray of hope for the water deficient state for which the government was pursuing the case for a long time. This would narrow down the gap between require and availability of water to some extent.

Table 3.18
Consumption of Pesticides in Haryana

(technical grade)

Year	*Quantity in Tonnes*
1966-67	273
1970-71	412
1980-81	2150
1990-91	5165
1999-00	5025
2002-03	4826
2003-04	4730
2004-05	4700
2006-06	4650

Sources : Statistical Abstract, Haryana 2005-06.

The state government has been making all out efforts by efficient distribution of water to make the optimum use of water resources. The internal clearance of irrigation channels is completed prior to the commencement of crop season and all possible steps taken to stop the pilferage of water to ensure the supply of canal water to the tail ends. Under Haryana Water Resources Consolidation Project which stands completed by December, 2001, the Government has taken all possible measures for the conservation of water by modernizing unlined canals, rehabilitation of old lined canals and replacement of old regulators and other irrigation structures. The main structures replaced/constructed under the project are hathnikund Barrage along with Link Channel, Pathrala Dam, Ch. Devi Lal Weir at Ottu, Budhera Complex and Sinchai Bhawan which is in advance stage of completion. Canal iirigation of 21.56 lakh hectares and 21.40 lakh hectares respectively was achieved during 1999-2000 and 2000-2001 despite prevailing dry conditions during both the years. This state served by the excellent network of irrigation in the state. The status of irrigation facilities available in the state is given in table 3.19. The table reveals that gross as well as net area irrigated is continuously increasing in the state since 1966-67. Percentage of gross irrigated area and gross cropped area from the year 1966-67 rose to 86.1 and 83.5 per cent in 2000-2001 respectively. Irrigation intensity during 2000-2001 was 177 in the state. The gross area irrigated in the state will further increase with the completion of S.Y.L. canal.

Table 3.19
Irrigation Facilities in Haryana

(000 Hectares)

Year	*Gross cropped Area*	*Gross Irrigated Area*	*Percentage*	*Net Cropped Area*	*Net Irrigated Area*	*Percentage*
1966-67	4599	1736	37.7	3423	1293	37.8
1970-71	4957	2230	45	3565	1532	43
1980-81	5462	3309	60.6	3602	2134	59.2
1990-91	5919	4237	71.6	3575	2600	72.7
1995-96	5974	4673	78.2	3586	2760	77
2000-01	6045	5202	86.1	3526	2958	83.89
2003-04	6338	5343	84.30	3534	2969	84.01
2004-05	6425	5434	84.57	3528	2954	83.73

Sources : Statistical Abstract, Haryana 2005-06.

It will be interesting to analyse the source-wise and cropwise irrigated area in Haryana. The source-wise irrigated area is shown in Table 3.20. The table shows that in Haryana, government canals and tubewells are the main source of irrigation. In 1966-67 the area irrigated by government canals was 991 thousand hectares which was 76.64% of total net irrigated area, while in 1999-2000 the area irrigated by government canals was 49.89 per cent of the total. The area irrigated by tubewells in 1999-2000 is 1432 hectares which is

49.58 per cent of total net irrigated area while it was nil in 1966-67. The extensive use of tubewells indicates exhaustive use of underground water resources which has resulted in lowering of water table in Haryana.

Crop-wise irrigated area in Haryana is shown in table 3.21. Table shows that gross area irrigated ahs increased in all the major crops. The gross area irrigated in case of rice has increased from 138 thousand hectares in 1966-67 to 1026 thousand hectares in 2001-2002, while incase of wheat it has increased from 512 thousand hectare in 1966-67 to 2280 thousand hectares in 2001-02. In case of cotton the gross area irrigated was 177 thousand hectares in 1966-67 while in 2000-01 it was 627 thousand hectares. The increase in gross irrigated area in all the major crops indicates extension of irrigation facilities in all the corners of the state, although extensive use of ground water resources is a cause of worry.

Table 3.20
Source-wise Net Irrigated Area in Haryana

(000' Hectares)

Year	*Government canals*	*Tanks*	*Wells*	*Tube wells*	*Other Source*	*Total*
1966-67	991	4	289	0	9	1293
1970-71	952	1	574	0	5	1532
1980-81	1161	0	26	941	6	2134
1990-91	1337	1	0	1248	14	2600
1995-96	1375	1	0	1352	32	2760
1999-00	1441	1	0	1432	14	2888
2000-01	1476	1	0	1467	14	2958
2002-03	1433	0	0	1522	11	2966
2003-04	1396	0	0	1561	12	2969
2004-05	1426	0	0	1514	14	2954

Sources : Statistical Abstract, Haryana 2005-06.

Table 3.21
Crop-wise Irrigated Area in Haryana

(000 Hectares)

Year	*Rice*	*Jawar*	*Bajra*	*Wheat*	*Gram*	*Sugarcane*	*Cotton*
1966-67	138	72	47	512	268	127	177
1970-71	235	55	88	914	238	133	189
1980-81	469	37	103	1378	311	103	311
1990-91	655	61	94	1805	141	142	488
2000-01	1052	70	147	2334	41	140	534
2002-03	905	77	175	2250	30	187	511
2003-04	1014	70	168	2292	26	159	523
2004-05	1022	71	176	2246	19	132	617

Sources : Statistical Abstract, Haryana 2005-06.

Conclusion

In conclusion, there are several point discussed in the strategy of national agricultural policy and agricultural development scenario of India as well as Haryana. No doubt, these all things are needed collectively to face the present changing situation of the world. Diversification of agriculture in favour of commercial and high value crops is in fact recognised as a powerful strategy to counter the emerging challenges. As a risk management device crop diversification towards the crops in which a country has comparative advantage as compared to imports was traditionally assumed to be efficient in facing international competition. But now it has become inevitable as free trade in agriculture mandated under WTO has posed a constant threat to the developing countries in the form of high market induced risks and fall in global prices for farm products that have adversely affected traditional crops and families depending upon them. The growth rate analysis shows that the initial years of reforms were somewhat favourable for agricultural growth, but the post-world trade organization period witnessed a sharp decline in the growth rate of almost all sub-sectors and commodity groups in the agricultural sector. At the state level, the growth rate has turned negative in four out of 20 major states while six states show a growth rate ranging between 0.10 and 0.95 per cent, further, the growth rate of agriculture in most of the low productivity states was much higher than the national average during 1984-85 to 1995-96. However, after 1995-96, their growth rates not only declined, but also turned out to be much lower than the national average. The main reasons for deceleration and stagnation in agricultural output after 1995-96 are a slowdown in growth of fertiliser use, irrigation, and energy (electric power) in some cases, stagnation or even a decline in other cases. Crop intensity and area under cultivation have also shown either a poor growth or a decline. Diversification towards high-value crops has also slowed down and in some cases farmers have been diversifying away from the high-value crops towards low-value, less risky and less input-demanding crops. Low level of input use and low productivity in most of the states offer some ray of hope to revive agricultural growth, but this would require simultaneous efforts on several fronts include ; stepping up invest-ments and putting in place suitable institutional mechanisms to exploit irrigation potential that exists in most of the states; increasing power supply to the sector; promoting fertilizer use by expanding the distribution network and improving credit facilities for farmers; establishing competitive seed markets and ensuring attractive prices for seeds; improvement in terms of trade for agriculture; and measures to mitigate risk in farming. Thus, the present scenario and growth rate of agricultural is witness to stress more and more on agricultural development in 11th plan.

Several points there has been try to examine and analyse for Haryana Agriculture, which is the mainstay of Haryana's economy. The total area under crops has increased considerably since 1970-71. The Gross Area Sown which was 45.99 lakh hectares during 1966-67 has increased to 49.57 lakh hectares in 1970-71 and further increased to 64.80 lakh hectares during 2004-05. During the year 2005-06 the Gross Area sown is likely to remain the same i.e. 64.80 lakh hectares. Cropping

Intensity in the state has enhanced from 139.0 in 1970-71 to 174.19 during 2004-05. The agriculture scene in the state is dominated by paddy- wheat rotation, causing degradation in soil fertility and further fall in the under ground water level. The percentage of area under these two crops (wheat and rice) to the total gross area sown in the State is increase from 28.20 percent during 1970-71 to 51.27 percent during 2005-06. The area under commercial crops i.e. sugarcane, cotton and oilseeds fluctuates every year but as compared to previous year, there will be a decrease of 12.31 percent under sugarcane and 6.60 percent under cotton during the year 2005-06 over 2001-02. However, the area under oilseeds has registered an increase.

A remarkable increase in foodgrains production is visible in Haryana since 1970-71. Production of total foodgrains is likely to increase from 47.71 lakh tonnes in 1970-71 to 138.11 lakh tonnes in 2005-06 showing an increase of 189.48 percent. Wheat and Rice played a major role in pushing up the agricultural production. Average Yield per hectare in kilograms of wheat and rice during 2005-06 in Haryana is estimated as 4200 and 3024 respectively. The average yield per hectare in respect of wheat and rice of all India during 2003-04 was 2713 kilograms and 2077 kilograms respectively, whereas in Haryana it was 3937 and 2749 respectively. The power of bio-technology to improve crop-yield today is being recognised the world over.

At the end that globalization offers both opportunities and challenges. The opportunities consist of contribution the benefits of world trade and growth. The challenges lie in enabling the sharing of these benefits not by a small minority of elite population but by the majority of working people in rural and urban India.

4

Data Interpretation and Inter-District Pattern of Agricultural Development

To reflect the real picture of economic development in any country, nation and state, there is need to access the level and pattern of that country economic development. No doubt it can be access through some statistical methods or technique with help of interpretation of some leading indicators of different sectors. In the present study there has been also tried to access the agricultural development pattern in Haryana during 1984-85 to 2004-05, for this purpose this present chapter is an empirical exercise of district wise measurement of level and pattern of agricultural development in the state. In the present work there have been selected ten variables or indicators to access the real seen of district wise agricultural development pattern of Haryana during 1984-85 to 2004-05. There have been estimated some results (C.V., Growth Rate, Factors Analysis, Correlation Matrix and Composite Index etc.) to reflect the real picture of agricultural development pattern of aforesaid time period in the state.

Haryana is a state where the agriculture play an important role, in view to access the district wise level and pattern of agricultural development during the years 1984-85 to 2004-05, there has been selected the following crops namely cereals, pulses and oilseeds, because these crops are generally grown in all of the 19 districts of Haryana or they are major crops. The crops selected for cereals; Rice, Jowar, Bajra, Maize,

Wheat, Barley etc ; Pulses; gram, Mash, Moong, Massar and etc; and the crops selected for oilseeds; Ground-nut, Sesamum, Rape Seed, Mustard and Linseed etc.

The data sequence of state records are available in very much heterogeneous manners like, from 1985 to 1989 there were only 12 districts from 1990 to 1999, there were 16 districts in the state and from 1999 to onwards there were 19 districts as per state records. As per availability of data, we merge the districts Yamuna Nagar, Kaithal, Panipat and Rewari into Ambala, Kurukshetra, Sonipat Mahendergarh respectively for the year 1989-90. In the year 1995-96 and 1996-97 we merge the districts Panchkula into Ambala and in year 1997-98, 1998-99, we merge the districts Panchkula Jhajjar, Fatehabad into Ambala, Rohtak, Hisar, respectively. Hence, this kind of sequence of districts continuously going to increase year by year and to meet out the fluctuations in agriculture sector there transformed the data in the form of Triennium Ending (TE). The Triennium Ending 1986-87 (i.e. 1984-85 through 1986-87) and Triennium ending 1989-90 (i.e. 1987-88 through 1989-90) have been computed for 12 district, and Triennium ending 1992-93, 1995-96, 1998-99 (i.e. 1990-01 through 1992-93, 1993-94 through 1995-96, 1996-97 through 1998-99) have been computed for 16 district, and Triennium ending 2001-02, 2004-05 (i.e. 1999-2000 through 2001-02, 2002-03 through 2004-05) have been computed for 19 districts.

District-wise Agricultural Area, Production and Productivity of Haryana

The district-wise interpretation of area, production and productivity of major crops or corps sown (cereal, pulses and oilseeds) sown in all districts of the state explained below.

District-wise Agricultural Area (Cereals, Pulses and Oilseeds)

The area under cereals in Haryana have been examined on the basis of district wise data during the year 1984-85 to 2004-

05 given in table 4.1. The data presented in table reflects the inter district variation in area under cereals generated from agriculture sector.

The area under cereals is the highest in Kurukshetra district, 461470 hectare followed by Karnal 437130 and the lowest in Feridabad district 175830 hectare the TE period 1986-87 (i.e. 1984-85 to 1986-87). However, Kurukshetra, Karnal, Hisar for TE period 1989-90 and Hisar, Karnal and Kaithal for TE period 1992-93, 1995-96 and 1998-99, Jind, Bhiwani, Kaithal for TE period 2001-02 and 2004-05 were the highest districts in the state during the study time period. Feridabad, Gurgaon for TE period 1989-90, Rewari for TE period 191-93, 1995-96, 1998-99, Panchkala, Rewari for TE period 2001-02, 2004-05 were the lowest districts in the state during the study period. Thus, the situation of area under cereals during the TE period 2004-05 remained more or less the same as in previous year. This kind of variations in area depends upon different types irrigation facilities for different years in the state. The area under cereals, in term of above (first category) and below (second category) the districts to the state average (mean) and standard deviation (S.D). The TE period 1986-87 in reference to mean, there are 6 districts (Kurukshetra, Karnal, Rohtak, Bhiwani, Jind and Hisar) in first category and 6 districts (Ambala, Sonipat, Feridabad, Gurgan, Mahendergerh, and Sirsa) in second category (below). In the sense of standard deviation, 12 districts are in first category (above) and none districts in the second category (below). There is marginal change in districts in reference to mean and standard deviation during TE 1989-90, TE 1992-93, TE 1995-96, TE 1998-99, TE 2001-02 and TE 2004-05 as compared the previous year. There are 6 district for TE period 1989-90, 7 district for TE period 1992-93 and 7 district for TE period 1995-96 and 7 districts for TE period 1998-99 and 9 districts for TE period 2001-02 and 9 districts for TE period 2004-05 are above the state average. The 6 districts for TE period 1989-90 and 9 districts for TE period 1992-93, 1995-96, 1998-99 and 10 districts for TE period 2001-02, 2004-05 are below

Table 4.1
District-wise Area under Cereals (Triennium Ending)

(thousand hectares)

Districts	TE 1986-87	TE 1989-90	Districts	TE 1992-93	TE 1995-96	TE 1998-99	Districts	TE 2001-02	TE 2004-05
Ambala	240.10	247.50	Ambala	169.47	170.63	177.97	Ambala	157.10	154.90
							Panchkula	32.60	33.70
			Yamuna Nagar	112.70	115.20	119.33	Yamuna Nagar	121.17	127.13
Kurukshetra	461.47	456.07	Kurukshetra	208.53	216.20	209.93	Kurukshetra	220.47	225.47
			Kaithal	296.60	306.70	318.00	Kaithal	334.07	343.57
Karnal	437.13	371.33	Karnal	293.80	325.20	323.87	Karnal	329.90	334.63
			Panipat	154.00	142.77	149.03	Panipat	156.13	153.43
Sonipat	193.13	224.00	Sonipat	161.67	203.03	219.03	Sonipat	234.00	211.07
Rohtak	282.10	278.80	Rohtak	291.33	245.53	307.87	Rohtak	160.87	141.53
							Jhajjar	176.33	155.67
Faridbad	175.83	172.43	Faridbad	167.77	179.97	190.50	Faridbad	197.90	186.50
Gurgoan	183.97	176.67	Gurgoan	171.33	178.27	200.50	Gurgoan	217.47	188.73
			Rewari	106.20	96.47	103.20	Rewari	113.97	99.53
Mahendragarh	227.70	204.43	Mahendragarh	132.57	125.83	133.43	Mahendragarh	146.37	127.57
Bhiwani	292.37	272.27	Bhiwani	247.73	236.57	299.07	Bhiwani	342.50	329.97
Jind	293.97	304.90	Jind	253.73	278.77	308.23	Jind	357.00	335.27
Hisar	351.43	339.20	Hisar	398.60	447.57	485.60	Hisar	296.93	297.33
							Fatehabad	248.50	252.73

Table 4.1 Continued

Table 4.1 Continued

Districts	*TE 1986-87*	*TE 1989-90*	*Districts*	*TE 1992-93*	*TE 1995-96*	*TE 1998-99*	*Districts*	*TE 2001-02*	*TE 2004-05*
Sirsa	178.83	181.97	Sirsa	212.23	240.87	266.23	Sirsa	291.17	297.87
Total	3318.03	3229.57		3378.27	3509.57	3811.80		4134.43	3996.60
For above 12 districts			For above 16 districts				For above 19 districts		
Average	276.50	269.13		211.14	219.35	238.24		217.60	210.35
Standard Deviation	97.75214	87.31909		80.2750	90.31008	99.6441440		90.13339666	92.10379
C.V.	35.353044	32.44488		38.0195	41.17207	41.8255480		41.42126378	43.78652

Source :Directorate of Land Records, Haryana, 1983-2007
Various issues of statistical Abstract, Haryana, 1983-2007.

the mean. On the other hand, the area under cereals, there 12 districts for TE period 1989-90 and 16 districts for TE period 1992-93, 1995-96, 1998-99 and 18 districts for TE period 2001-02, 2004-05 are above and 1 districts for TE period 2001-02 and 2004-05 is below the standard deviation.

Thus, during, the 21year period (between 1984-85 and 2004-05) the mode of area has not shown any big changes but the variation among districts at the seven points of time reflects a mixed picture of decrease and increase in C.V but, overall during this time period the variation increases. The coefficient of variance for the cereals in the TE year 1986-87 was 35.353 which increased to 43.786 during TE period 2004-05. Thus, the disparity among districts in area under cereals has increased. This is also evident from the coefficient of variation indicated that inter-district disparities in area under cereals declined during the TE period 1986-87 to 1989-90, from 35.35 to 32.444 but increases later on continuously. The more details are in table 4.1.

Table 4.2 reveals the growth pattern of district during the year 1984-85 to 2004-05.The district wise compound growth rate of area of (Triennium Ending) TE 1986-87 to TE 2004-05. In the TE year 1986-87 to 1989-90 the area under cereals has declined in 8 districts namely, Kurukshetra, Karnal, Mahendragarh, Rohtak, Faridabad, Gurgaon, Hisar, Bhiwani and it has increased in 4 districts namely, Ambala, Sirsa, Jind Sonipat. The increase in area under cereals is the highest in Sonipat district 1.94 percent, but the highest decline in the area in Gurgaon district - 1.38 percent. In the TE period 1992-93 to 1995-96, the area under cereals has declined in 5 districts and increased in 11 districts. The area under cereals is the highest in Sonipat district 2.9 percent for TE period 1992-93 to 1995-96 and Bhiwani district 3.08 percent for TE period 1995-96 to 1998-99 and Yamunanagar 0.62 percent for the TE period 2001-02 to 2004-05. The highest decline in Rohtak district -2.14 for TE period 1992-93 to 1995-96 and Rewari district -1.74 percent in TE year 2001-02 to 2004-05.

Table 4.2
District-wise Growth Rates of area under Cereals

(Triennium Ending)

Districts	*TE 1986-87 to TE 1989-90*	*Districts*	*TE 1992-93 to TE 1995-96*	*TE 1995-96 to TE 1998-99*	*Districts*	*TE 2001-02 to TE 2004-05*
Ambala	0.394457	Ambala	0.088509	0.547725	Ambala	-0.18273
					Panchkula	0.431317
		Yamuna Nagar	0.284953	0.457859	Yamuna Nagar	0.624667
Kurukshetra	-0.15254	Kurukshetra	0.469559	-0.38095	Kurukshetra	0.291261
		Kaithal	0.435226	0.470345	Kaithal	0.364322
Karnal	-2.09356	Karnal	1.325615	-0.05314	Karnal	0.184798
		Panipat	-0.97719	0.558094	Panipat	-0.22599
Sonipat	1.941714	Sonipat	2.998409	0.988632	Sonipat	-1.32862
Rohtak	-0.15249	Rohtak	-2.1938	2.977866	Rohtak	-1.64744
					Jhajjar	-1.60321
Faridabad	-0.25292	Faridabad	0.914544	0.74018	Faridabad	-0.76652
Gurgaon	-0.52373	Gurgaon	0.516305	1.535747	Gurgaon	-1.8215
		Rewari	-1.2385	0.878436	Rewari	-1.74167
Mahendragarh	-1.38839	Mahendragarh	-0.67443	0.76348	Mahendragarh	-1.76711
Bhiwani	-0.91949	Bhiwani	-0.59604	3.087105	Bhiwani	-0.48219
Jind	0.474577	Jind	1.228093	1.311398	Jind	-0.81115
Hissar	-0.45832	Hissar	1.514147	1.06328	Hissar	0.017461
					Fatehabad	0.219145
Sirssa	0.225999	Sirssa	1.655278	1.306721	Sirssa	0.295483

Source: Table 4.1

Table 4.3 shows the data on area under pluses. The area under pluses is the highest in Bhiwani district 183370 hectare for the TE period 1986-87, 158300 hectare for the TE period 1989-90, 162200 hectare for TE period 1991-93, 152230 hectare for TE period 1995-96 and 63400 hectare for TE period 2004-05. The area is lowest in Kurakshetra district 7700 hectare during the TE period 1986-87 and Karnal for TE period 1989-90, Kurukshetra 2300 hectare for TE period 1992-93 and Kaithal 770 hectare, 630 hectare and 600 hectare during the TE period 1998-99, 2001-02 and 2004-05. It is clear from above analysis the pattern of area under pluses have wide variation.

There employed C.V. to analyze the disparities among districts in area under pulses. Co efficient of variation figures indicated that inter-district disparities in the area widened during TE period 2001-02 but declined marginally during the TE period 2004-05. In case of area under pluses, C. V. was 95.106 for TE period 1986-87 to increased 201.77 for the TE period 2001-02 which shows the disparities among districts have been increased but declined 164.41 during TE period 2004-05, which is again the indication of decrease the disparities among districts.

Table 4.3 presents the data regarding the situation of district which exist in above and below the state average (mean) and standard deviation during the years TE period 1986-87 to 2004-05. The districts in reference to area under pluses there are 5 districts (Rohtak, Mahendragarh, Bhiwani, Hisar, Sirsa) for TE period 1986-1987 and 4 district for TE period 1989-90, 1992-93, 1995-96, 1998-99, 2001-02 and 5 districts for TE period 2004-05 in above. There are 7 districts for TE period 1986-87 and 8 districts for TE period 1989-90 and 14 districts TE period 2004-05 below the state average. There are 5 districts for TE period 1986-87, 4 districts for TE period 1989-90, 3 districts for TE period 1992-93, 1995-96, 1998-99, 1 districts TE period 2001-02 and 3 districts for TE period 2004-05 in above. There are 7 districts for TE period 1986-87, 8 districts for TE period 1989-90 and 13 districts for TE period 1992-93, 1995-96, 1998-99, 18 districts for TE period

Table 4.3
District-wise area under Pulses (Triennium Ending)

(thousand hectares)

Districts	*TE 1986-87*	*TE 1989-90*	*Districts*	*TE 1992-93*	*TE 1995-96*	*TE 1998-99*	*Districts*	*TE 2001-02*	*TE 2004-05*
Ambala	26.13	16.83	Ambala	11.00	8.13	8.07	Ambala	2.63	3.03
							Panchkula	2.40	1.80
			Yamuna Nagar	5.93	4.76	3.60	Yamun Nagar	2.70	2.97
Kurukshetra	7.70	6.83	Kurukshctra	2.30	1.97	1.07	Kurukshetra	1.23	0.97
			Kaithal	5.93	2.57	0.77	Kaithal	0.63	0.60
Karnal	8.53	5.63	Karnal	4.20	3.37	3.10	Karnal	1.83	1.40
			Panipat	3.53	2.33	1.63	Panipat	1.00	0.63
Sonipat	9.40	8.10	Sonipat	12.77	19.97	18.63	Sonipat	2.07	6.90
Rohtak	67.37	37.10	Rohtak	36.43	30.23	19.23	Rohtak	7.03	12.57
							Jhajjar	6.53	7.47
Faridbad	12.83	5.38	Faridbad	9.23	7.83	5.80	Faridbad	4.90	7.37
Gurgoan	31.93	6.97	Gurgoan	12.77	8.83	9.00	Gurgoan	5.03	2.67
			Rewari	10.93	5.97	4.50	Rewari	1.50	0.77
Mahendragarh	81.53	51.73	Mahendragarh	29.73	24.50	26.70	Mahendragarh	9.70	10.80
Bhiwani	183.37	158.30	Bhiwani	161.20	152.23	168.34	Bhiwani	76.67	63.40
Jind	50.60	32.00	Jind	25.33	15.37	8.63	Jind	1.40	1.57
Hisar	136.40	95.07	Hisar	124.53	122.77	75.87	Hisar	15.40	23.23
							Fatehabad	3.77	3.27

Table 4.3 Continued

Table 4.3 Continued

Districts	*TE 1986-87*	*TE 1989-90*	*Districts*	*TE 1992-93*	*TE 1995-96*	*TE 1998-99*	*Districts*	*TE 2001-02*	*TE 2004-05*
Sirsa	123.40	82.40	Sirsa	75.03	56.53	46.20	Sirsa	14.30	17.40
Total	739.20	506.35		530.87	467.36	401.14		160.73	168.80
For above 12 districts			For above 16 districts				For above 19 districts		
Average	61.60	42.20		33.18	29.21	25.07		8.46	8.88
Standard Deviation	58.5858327	47.7706346		46.99015	44.89337	43.129987		17.06882	14.60663
C.V.	95.1068713	113.2124793		141.6255	153.6918	172.02966		201.7675	164.41111

Source: Various issues of statistical abstract, Haryana 1983-2007
Directorate of Land Records, Haryana 1984-2007.

2001-02 and 16 districts for TE period 2004-05 in below the standard deviation.

The compound growth rates of area under pluses during the year 1984-85 to 2004-05 show more ups and downs. Table 4.4 reflects the compound growth rates of the area under pulses decrease in all districts namely Ambala, Kurukshetra, Karnal, Sonipat, Rohtak, Faridabad, Gurgaon, Mahendragarh, Bhiwani, Jind, Hisar Sirsa for TE period 1986-87 to 1989-90, 15 districts for TE period 1992-93 to 1995-96 and 9 districts for TE period 2001-02 to 2003-05. The compound growth rate of area under pulses is only increased in Sonipat district for TE period 1992-93 to 1995-96 and for TE period 1995-96 to 1998-99 there are only three districts. During the TE period 2001-02 to 2004-05, there are 9 districts they have positive compound growth rate. Thus there is certain improvement in the area under pulses during TE period 2001-02 to 2004-05.

The area under oilseeds during the year 1984-85 to 2004-05 is depicted by table 4.5. The area under oilseeds is the highest in Hisar District 81900 hectare which is 24.05 percent of total in the state followed by Sirsa District, Mahendragarh. However, Mahendragarh for TE period 1989-90 and Hisar for TE period 1992-93 and Bhiwani for TE period 1995-96, 1998-99, 2001-02 and 2004-05 are the highest districts in the state. Karnal district for TE period 1989-90 and Panipat for TE period 1992-93, 1995-96, 1998-99, 2001-02 and 2004-05 are the lowest districts in the state. Data reveals above and below the state average and standard deviation during the study period. In the TE period 1986-87, the districts in reference to area under oilseeds there are 5 districts in above and 7 districts in below the state average and 7 districts above and 5 districts below the standard deviation. However, 6 districts for TE period 1989-90 and 7 districts for TE period 1992-93, 1995-96, 1998-99, 2001-02 and 2004-05 are in above. There are 6 districts for TE period 1989-90 and 9 districts for TE period 1992-93, 1995-96 and 1998-99 and 12 districts for TE period 2001-02 and 2004-05 are below the state average and standard deviation.

Table 4.4
District-wise Growth Rates of area under Pulses (Triennium Ending)

Districts	*TE 1986-87 to TE 1989-90*	*Districts*	*TE 1992-93 to TE 1995-96*	*TE 1995-96 to TE 1998-99*	*Districts*	*TE 2001-02 to TE 2004-05*
Ambala	-5.54571	Ambala	-3.84515	-0.096022	Ambala	1.853123
					Panchkula	-3.66226
		Yamuna Nagar	-2.81008	-3.55765	Yamuna Nagar	1.243767
Kurukshetra	-1.54292	Kurukshetra	-1.98857	-7.61085	Kurukshetra	-3.03289
		Kaithal	-10.2765	-14.4709	Kaithal	-0.63077
Karnal	-5.24583	Karnal	-2.81507	-1.07722	Karnal	-3.41407
		Panipat	-5.24522	-4.52802	Panipat	-5.81622
Sonipat	-1.91189	Sonipat	5.970382	-0.89677	Sonipat	16.89963
Rohtak	-7.44545	Rohtak	-2.39047	-5.698005	Rohtak	7.82802
					Jhajjar	1.759501
Faridabad	-10.6595	Faridabad	-2.11079	-3.81734	Faridabad	5.436422
Gurgaon	-17.9123	Gurgaon	-4.67223	0.247623	Gurgaon	-7.88563
		Rewari	-7.5436	-3.59961	Rewari	-8.28483
Mahendragarh	-5.72943	Mahendragarh	-2.4781	1.121468	Mahendragarh	1.402903
Bhiwani	-1.88859	Bhiwani	-0.73978	1.313159	Bhiwani	-2.43462
Jind	-5.76955	Jind	-6.27361	-7.21217	Jind	1.497413
Hissar	-4.5737	Hissar	-0.18443	-6.051138	Hissar	5.47601
					Fatehabad	-1.8284
Sirssa	-5.10275	Sirssa	-3.6052	-2.58313	Sirssa	2.577347

Source: Table 4.3

Table 4.5
District-wise area under Oil Seeds (Triennium Ending)

(thousand hectares)

Districts	*TE 1986-87*	*TE 1989-90*	*Districts*	*TE 1992-93*	*TE 1995-96*	*TE 1998-99*	*Districts*	*TE 2001-02*	*TE 2004-05*
Ambala	13.90	12.30	Ambala	8.63	12.73	10.10	Ambala	1.87	2.73
							Panchkula	1.77	2.00
			Yamun Nagar	3.70	7.20	3.80	Yamun Nagar	1.87	2.67
Kurukshetra	10.33	11.53	Kurukshetra	5.93	8.57	27.57	Kurukshetra	2.07	2.37
			Kaithal	9.40	6.13	7.30	Kaithal	2.20	1.47
Karnal	3.30	2.33	Karnal	3.73	3.57	6.30	Karnal	0.93	0.83
			Panipat	2.20	1.77	1.03	Panipat	1.00	0.77
Sonipat	6.70	5.57	Sonipat	11.17	8.00	6.53	Sonipat	4.10	5.53
Rohtak	32.80	48.17	Rohtak	76.03	70.87	52.47	Rohtak	11.83	21.13
							Jhajjar	25.23	47.07
Faridbad	12.77	11.97	Faridbad	19.27	10.50	8.60	Faridbad	5.13	6.00
Gurgoan	30.83	46.73	Gurgoan	61.80	61.80	47.37	Gurgoan	45.70	59.57
			Rewari	59.63	66.17	65.20	Rewari	60.80	67.97
Mahendragarh	52.07	77.77	Mahendragarh	72.37	85.23	83.63	Mahendragarh	85.90	85.80
Bhiwani	27.77	41.03	Bhiwani	88.27	96.80	118.37	Bhiwani	117.30	167.83
Jind	25.57	18.40	Jind	20.60	18.87	14.83	Jind	5.57	11.57
Hisar	81.90	72.57	Hisar	94.57	94.80	93.00	Hisar	42.07	66.47
							Fatehabad	14.43	18.30

Table 4.5 Continued

Table 4.5 Continued

Districts	*TE 1986-87*	*TE 1989-90*	*Districts*	*TE 1992-93*	*TE 1995-96*	*TE 1998-99*	*Districts*	*TE 2001-02*	*TE 2004-05*
Sirsa	42.50	39.73	Sirsa	55.77	55.37	50.97	Sirsa	43.93	86.10
Total	340.43	388.10		593.07	608.37	597.07		473.70	656.17
For above 12 districts			For above 16 districts				For above 19 districts		
Average	28.37	32.34		37.07	38.02	37.32		24.93	34.54
Standard Deviation	22.4354133	25.81539406		34.06364	36.19021	36.9916		33.244193	44.778702
C.V.	79.0830195	79.82085256		91.89832	95.18	99.1290		133.34171	129.66147

Source: Various issues of statistical abstract, Haryana 1983-2007
Directorate of Land Records, Haryana 1984-2007.

Table 4.6 depicts the district wise compound growth rate of area under oilseeds during the study period. The area under oilseeds has increased in 5 districts namely Kurukshetra, Rohtak, Gurgaon, Mahendragarh, Bhiwani for TE period 1986-87 to 1989-90 and 7 districts for TE period 1992-93 to 1995-96 and 4 districts for TE period 1995-96 to 1998-99 and 15 districts for TE period 2001-02 to 2004-05 and remained districts have decreasing trends during the aforesaid time period. The increase in area under oilseeds is the highest in Kurushetra 16.36 percent during the TE period 1995-96 to 1998-99, but the highest decline in Faridabad district -7.57 percent for TE period 1992-93 to 1995-96. The increase and decrease in area under cereals, pulses, oilseeds, because of expansion of cultivated area may have been a less costly measure for increasing the crop production initially, but the scope for brining more area under cultivation seems to have been exhausted due to the high cost of preparation and improvement of new lands for cultivation. Another factors, the substitution of one crop to another, based on profitability, as substitution of inferior cereals like Bajra, Jowar for course cereals pulses by the more remunerative cereals and oilseeds.

To examine the disparities level among districts in area under oilseeds the C.V. was 79.08 for TE period 1986-87, 79.82 for TE period 1989-90 and 99.25 for TE period 1998-99, 133.34 for TE period 2001-02 and 129.66 for TE 2004-05. Thus, Coefficient of variation figures indicated that inter district disparities in area widened up to during TE period 2001-02 but declined during the TE period 2004-05.

Thus, the disparities among districts in area under cereals, pulses and oilseeds crops has increased during TE 1984-85 to TE 2001-02, and disparities decline during TE 2004-05 as compared the previous year. There increased and decreased in disparities among districts in area under crops during aforesaid time period, because of extension of irrigation facilities by canals, wells and tube-wells in the some districts (southern western region) in the state.

Table 4.6
District-wise Growth Rates of Area under Oil Seeds (Triennium Ending)

Districts	*TE 1986-87 to TE 1989-90*	*Districts*	*TE 1992-93 to TE 1995-96*	*TE 1995-96 to TE 1998-99*	*Districts*	*TE 2001-02 to TE 2004-05*
Ambala	-1.57349	Ambala	5.170581	-2.956812	Ambala	5.029453
					Panchkula	1.597033
		Yamuna Nagar	9.017925	-7.95416	Yamuna Nagar	4.727177
Kurukshetra	1.43552	Kurukshetra	4.891699	16.36247	Kurukshetra	1.770763
		Kaithal	-5.39361	2.291309	Kaithal	-5.09475
Karnal	-4.41362	Karnal	-0.89571	7.64438	Karnal	-1.46453
		Panipat	-2.78111	-6.78093	Panipat	-3.33288
Sonipat	-2.3671	Sonipat	-4.23662	-2.59883	Sonipat	3.956662
Rohtak	5.11046	Rohtak	-0.90734	-3.823593	Rohtak	7.813041
					Jhajjar	8.423658
Faridabad	-0.83553	Faridabad	-7.57249	-2.5556	Faridabad	2.052452
Gurgaon	5.54198	Gurgaon	0	-3.3898	Gurgaon	3.497298
		Rewari	1.358832	-0.19134	Rewari	1.456263
Mahendragarh	5.340531	Mahendragarh	2.14392	-0.24548	Mahendragarh	-0.01511
Bhiwani	5.19282	Bhiwani	1.20355	2.643322	Bhiwani	4.755388
Jind	-4.17797	Jind	-1.13118	-3.07624	Jind	9.94471
Hissar	-1.55635	Hissar	0.031509	-0.248309	Hissar	6.111805
					Fatehabad	3.129337
Sirssa	-0.87028	Sirssa	-0.09331	-1.06811	Sirssa	9.119259

Source : Table 4.5

Districts wise Agricultural Production (Cereals, Pluses, Oilseed)

Table 4.7 presents the data regarding to output, covering three years average of production of cereals. The production of cereals is the highest in Kurukshetra district 1299000 tonnes which is 18.48 percent of total cereals in the state and the lowest in Bhiwani district, 234670 tonnes which is only 3.33 percent for TE period 1986-87. However Kurukshetra district 1372330 tonnes for TE period 1989-90 and Hisar 1297670 tonnes for TE period 1992-93 and Karnal 1210000 tonnes for TE period 2001-02 and 1210670 tonnes for TE period 2004-05. The production is lowest in the Gurgaon 282330 tonnes for TE period 1989-90 and Mahendergarh for TE period 1992-93 and Rewari for TE period 1995-96 and 1998-99 and Panchkula for TE period 2000-05. It is clear from above analysis the level and pattern of production of cereals have variation. Table shows the district which exist in above and below the state average and standard deviation during the study period. In the TE period 1986-87, the districts in reference to production of cereals, there are 4 districts (Kurukshetra, Karnal, Jind and Hisar) to above the state average and 8 districts are above to standard deviation and 8 districts are below to state average and 4 distract are below to standard deviation. However, 4 districts for TE period 1989-90 and 6 district for TE period 1992-93, 1995-96 and 1998-99 and 8 districts for TE period 2001-02 and 2004-05 are to above and 10 districts for TE period 1992-93, 1995-96 and 1998-99, 11 districts for TE period 2001-02 and 2004-05 are to below the state average.

Data given in table 4.8 presents inter-district compound growth rate of production of cereals during the years 1985 to 2005, shows up sand downs. The compound growth rate of cereals production is positive in all of the districts except Karnal for TE period 1986-87 to 1989-90. In the TE period 1992-93 to 1995-96 there are 11 districts, 13 districts for TE period 1995-96 to 1998-99 and 6 districts for TE period 2001-02 to 2004-05 have positive growth rates. Other hand, the 5 districts for TE period 1992-93 to 1995-96, 3 districts for TE

Table 4.7
District-wise Production of Cereals (Triennium Ending)

(thousand tonnes)

Districts	*TE 1986-87*	*TE 1989-90*	*Districts*	*TE 1992-93*	*TE 1995-96*	*TE 1998-99*	*Districts*	*TE 2001-02*	*TE 2004-05*
Ambala	521.00	607.67	Ambala	443.00	445.00	528.67	Ambala	530.67	496.33
							Panchukala	84.33	85.33
			Yamuna Nagar	333.33	343.00	376.67	Yamuna Nagar	411.67	418.33
Kurukshetra	1299.00	1372.33	Kurukshetra	713.00	703.67	722.00	Kurukshetra	853.67	856.00
			Kaithal	964.67	938.00	1040.33	Kaithal	1133.67	1153.67
Karnal	1253.33	1103.33	Karnal	947.67	993.00	1034.00	Karnal	1210.00	1210.67
			Panipat	489.00	432.67	463.00	Panipat	534.00	518.33
Sonipat	438.00	581.00	Sonipat	472.33	587.33	615.67	Sonipat	730.67	672.00
Rohtak	457.67	546.67	Rohtak	573.00	594.00	728.00	Rohtak	416.67	387.33
							Jhajjar	453.33	405.00
Faridbad	334.00	379.67	Faridbad	434.33	508.67	550.67	Faridbad	639.33	600.67
Gurgoan	273.00	282.33	Gurgoan	326.67	391.33	491.67	Gurgoan	567.67	517.33
Rewari			Rewari	231.00	215.67	243.33	Rewari	298.00	261.33
Mahendragarh	235.33	379.00	Mahendragarh	196.00	227.33	282.33	Mahendragarh	300.00	292.33
Bhiwani	234.67	317.00	Bhiwani	335.00	377.00	520.00	Bhiwani	663.67	646.67
Jind	626.33	642.00	Jind	724.00	840.33	966.67	Jind	1151.67	1095.67
Hisar	844.33	986.00	Hisar	1297.67	1152.67	1681.67	Hisar	1025.33	997.33
							Fatehabad	951	974.00

Table 4.7 Continued

Table 4.7 Continued

Districts	*TE 1986-87*	*TE 1989-90*	*Districts*	*TE 1992-93*	*TE 1995-96*	*TE 1998-99*	*Districts*	*TE 2001-02*	*TE 2004-05*
Sirsa	512.33	542.00	Sirsa	873.00	898.67	1032.00	Sirsa	1155.33	1140.33
Total	7029.00	7739.00		9353.67	9648.33	11276.67		13110.67	12728.67
For above 12 districts			For above 16 districts				For above 19 districts		
Average	585.75	644.92		584.60	603.02	704.79		690.04	669.93
Standard Deviation	366.55216	338.63499		309.44484	287.30612	369.82534		337.85748	342.34333
C.V.	62.578261	52.508333		52.932369	47.644477	52.173001		48.962363	51.101372

Source: Various issues of statistical abstract, Haryana 1983-2007
Directorate of Land Records, Haryana 1984-2007.

Table 4.8

District-wise Growth Rates of Production of Cereals (Triennium Ending)

Districts	*TE 1986-87 to TE 1989-90*	*Districts*	*TE 1992-93 to TE 1995-96*	*TE 1995-96 to TE 1998-99*	*Districts*	*TE 2001-02 to TE 2004-05*
Ambala	2.015771	Ambala	0.058437	2.25961	Ambala	-0.86388
					Panchkula	0.153003
		Yamuna Nagar	0.371574	1.221826	Yamuna Nagar	0.208353
Kurukshetra	0.714749	Kurukshetra	-0.17068	0.334068	Kurukshetra	0.035356
		Kaithal	-0.36295	1.35193	Kaithal	0.227063
Karnal	-1.63961	Karnal	0.607816	0.526105	Karnal	0.00718
		Panipat	-1.57473	0.882557	Panipat	-0.38553
Sonipat	3.732168	Sonipat	2.866415	0.613035	Sonipat	-1.0797
Rohtak	2.331346	Rohtak	0.467899	2.673323	Rohtak	-0.94251
					Jhajjar	-1.45142
Faridabad	1.676041	Faridabad	2.070202	1.034238	Faridabad	-0.80569
Gurgaon	0.436778	Gurgaon	2.36989	3.004555	Gurgaon	-1.19709
		Rewari	-0.88662	1.57729	Rewari	-1.68856
Mahendragarh	6.375418	Mahendragarh	1.941788	2.84994	Mahendragarh	-0.33533
Bhiwani	3.977166	Bhiwani	1.543644	4.258873	Bhiwani	-0.33597
Jind	0.320995	Jind	1.951244	1.833096	Jind	-0.64439
Hissar	2.03206	Hissar	-1.52496	5.020507	Hissar	-0.35845
					Fatehabad	0.310409
Sirssa	0.732799	Sirssa	0.376559	1.810323	Sirssa	-0.16934

Source : Table 4.7

period 1995-96 to 1998-99 and 13 districts for TE 2001-02 to 2004-05 have negative growth rates. The highest increase in growth rate of cereals in Mahendragarh district 6.37 percent for TE period 1986-87 to 1989-90 and Sonipat district 2.86 percent for TE period 1992-93 to 1995-96 and Fatehabad 0.31 percent for TE period 2001-02 to 2004-05. The coefficient of variance of production of cereals has declined from 62.57 in the TE period 1986-87 to 48.96 in the TE period 2001-02, but C. V. has increased in TE 2004-05.

Table 4.9 provides the data of production of pluses. The production of pluses is the highest in Bhiwani district 1036700 tonnes during the period TE 1986-87, 111730 tonnes for TE period 1989-90, 118670 tonnes for TE period 1992-93 and 43300 tonnes for TE period 2004-05 respectively. The production is lowest in Karnal 5300 tonnes, Feridabad, Kurukshetra and Kaithal districts during the TE periods of the study.

Data presented in table 4.9 shows the districts which exist in above and below the state average and standard deviation. In the TE period 1986-87 the districts in reference to production of pluses, there are 5 district in above and 7 districts are below the state average and 6 districts are above and 6 districts are below the standard deviation However, 4 districts for TE period 1989-90, 1992-93 and 1995-96 and 3 districts for TE period 2001-02 and 1998-99 and 7 districts for TE period 1989-90 and 16 districts for TE period 2001-02 and 12 districts for TE period 2004-05 are below the state average. The 4 districts for TE period 1989-90 and 3 districts for TE period 1992-93, 1995-96, 1998-99 and 2004-05 and 1 district for TE period 2001-02 and 16 district for TE period 2004-05 are below the standard deviation.

Data given in table 4.10 depicts, the picture regarding the situation of compound growth rate of districts. The compound growth rate of pulses are negative in all of the districts except Sonipat, Mahendragarh, Bhiwani for TE period 1986-87 to 1989-90, 10 districts for TE period 1992-93 to 1995-96, 13 districts for TE period 1995-96 to 1998-99 and 10 districts for TE period 2001-02 to 2004-05 have their declined trends

Table 4.9
District-wise Production of Pulses (Triennium Ending)

(thousand tonnes)

Districts	*TE 1986-87*	*TE 1989-90*	*Districts*	*TE 1992-93*	*TE 1995-96*	*TE 1998-99*	*Districts*	*TE 2001-02*	*TE 2004-05*
Ambala	21.83	10.97	Ambala	7.13	6.70	6.43	Ambala	1.73	1.63
							Panchkula	1.73	1.57
			Yamun Nagar	3.47	3.20	3.33	Yamun Nagar	1.70	1.77
Kurukshetra	5.73	4.97	Kurukshetra	1.67	1.57	1.23	Kurukshetra	1.10	0.90
Kaithal			Kaithal	6.03	2.80	0.83	Kaithal	0.43	0.40
Karnal	5.30	4.33	Karnal	3.83	3.43	3.37	Karnal	1.67	1.10
			Panipat	3.53	2.47	1.60	Panipat	1.00	0.60
Sonipat	8.17	9.63	Sonipat	17.47	30.00	19.47	Sonipat	2.67	8.57
Rohtak	53.57	28.07	Rohtak	26.33	28.53	20.37	Rohtak	4.53	9.40
							Jhajjar	4.67	6.73
Faridbad	6.67	3.43	Faridbad	6.50	5.50	5.63	Faridbad	2.77	4.00
Gurgoan	22.97	3.80	Gurgoan	6.67	6.07	9.63	Gurgoan	3.13	2.33
			Rewari	7.33	6.10	3.97	Rewari	1.37	0.73
Mahendragarh	45.13	54.40	Mahendragarh	19.70	23.40	20.83	Mahendragarh	7.70	9.07
Bhiwani	103.67	111.73	Bhiwani	118.67	158.30	150.13	Bhiwani	48.53	43.30
Jind	39.77	28.47	Jind	20.93	15.93	8.10	Jind	1.20	1.67
Hisar	102.83	81.50	Hisar	82.30	129.80	69.53	Hisar	9.70	12.87
							Fatehabad	3.33	2.40

Table 4.9 Continued

Table 4.9 Continued

Districts	*TE 1986-87*	*TE 1989-90*	*Districts*	*TE 1992-93*	*TE 1995-96*	*TE 1998-99*	*Districts*	*TE 2001-02*	*TE 2004-05*
Sirsa	87.90	61.03	Sirsa	48.73	54.77	42.70	Sirsa	9.80	11.23
Total	503.53	402.33		380.30	478.57	367.17		108.77	120.27
For above 12 districts			For above 16 districts				For above 19 districts		
Average	41.96	33.53		23.77	29.91	22.95		5.72	6.33
Standard Deviation	37.6383746	35.93239115		32.94977	47.11357	38.53548239		10.74365068	9.8204869
C.V.	89.6982314	107.1720034		138.6264	157.5156	167.9258424		187.6763986	155.14627

Source: Various issues of statistical abstract, Haryana 1983-2007
Directorate of Land Records, Haryana 1984-2007.

in growth rates. The 6 districts for TE period 1992-93 to 1995-96, 9 districts for TE period 2001-02 to 2004-05 have their positive growth rates. The highest increase in growth rates of pulses in Sonipat district 16.32 percent for TE period 2001-02 to 2004-05 and highest decrease in Gurgaon -20.81 percent during the TE period 1986-1987 to 1989-90.

To explain the disparities level among districts in production of pulses the C. V. indicates that the inter-district disparities in the production of pluses widened during TE 2001-02 but declined for TE period 2004-05. The C. V. was 89.69 for TE period 1986-87 increased to 187.67 for TE period 2001-02 which shows the disparities have been increased.

Data presented in table 4.11 reflects the inter-district variation of production of oilseeds. The production of oilseeds is the highest in Hisar 62130 tonnes and 80070 tonnes, Bhiwani 95570 tonnes, 213100 tonnes. The districts Karnal 3100 tonnes and 2170 tonnes, 3430 tonnes, 2770 tonnes and 1130 tonnes, again Karnal 700 tonnes and 1000 tonnes, are lowest during the study time period.

Table 4.11 shows the situation of district which exist in above and below the state average and standard deviation during certain parts of the study period. In TE period 1986-87 the districts in reference to production of oilseeds there are 4 districts above the state average and 6 districts are above the standard deviations 8 districts are below the state average and 6 districts are below the standard deviation. However, 6 districts for TE period 1989-90, and 7 districts for TE period 1995-96, 1998-99, 2001-02, and 2004-05 are above and 6 district for TE period 1998-90 and 9 districts for TE period 1992-93, 1995-96 and 1998-99 and 12 districts for TE period 2001-02 and 2004-05 are below in the state average.

Data in Table 4.12 depicts the compound growth rate of districts. The compound growth rate of oilseeds are positive in 8 districts for TE period 1986-87 to 1989-90, 11 districts for TE period 1992-93 to 1995-96 and 3 districts for TE period 1995-96 to TE 1998-99 and all districts for TE period 2001-02

Table 4.10
District-wise Growth Rates of Production of Pulses (Triennium Ending)

Districts	*TE 1986-87 to TE 1989-90*	*Districts*	*TE 1992-93 to TE 1995-96*	*TE 1995-96 to TE 1998-99*	*Districts*	*TE 2001-02 to TE 2004-05*
Ambala	-8.53773	Ambala	-0.80349	-0.532041	Ambala	0.76923
					Panchkula	-1.25072
		Yamuna Nagar	-1.04505	0.517788	Yamuna Nagar	0.524695
Kurukshetra	-1.82854	Kurukshetra	-0.79762	-3.11571	Kurukshetra	-2.56896
		Kaithal	-9.47012	-14.5893	Kaithal	-0.93356
Karnal	-2.58752	Karnal	-1.42038	-0.22861	Karnal	-5.27082
		Panipat	-4.52544	-5.47578	Panipat	-6.41031
Sonipat	2.155217	Sonipat	7.264331	-5.45258	Sonipat	16.32819
Rohtak	-8.04016	Rohtak	1.046175	-4.275152	Rohtak	9.929985
					Jhajjar	4.853242
Faridabad	-8.26377	Faridabad	-2.14325	0.303437	Faridabad	4.880864
Gurgaon	-20.8116	Gurgaon	-1.21505	6.168365	Gurgaon	-3.7557
		Rewari	-2.35412	-5.41825	Rewari	-7.83998
Mahendragarh	2.452454	Mahendragarh	2.257323	-1.49753	Mahendragarh	2.146441
Bhiwani	0.975765	Bhiwani	3.807716	-0.68489	Bhiwani	-1.46799
Jind	-4.24248	Jind	-3.47838	-8.39788	Jind	4.379534
Hissar	-2.97	Hissar	6.087145	-7.776795	Hissar	3.735414
					Fatehabad	-4.15851
Sirssa	-4.62141	Sirssa	1.526961	-3.17703	Sirssa	1.782181

Source: Table 4.9

Table 4.11
District-wise Production of Oil Seeds (Triennium Ending)

(thousand tonnes)

Districts	*TE 1986-87*	*TE 1989-90*	*Districts*	*TE 1992-93*	*TE 1995-96*	*TE 1998-99*	*Districts*	*TE 2001-02*	*TE 2004-05*
Ambala	9.53	7.43	Ambala	8.90	15.47	11.33	Ambala	2.00	3.77
							Panchkula	1.37	1.70
			Yamuna Nagar	4.17	10.60	3.27	Yamun Nagar	2.17	2.97
Kurukshetra	8.90	9.97	Kurukshetra	9.43	15.43	45.87	Kurukshetra	1.83	3.80
			Kaithal	9.40	6.60	8.83	Kaithal	2.97	2.10
Karnal	3.10	2.17	Karnal	6.50	5.73	10.47	Karnal	0.70	1.00
			Panipat	3.43	2.77	1.13	Panipat	1.40	1.00
Sonipat	4.67	4.33	Sonipat	13.30	8.27	6.27	Sonipat	4.67	6.07
Rohtak	24.43	53.53	Rohtak	77.93	91.17	52.13	Rohtak	15.00	26.33
							Jhajjar	38.70	62.00
Faridbad	9.97	14.80	Faridbad	22.70	14.80	9.77	Faridbad	7.43	8.07
Gurgoan	22.10	49.20	Gurgoan	61.10	77.63	52.20	Gurgoan	66.60	73.97
			Rewari	69.07	99.80	86.37	Rewari	99.73	100.13
Mahendragarh	48.40	91.13	Mahendragarh	87.03	119.03	97.70	Mahendragarh	117.70	111.53
Bhiwani	22.53	46.13	Bhiwani	95.57	133.73	132.70	Bhiwani	147.67	213.10
Jind	18.30	16.10	Jind	19.00	20.37	13.57	Jind	6.73	15.13
Hisar	62.13	80.07	Hisar	93.83	129.07	100.23	Hisar	61.80	84.50
							Fatehabad	21.13	23.00

Table 4.11 Continued

Table 4.11 Continued

Districts	*TE 1986-87*	*TE 1989-90*	*Districts*	*TE 1992-93*	*TE 1995-96*	*TE 1998-99*	*Districts*	*TE 2001-02*	*TE 2004-05*
Sirsa	37.93	42.80	Sirsa	59.13	71.70	66.23	Sirsa	58.00	99.10
Total	272.00	417.67		640.50	822.17	698.07		657.60	839.27
For above 12 districts			For above 16 districts				For above 19 districts		
Average	22.67	34.81		40.03	51.39	43.63		34.61	44.17
Standard Deviation	18.3540214	30.27409411		35.89557	49.85286	42.25672136		45.204008	57.097453
C.V.	80.9736238	86.98063752		89.66886	97.01754	96.85429401		130.60769	129.26185

Source: Various issues of statistical abstract, Haryana 1983-2007
Directorate of Land Records, Haryana 1984-2007.

to 2004-05 except Kairthal, Panipat and Mahendragarh. The 4 districts for TE period 1986-87 to 1989-90, 5 districts for TE period 1992-93 to 1995-96 and 13 districts for TE period 1995-96 to 1998-99 have their negative growth rates. The highest growth rate increase in Yamunaganar district which is 12.86 percent during the TE period 1986-87 to 1989-90.

The disparities among districts in the production of oilseeds has increased from 80.97 for TE period 1986-87 to 130.60 for TE period 2001-02 but declined 129.26 for TE 2004-05 which shows the disparities in the production of oilseeds has increased among districts in the state during 1986 to 2002 and decrease from 2001-02 to 2004-05.

District-wise Agricultural Productivity (Cereals, Pluses, Oilseed)

The productivity of cereals during the years 1984-85 to 2004-05 is depicted in table 4.13. The productivity of cereals is the highest in Karnal district (2867 kg/ha.) and the lowest in Bhiwani only (804 kg/ha.) during the TE period 1986-87. However, Kurukshetra (3002 kg/ha.) for TE period 1989-90 and Sirsa (3665 kg/ha.) for TE period 1992-93, Ambala (4643 kg/ha.) for TE period 1998-99 and Fatehabad (3852 kg/ha.) for TE periods 2004-05 districts are in highest position and Bhiwani remained lowest during the aforesaid time periods.

The situation of districts which exist in above and below the state average and standard deviation during the study time period explained as there are 7 districts, 9 districts, 12 districts and again 12 districts above the state average and 5 districts, 7 districts and again 7 districts, 6 districts and 7 districts are below the state average during the study TE periods. There are 12 districts, 16 district and 19 districts, above the standard deviation during the study TE periods.

Data presented in table 4.14 reveals the growth pattern among the districts in the term of productivity of cereals. The growth rate of productivity of cereals is positive in all of the districts for TE period 1986-87 to 1989-90 and 10 districts

Table 4.12
District-wise Growth Rates of Production of Oil Seeds (Triennium Ending)

Districts	*TE 1986-87 to TE 1989-90*	*Districts*	*TE 1992-93 to TE 1995-96*	*TE 1995-96 to TE 1998-99*	*Districts*	*TE 2001-02 to TE 2004-05*
Ambala	-3.17672	Ambala	7.433335	-3.958745	Ambala	8.568952
					Panchkula	2.838517
		Yamuna Nagar	12.86187	-14.1463	Yamuna Nagar	4.154149
Kurukshetra	1.483276	Kurukshetra	6.594588	15.1769	Kurukshetra	9.939928
		Kaithal	-4.48284	3.847304	Kaithal	-4.39589
Karnal	-4.52043	Karnal	-1.62194	8.131519	Karnal	4.734443
		Panipat	-2.73362	-10.9779	Panipat	-4.26993
Sonipat	-0.97557	Sonipat	-5.97603	-3.52693	Sonipat	3.458993
Rohtak	10.70892	Rohtak	2.055907	-6.993039	Rohtak	7.570071
					Jhajjar	6.302977
Faridabad	5.256952	Faridabad	-5.39635	-5.24375	Faridabad	1.077375
Gurgaon	10.93724	Gurgaon	3.154089	-5.01688	Gurgaon	1.370488
		Rewari	4.889035	-1.85695	Rewari	0.051927
Mahendragarh	8.552893	Mahendragarh	4.144531	-2.52856	Mahendragarh	-0.6959
Bhiwani	9.739505	Bhiwani	4.453497	-0.10023	Bhiwani	4.871812
Jind	-1.6474	Jind	0.907059	-5.13175	Jind	11.07816
Hissar	3.34464	Hissar	4.222191	-3.226543	Hissar	4.140823
					Fatehabad	1.105862
Sirssa	1.578959	Sirssa	2.531349	-1.02392	Sirssa	7.194438

Source: Table 4.11

Table 4.13
District-wise Productivity of Cereals (Triennium Ending)

(Kgs/ hectare)

Districts	TE 1986-87	TE 1989-90	Districts	TE 1992-93	TE 1995-96	TE 1998-99	Districts	TE 2001-02	TE 2004-05
Ambala	2165.67	2430.67	Ambala	2614.00	2608.00	4643.00	Ambala	3377.00	3205.67
							Panchkula	2586.00	2529.67
			Yamuna Nagar	2959.33	2979.33	3160.67	Yamun Nagar	3396.67	3291.67
Kurukshetra	2825.33	3001.67	Kurukshetra	3420.00	3251.67	3443.00	Kurukshetra	3871.67	3802.00
			Kaithal	3251.33	3062.33	3273.67	Kaithal	3392.67	3811.67
Karnal	2867.00	2985.67	Karnal	3230.33	3051.33	3193.33	Karnal	3667.33	3616.00
			Panipat	3235.33	3030.33	3105.67	Panipat	3416.67	3402.33
Sonipat	2275.33	2513.00	Sonipat	2905.67	2901.67	2810.00	Sonipat	3236.33	3196.00
Rohtak	1635.00	1948.00	Rohtak	2218.67	2439.33	3938.67	Rohtak	2591.00	2737.00
							Jhajjar	2570.67	2598.00
Faridbad	1915.00	2195.67	Faridbad	2593.67	2826.00	2893.67	Faridbad	3424.67	3269.33
Gurgoan	1500.67	1590.33	Gurgoan	1906.00	2192.67	2485.33	Gurgoan	2611.67	2741.67
			Rewari	2169.00	2227.33	2354.00	Rewari	2614.00	2615.33
Mahendr-agarh	1037.00	1472.67	Mahendr-agarh	1474.00	1791.67	2115.67	Mahendragarh	2049.67	2273.33
Bhiwani	804.00	1136.67	Bhiwani	1349.33	1569.67	1742.00	Bhiwani	1945.33	1954.00
Jind	2132.33	2576.33	Jind	2849.00	3015.00	3139.67	Jind	3225.33	3267.67

Table 4.13 Continued

Table 4.13 Continued

Districts	TE 1986-87	TE 1989-90	Districts	TE 1992-93	TE 1995-96	TE 1998-99	Districts	TE 2001-02	TE 2004-05
Hisar	2405.33	2745.00	Hisar	3251.00	3320.33	5784.00	Hisar	3451.67	3352.33
							Fatehabad	3824.33	3852.67
Sirsa	2862.00	2964.33	Sirsa	3665.00	3729.67	3876.00	Sirsa	3968.00	3827.00
Total	24424.67	27560.00		43091.67	43996.33	51958.33		59220.67	59343.33
For above 12 districts			For above 16 districts				For above 19 districts		
Average	2023.55	2284.48		2698.51	2759.22	3154.36		3102.43	3118.76
Standard Deviation	719.374331	663.1109236		719.1022	594.3702	944.94757		615.8314	578.08498
C.V.	35.5501938	29.02671576		26.64811	21.54122	29.956914		19.84999	18.535736

Source: Various issues of statistical abstract, Haryana 1983-2007
Directorate of Land Records, Haryana 1984-2007.

Table 4.14
District-wise Growth Rates of Productivity of Cereals (Triennium Ending)

Districts	*TE 1986-87 to TE 1989-90*	*Districts*	*TE 1992-93 to TE 1995-96*	*TE 1995-96 to TE 1998-99*	*Districts*	*TE 2001-02 to TE 2004-05*
Ambala	1.508389	Ambala	-0.0298	7.767215	Ambala	-0.67299
					Panchkula	-0.28522
		Yamuna Nagar	0.087393	0.769236	Yamuna Nagar	-0.40641
Kurukshetra	0.788292	Kurukshetra	-0.65244	0.744262	Kurukshetra	-0.23523
		Kaithal	-0.77369	0.869263	Kaithal	1.521726
Karnal	0.52739	Karnal	-0.7366	0.591669	Karnal	-0.18264
		Panipat	-0.84536	0.319004	Panipat	-0.05453
Sonipat	1.296854	Sonipat	-0.01786	-0.41547	Sonipat	-0.1625
Rohtak	2.297687	Rohtak	1.237272	6.410911	Rohtak	0.713485
					Jhajjar	0.137248
Faridabad	1.789616	Faridabad	1.118819	0.307365	Faridabad	-0.60022
Gurgaon	0.755439	Gurgaon	1.833765	1.638123	Gurgaon	0.631998
		Rewari	0.344761	0.719937	Rewari	0.006597
Mahendragarh	4.653928	Mahendragarh	2.563481	2.179187	Mahendragarh	1.35224
Bhiwani	4.593055	Bhiwani	1.981051	1.360147	Bhiwani	0.05769
Jind	2.483467	Jind	0.737172	0.526867	Jind	0.169286
Hissar	1.72791	Hissar	0.274045	7.463713	Hissar	-0.37802
					Fatehabad	0.095799
Sirssa	0.456652	Sirssa	0.227107	0.500353	Sirssa	-0.46814

Source: Table 4.13

for TE period 1992-93 to 1995-96, 13 districts for TE period 1995-96 to 1998-99 and 9 districts for TE period 2001-02 to 2004-05. The 6 districts for TE period 1992-93 to 1995-96 and 2 districts for TE period 1995-96 to 1998-99 and 10 districts for TE period 2001-02 to 2004-05 have their negative growth rates. The highest increase in growth rate of cereals occurs in Mahendragarh district 4.65 percent and highest decrease in Kairthal district -0.77% during the study period. To measure the disparities level among districts in productivity of cereals the C.V. figures indicated that the inter-district disparities continuously declined (35.55 to 18.53) during the study period. Thus, the productivity point of view, the variation among districts during the whole study period decreases.

Table 4.15 provides the data of productivity of pluses. The productivity of pluses is highest in Rohtak (854kg/ha.) for TE period 1986-87, Sonipat remained highest on all TE time period. There are districts Mahendragarh (517kg/ha.), Gurgaon (488kg/ha.), again Gurgaon (522kg/ha.), Yamunanagar (673 kg/ha.), Fariradabad (573 kg/ha.) and Hisar (593 kg/hg.) and again Hisar (539 kg/ha.) remained lowest in difference TE time period respectively.

The districts which exist above and below the state average and standard deviation during the TE time period 1986-87 in reference to productivity of pluses, the 7 districts are above and 5 districts are below the mean and 12 districts are above the standard deviation. However, 6 districts for TE period 1989-90, 5 districts for TE period 1992-93, 9 districts for TE period 1995-96, 2004-05, 6 districts for TE period 1998-99 and 8 district for TE period 2001-02 are above and 6 districts for TE period 1989-90, 11 districts for TE period 1992-93, 2001-02, 7 districts for TE period 1995-96 and 10 districts for period 2004-05 are below the state average. The growth pattern among districts in the term of productivity of pluses during the 1984 to 2005 explained through table 4.16. The compound growth rate of productivity of pulses is positive in 5 districts for TE period 1986-87 to 1989-90 and 15 districts for TE period 1992-93 to 1995-96, 9 districts for TE period 1995-96 to 1998-

Table 4.15
District-wise Productivity of Pulses (Triennium Ending)

(Kgs/ hectare)

Districts	*TE 1986-87*	*TE 1989-90*	*Districts*	*TE 1992-93*	*TE 1995-96*	*TE 1998-99*	*Districts*	*TE 2001-02*	*TE 2004-05*
Ambala	848.33	624.00	Ambala	607.33	828.00	1270	Ambala	657.33	540.00
							Panchkula	771.00	880.67
			Yamuna Nagar	598.33	673.33	862.67	Yamun Nagar	629.67	594.00
Kurukshetra	727.00	736.67	Kurukshetra	709.33	797.00	888.67	Kurukshetra	892.33	892.00
Kaithal			Kaithal	1022.33	1080.00	717.67	Kaithal	700.00	649.00
Karnal	611.33	731.33	Karnal	913.67	1025.00	1172.00	Karnal	905.33	786.33
			Panipat	1001.67	1056.67	1251.33	Panipat	989.67	952.33
Sonipat	847.00	814.67	Sonipat	1361.00	1500.33	1507.00	Sonipat	1279.33	1242.33
Rohtak	854.67	762.00	Rohtak	718.33	942.33	1233.67	Rohtak	623.00	1349.67
							Jhajjar	704.00	912.67
Faridbad	770.33	667.67	Faridbad	708.33	700.67	573.33	Faridbad	737.00	539.67
Gurgoan	657.67	488.33	Gurgoan	522.00	691.67	892.33	Gurgoan	615.67	853.33
			Rewari	692.00	1007.67	678.00	Rewari	928.00	336.00
Mahendr-agarh	517.33	600.50	Mahendra-garh	681.67	952.67	896.67	Mahendragarh	794.33	794.33
Bhiwani	563.33	589.33	Bhiwani	710.33	1040.33	802.67	Bhiwani	613.33	671.00
Jind	774.67	662.33	Jind	831.33	1031.00	716.33	Jind	981.67	1052.00

Table 4.15 Continued

Table 4.15 Continued

Districts	*TE 1986-87*	*TE 1989-90*	*Districts*	*TE 1992-93*	*TE 1995-96*	*TE 1998-99*	*Districts*	*TE 2001-02*	*TE 2004-05*
Hisar	744.67	749.67	Hisar	655.67	1056.00	1314.67	Hisar	593.67	539.00
							Fatehabad	889.33	738.33
Sirsa	715.67	683.67	Sirsa	668.33	968.00	837.00	Sirsa	681.33	661.67
Total	8632	8110.17		12401.67	15350.67	15614		14986.00	14984.33
For above 12 districts			For above 16 districts				For above 19 districts		
Average	719.33	675.85		775.10	959.42	975.88		788.74	788.65
Standard Deviation	112.1032	90.5750835		209.6106	201.4553	274.7055		178.0362	251.26228
C.V.	15.58432	13.4017098		27.0429	20.9976	28.14966		22.57232	31.859832

Source: Various issues of statistical abstract, Haryana 1983-2007
Directorate of Land Records, Haryana 1984-2007.

Table 4.16
District-wise Growth Rates of Productivity of Pulses (Triennium Ending)

Districts	*TE 1986-87 to TE 1989-90*	*Districts*	*TE 1992-93 to TE 1995-96*	*TE 1995-96 to TE 1998-99*	*Districts*	*TE 2001-02 to TE 2004-05*
Ambala	-3.90481	Ambala	4.101564	5.70445674	Ambala	-2.51773
					Panchkula	1.739793
		Yamuna Nagar	1.54336	3.265919	Yamuna Nagar	-0.75347
Kurukshetra	0.171516	Kurukshetra	1.522828	1.421988	Kurukshetra	-0.0048
		Kaithal	0.714245	-5.16256	Kaithal	-0.97629
Karnal	2.351666	Karnal	1.50235	1.753312	Karnal	-1.81106
		Panipat	0.695662	2.21711	Panipat	-0.49755
Sonipat	-0.50346	Sonipat	1.272069	0.057546	Sonipat	-0.37989
Rohtak	-1.47744	Rohtak	3.582872	3.555561	Rohtak	10.54591
					Jhajjar	3.424066
Faridabad	-1.83782	Faridabad	-0.14092	-2.56776	Faridabad	-3.96101
Gurgaon	-3.78749	Gurgaon	3.717499	3.358778	Gurgaon	4.324495
		Rewari	4.994682	-5.00921	Rewari	-12.3446
Mahendragarh	1.952281	Mahendragarh	4.436687	-0.7826	Mahendragarh	0
Bhiwani	0.586894	Bhiwani	5.073057	-3.30761	Bhiwani	1.172307
Jind	-2.01142	Jind	2.83105	-4.61286	Jind	0.901418
Hissar	0.086827	Hissar	6.375948	2.88227273	Hissar	-1.24511
					Fatehabad	-2.38439
Sirssa	-0.5915	Sirssa	4.92172	-1.86815	Sirssa	-0.37902

Source: Table 4.15

99 and 7 districts for TE period 2001-02 to 2004-05. The 7 districts, 1 districts, 7 districts and 12 districts have their negative growth rates during the aforesaid TE time period.

The district-wise coefficients of variations of productivity of pluses are presented in table 4.15. The C.V. results for whole time period increased from 15.58 TE period 1986-87 to 31.85 TE period with fluctuation for different TE period, but the trends shows there increase in variation during the whole TE time period.

Table 4.17 shows the data of productivity of oilseeds. The productivity of oilseeds is highest in the districts namely, Mahendergarh (927 kg/ha.), Rohtak (1269.67 kg./ha.), again Rohtak (1552 kg./ha.), Karnal (1602.67 kg/ha.), Ambala (1739 kg/ha.) and Rewari (1642.67 kg/ha.) and Rewari (1642.67 kg/ha.) during the different- different TE time period respectively. The productivity of oilseeds is lowest in the district namely, Ambala (662 kg/ha.), again Ambala (601.33 kg/ha.), Jind (920.33kg/ha.), again Jind (1076 kg/ha.), Panipath (833 kg/ha.), Panckula (844 kg/ha.) and again Panckula (772 kg/ha.) for all TE time period respectively. Data in table (4.17) depicts the picture of districts which exist above and below the state average and standard deviation. There are 5 districts for TE period 1986-87, 7 districts for TE period 1998-99, 12 districts for TE period 2001-02 and 10 districts for TE period 2004-05 are above and 5 districts for TE period 1989-90 and 10 districts for TE period 1992-93 and 7 district for TE period 2001-02 and 9 district for TE period 2004-05 are below the state average. Similarly, the oilseeds productivity of all districts is above the standard deviation during the all TE time period.

Table 4.18 shows that the compound growth rates of productivity of oilseeds during the study period. The highest increase in growth rate of productivity of oilseeds in Rohtak 6.94 percent for TE period 1986-87 to 1989-90, Hisar 3.49 percent for TE period 1992-93 to 1995-96, Ambala 4.35 percent for TE period 1995-96 to 1998-99 and Karnal 7.90 percent for TE period 2001-02 to 2004-05. The highest decrease in Karnal

Table 4.17
District-wise Productivity of Oil Seeds (Triennium Ending)

(Kgs/ hectare)

Districts	*TE 1986-87*	*TE 1989-90*	*Districts*	*TE 1992-93*	*TE 1995-96*	*TE 1998-99*	*Districts*	*TE 2001-02*	*TE 2004-05*
Ambala	662.00	601.33	Ambala	986.00	1251.67	1739.00	Ambala	1033.67	1334.00
							Panchkula	772.00	844.00
			Yamun Nagar	1137.67	1474.67	987.00	Yamun Nagar	1133.00	1125.33
Kurukshetra	852.67	866.00	Kurukshetra	1353.00	1446.33	1678.67	Kurukshetra	1330.33	1537.33
			Kaithal	940.67	1089.33	1203.00	Kaithal	1375.67	1383.33
Karnal	889.67	678.67	Karnal	1552.00	1602.67	1469.33	Karnal	669.67	1203.67
			Panipat	1490.33	1681.33	833.33	Panipat	1410.33	1322.33
Sonipat	716.33	795.67	Sonipat	1103.67	1028.00	929.67	Sonipat	1106.67	1097.00
Rohtak	756.33	1269.67	Rohtak	989.33	1282.00	1482.00	Rohtak	1240.67	1253.67
							Jhajjar	1197.33	1316.00
Faridbad	771.33	1236.67	Faridbad	1160.33	1406.67	1121.00	Faridbad	1461.67	1336.33
Gurgoan	771.33	1059.67	Gurgoan	985.33	1255.67	1092.67	Gurgoan	1448.33	1249.67
			Rewari	1173.67	1428.33	1322.00	Rewari	1642.67	1476.00
Mahendr-agarh	927.00	1178.67	Mahendr-agarh	1228.00	1405.33	1158.33	Mahendr-agarh	1364.00	1294.00
Bhiwani	811.67	1102.00	Bhiwani	1128.00	1384.33	1115.67	Bhiwani	1250.00	1263.67
Jind	712.67	884.00	Jind	920.33	1076.00	921.33	Jind	1199.67	1321.00

Table 4.17 Continued

Table 4.17 Continued

Districts	*TE 1986-87*	*TE 1989-90*	*Districts*	*TE 1992-93*	*TE 1995-96*	*TE 1998-99*	*Districts*	*TE 2001-02*	*TE 2004-05*
Hisar	752.67	1094.67	Hisar	1057.67	1378.67	1652.33	Hisar	1450.00	1274.67
							Fatehabad	1468.00	1268.33
Sirsa	900.67	1000.00	Sirsa	1126.00	1298.00	1294.00	Sirsa	1310.67	1181.67
Total	9524.33	11767.00		18332.00	21489.00	19999.33		22864.33	24082.00
For above 12 districts			For above 16 districts				For above 19 districts		
Average	793.69	980.58		1145.75	1343.06	1249.96		1203.39	1267.47
Standard Deviation	83.2289599	259.40		185.0006	179.7567	284.87034		319.7418	146.90046
C.V.	10.4862722	26.45370149		16.14668	13.38409	22.790387		26.57018	11.59002

Source: Various issues of statistical abstract, Haryana 1983-2007
Directorate of Land Records, Haryana 1984-2007.

Table 4.18
District-wise Growth Rates of Productivity under Oil Seeds (Triennium Ending)

Districts	*TE 1986-87 to TE 1989-90*	*Districts*	*TE 1992-93 to TE 1995-96*	*TE 1995-96 to TE 1998-99*	*Districts*	*TE 2001-02 to TE 2004-05*
Ambala	-1.23888	Ambala	3.142524	4.356922	Ambala	3.363326
					Panchkula	1.163148
		Yamuna Nagar	3.422133	-5.07412	Yamuna Nagar	-0.08806
Kurukshetra	0.201385	Kurukshetra	0.868862	1.950837	Kurukshetra	22.0705
Kaithal		Kaithal	1.921134	1.295586	Kaithal	0.072041
Karnal	-3.45004	Karnal	0.417525	-1.12024	Karnal	7.901031
Panipat		Panipat	1.576216	-8.70116	Panipat	-0.8321
Sonipat	1.371652	Sonipat	-0.91692	-1.29547	Sonipat	-0.11376
Rohtak	6.949317	Rohtak	3.418066	1.897945	Rohtak	0.135278
Jhajjar					Jhajjar	1.233165
Faridabad	6.313545	Faridabad	2.52827	-2.90114	Faridabad	-1.15599
Gurgaon	4.204975	Gurgaon	3.19431	-1.78714	Gurgaon	-1.89518
Rewari		Rewari	2.579471	-0.99828	Rewari	-1.37796
Mahendragarh	3.164074	Mahendragarh	1.764744	-2.47569	Mahendragarh	-0.68093
Bhiwani	4.045512	Bhiwani	2.69128	-2.75946	Bhiwani	0.141161
Jind	2.833463	Jind	2.047417	-1.99254	Jind	1.257323
Hissar	4.977952	Hissar	3.497259	2.376083	Hissar	-1.65753
Fatehabad					Fatehabad	-1.87823
Sirssa	1.366035	Sirssa	1.860709	-0.04002	Sirssa	-1.33475

Source: Table 4.17

-3.4 percent for TE period 1986-87 to 1989-90, Sonipat -0.91 percent for TE period 1992-93 to 1995-96, Yamunagar -5.07 percent for TE period 1995-96 to 1998-99 and Fatehabad -1.87 percent for TE period 2001-02 to 2004-05. The growth rate of productivity of oilseeds remains positive in all of the districts except to Ambala and Karnal during the TE period 1986-87 to 1989-90.

The measure the disparities among districts in the productivity of oilseeds with help of C.V. indicated very much heterogeneous mode of disparities among districts during the all TE time period. The C.V. is 10.48, 26.45, 16.14, 13.38, 23, 27 and 12 for different TE time period.

Impact of Inputs on Agriculture Development in Haryana

On the eve of economic planning, Indian agriculture was carried on the traditional lines. The use of improved agricultural machinery etc was negligible. With the adoption of economic planning, the principal technical programmers for increasing agricultural production have put emphasis on the use of fertilizers, manure's, multiplication and distribution of improved seeds. The impact of these programme was slow in the early years of planning but it gained momentum in the long run. However, the modern inputs have shown wide variation among the districts in Haryana. The disparities in agricultural productivity and income across different districts can be attributed to the use of these inputs on the one hand and other factors such as agro-climatic conditions, resource base and the nature of technological change on the others.

Growth of Inputs

Present day farmer is more conscious, judicious, awakened, knowledgeable and flexible for change if convinced and some times willing to take the risk gain experience and gets set for transformation. Adoption of new inputs, technology and farm operations are accepted and later on adopted. Government, on the other hand is also aware about the food problem and introduced several measures for the development of agriculture such as adequate provision in the union government as well as state budget for the development of agricultural sector, supply of inputs, liberal credit facilities for the farmers, subsidies, particularly to the weaker sections, large scale irrigation projects, use of modern inputs, HYV seeds, chemical fertilizers, insecticides and pesticides, machinery for the farm operation etc. So the Haryana agriculture has undergone some dynamic change because of the adoption of new technology, extended irrigation facilities and the infrastructure built by the state. The farmers of Haryana have switched over to high yielding varieties and high price crops by discarding inferior crops with lower yield. The basis of approach in the new technology was to devise the ways and means which will be able to bring about significant improvements in the agricultural productivity.

District-wise Land Utilization

Land use pattern among districts during the years 1984-85 to 2004-05 presented in tables 4.19 to 4.28. There are five indicators namely forest area as a percentage of total reporting area, cropping intensity, net area sown, gross cropped area and sown area as a percentage of reporting area have been taken for explanation.

Table 4.19 presents data regarding forest area as a parentage of reporting area. The forest area as a percentage of reporting area is the highest in Ambala district 15.68 percentage for TE period 1986-87, again Ambala 17.10 percentage for TE period 1989-90, again Ambala 21.08 percentage for TE period 1992-930 and again Ambala 9.69 percentage for TE period 1998-99 and Panchkula 19.30 percentage for TE period 2001-02 and again Panchkula 2.33 percentage for TE period 2004-05. The forest area is lowest in Sirsa district 1.40 percentages for TE period 1986-87, Hisar 1.5 percentage for TE period 1989-90, again Sirsa 1.17 percentage for TE period 1992-93, 1995-96 and 1998-99. The

Table 4.19
District-wise Forest Area as a Percentage of total Reporting Area (Triennium Ending)

(percentage)

Districts	*TE 1986-87*	*TE 1989-90*	*Districts*	*TE 1992-93*	*TE 1995-96*	*TE 1998-99*	*Districts*	*TE 2001-02*	*TE 2004-05*
Ambala	15.68	17.19	Ambala	21.08	15.45	9.69	Ambala	1.54	0.64
							Panchkula	19.30	2.33
			Yamuna Nagar	13.69	7.36	7.55	Yamuna Nagar	7.94	8.72
Kurukshetra	2.78	2.77	Kurukshetra	2.67	1.59	1.78	Kurukshetra	1.38	0.39
			Kaithal	3.12	2.05	1.31	Kaithal	1.31	1.02
Karnal	3.40	3.72	Karnal	3.24	2.98	2.83	Karnal	2.02	0.40
			Panipat	3.32	3.14	3.11	Panipat	2.84	2.30
Sonipat	3.62	3.95	Sonipat	4.47	3.43	3.28	Sonipat	2.34	0.46
Rohtak	2.26	2.17	Rohtak	2.10	2.26	2.25	Rohtak	1.85	0.51
							Jhajjar	1.39	0.00
Faridbad	1.90	2.23	Faridbad	3.04	2.08	1.44	Faridbad	1.12	0.48
Gurgoan	4.39	4.40	Gurgoan	5.33	2.44	1.11	Gurgoan	1.73	2.96
			Rewari	2.80	2.14	2.62	Rewari	2.20	1.32
Mahendragarh	2.49	2.68	Mahendragarh	2.92	2.05	1.03	Mahendragarh	1.03	1.03
Bhiwani	2.17	2.10	Bhiwani	2.05	1.77	1.93	Bhiwani	1.50	0.64
Jind	2.38	2.64	Jind	2.53	2.27	2.15	Jind	1.55	0.35
Hisar	1.46	1.51	Hisar	1.52	1.68	1.53	Hisar	1.49	0.00
							Fatehabad	1.07	0.00

Table 4.19 Continued

Table 4.19 Continued

Districts	TE 1986-87	TE 1989-90	Districts	TE 1992-93	TE 1995-96	TE 1998-99	Districts	TE 2001-02	TE 2004-05
Sirsa	1.40	1.55	Sirsa	1.17	1.17	1.17	Sirsa	0.93	0.46
For above 12 districts			For above 16 districts				For above 19 districts		
Average	3.66	3.91		4.69	3.37	2.80		2.87	1.26
Standard Deviation	3.88677	4.27995		5.23384	3.51603	2.41105		4.26292	1.9886758
C.V.	106.172	109.485		111.596	104.449	86.162		148.488	157.32758

Source: Various issues of statistical abstract, Haryana 1983-2007
Directorate of Land Records, Haryana 1984-2007.

districts Faridabad, Hisar, Jhajjar have 0.00 percentage of forest area for TE period 2004-05.

Table 4.19 presents the picture regarding the situation of districts which exist in above and below the state average and standard deviation. In the TE period 1986-87, the districts in the reference to forest area, there are 2 districts above and 10 districts below the state average and standard deviation. However, 3 districts for TE period 1989-90, 1992-93, 1995-96, 1998-99 and 1 district for TE period 2004-05 are in above and 9 districts for TE period 1989-90, 13 districts for TE period 1992-93, 1995-96, 1998-99 and 18 districts for TE period 2004-05 are above the state average. The 2 districts for TE period 1989-90, 1995-96, 2001-02, 3 districts for TE period 1992-93, 1998-99 are above and 13 districts for TE period 1992-93, 1998-99 and 14 districts for TE period 2004-05 are below the standard deviation.

To measure the disparities level among districts in the forest area the C.V. has increased from 106.17 in TE period 1986-87 to 157.32 in TE period 2004-05, but declined in 86.16 during TE period 1998-99, which shows the overall disparities in the forest area has increased, except to the TE period 1995-96 to 1998-99.

Table 4.20 provides the data on compound growth rate of forest area as percentage of reporting area of study period. The growth rate of forest area as a percentage of reporting area is positive in all of the districts except Kurukshetra, Rohtak, Bhiwani, for TE period 1986-87 to TE 1989-90 and all of the districts except Hisar and Rohtak have their negative growth rates during TE period 1992-93 to 1995-96. However, 4 districts and 2 districts have their positive growth rates for TE period 1995-96 to 2004-05.

In case of cropping intensity (i.e. gross cropped area as a percentage of net sown area, table 4.21) is the highest in Jind district for TE period 1986-87, 1989-90, Karnal 191.12 for TE period 1992-93 and Panipat 200.79 for TE period 2004-05. The districts Sirsa 137.69, Rohtak 132.97, again Rohtak 154.48 have lowest cropping intensity during the study period.

Table 4.20

District-wise Growth Rates of Forest Area as a percentage of total Reporting Area (Triennium Ending)

Districts	*TE 1986-87 to TE 1989-90*	*Districts*	*TE 1992-93 to TE 1995-96*	*TE 1995-96 to TE 1998-99*	*Districts*	*TE 2001-02 to TE 2004-05*
Ambala	1.199548	Ambala	-3.94962	-5.87092	Ambala	-10.7634
					Panchkula	-23.9819
		Yamuna Nagar	-7.73336	0.331101	Yamuna Nagar	1.222705
Kurukshetra	-0.04672	Kurukshetra	-6.50153	1.474722	Kurukshetra	-15.1165
		Kaithal	-5.30128	-5.64233	Kaithal	-3.19312
Karnal	1.173386	Karnal	-1.07901	-0.66758	Karnal	-18.9433
		Panipat	-0.72032	-0.12443	Panipat	-2.69807
Sonipat	1.137877	Sonipat	-3.37629	-0.57826	Sonipat	-19.0199
Rohtak	-0.52565	Rohtak	0.956843	-0.0575	Rohtak	-15.3895
					Jhajjar	0
Faridabad	2.098705	Faridabad	-4.80252	-4.65716	Faridabad	-10.4065
Gurgaon	0.029513	Gurgaon	-9.63699	-9.71061	Gurgaon	7.213645
		Rewari	-3.42622	2.6593	Rewari	-6.41031
Mahendragarh	0.958239	Mahendragarh	-4.48412	-8.53963	Mahendragarh	0
Bhiwani	-0.42435	Bhiwani	-1.88663	1.128681	Bhiwani	-10.4583
Jind	1.353706	Jind	-1.39653	-0.70191	Jind	-17.5511
Hissar	0.437669	Hissar	1.306462	-1.20563	Hissar	
					Fatehabad	0
Sirssa	1.32879	Sirssa	0	0	Sirssa	-8.7254

Source: Table 4.19

Table 4.21 shows the picture regarding he situation of districts which exist in the above and below the standard deviation and state average during the study period. The disparities among the districts in cropping intensity did not change much during the study period but overall there is an increase. The coefficient of variation was 8.44 in TE period 1986-87, increased to 9.68 in TE period 2004-05.

The compound growth rate of cropping intensity (Table 4.22) is positive in 5 districts for TE period 1986-87 to 1989-90, 12 districts for TE period 1992-93 to 1995-96, 9 districts for TE period 1995-96 to 1998-99 and 11 districts for TE period 2001-02 to 2004-05. There are 8 districts for TE period 1986-87 to 1989-90, 7 districts for TE period 1992-93 to 1995-96 and 11 districts for TE period 2001-02 to 2004-05 have negative growth rates. The highest increase in growth rate of cropping intensity occurs in Panchakula 3.53 percent in TE period 2001-02 to 2004-05 and the highest decrease in Ambala - 1.24 percent in TE period 2001-02 to 2004-05.

Table 4.23 presents data, net area sown. Which is the highest in Hisar 561.00 thousand hectare for TE period 1986-87, 520 thousand hectare for TE period 1989-90 and 575 thousand hectare for TE period 1992-93, Bhiwani 399 thousand hectare for TE period 2001-02 again Bhiwani 400 thousand hectare during TE period 2004-05. However, it is lowest in Faridabad district 164 thousand hectare for TE period 1986-87, Panipat 115 thousand hectares for TE period 1992-93 and Panchkula 23.66 thousand hectares during TE period 2004-05. The picture regarding the situation of districts which exists in the above and below the state average and standard deviation during the study period shown in table 4.23.

The disparities level among the districts in the net area sown computed by C.V. The C.V. has increased from 37.84 for TE period 86-87 to 51.46 for TE period 2004-05 which shows the overall disparities in net area sown has increased.

The compound growth rate of net area sown (Table 4.24) is positive in 6 districts for TE period 1996-97, 9 districts for

Table 4.21
District-wise cropping intensity (Triennium Ending)

(percentage)

Districts	*TE 1986-87*	*TE 1989-90*	*Districts*	*TE 1992-93*	*TE 1995-96*	*TE 1998-99*	*Districts*	*TE 2001-02*	*TE 2004-05*
Ambala	159.20	163.65	Ambala	162.91	163.99	156.70	Ambala	165.37	150.11
							Panchkula	144.41	188.76
			Yamun Nagar	155.70	158.93	156.16	Yamun Nagar	154.13	158.93
Kurukshetra	166.89	164.86	Kurukshetra	183.51	178.50	189.86	Kurukshetra	179.62	179.77
			Kaithal	174.05	191.64	186.96	Kaithal	189.68	195.09
Karnal	161.88	176.20	Karnal	191.12	193.73	184.42	Karnal	192.21	197.96
			Panipat	172.86	187.23	185.72	Panipat	200.90	200.79
Sonipat	147.48	145.26	Sonipat	153.01	160.95	168.53	Sonipat	165.05	178.80
Rohtak	139.77	132.97	Rohtak	133.57	136.51	144.10	Rohtak	155.75	154.48
							Jhajjar	151.93	150.11
Faridbad	146.16	147.04	Faridbad	153.71	155.95	160.33	Faridbad	164.96	181.26
Gurgoan	150.01	142.19	Gurgoan	155.18	148.93	143.45	Gurgoan	157.12	176.23
			Rewari	152.32	144.78	152.65	Rewari	158.15	148.85
Mahendragarh	155.49	153.39	Mahendragarh	164.67	169.72	172.46	Mahendragarh	177.61	170.70
Bhiwani	153.96	149.66	Bhiwani	159.88	160.67	174.23	Bhiwani	166.88	191.03
Jind	186.39	182.68	Jind	184.70	188.34	181.48	Jind	188.77	185.64
Hisar	154.82	164.56	Hisar	168.04	177.77	184.83	Hisar	184.43	195.95
							Fatehabad	185.90	183.79

Table 4.21 Continued

Table 4.21 Continued

Districts	*TE 1986-87*	*TE 1989-90*	*Districts*	*TE 1992-93*	*TE 1995-96*	*TE 1998-99*	*Districts*	*TE 2001-02*	*TE 2004-05*
Sirsa	137.69	158.39	Sirsa	167.46	163.49	167.31	Sirsa	171.86	174.65
For above 12 districts			For above 16 districts				For above 19 districts		
Average	154.98	156.74		164.54	167.57	168.94		171.30	176.99
Standard Deviation	13.0878	14.4388		14.612	17.2667	16.0117		15.9754	17.150274
C.V.	8.44492	9.21203		8.88036	10.3041	9.47792		9.32597	9.6897084

Source: Various issues of statistical abstract, Haryana 1983-2007
Directorate of Land Records, Haryana 1984-2007.

Table 4.22
District-wise Growth Rates of Cropping Intensity (Triennium Ending)

Districts	*TE 1986-87 to TE 1989-90*	*Districts*	*TE 1992-93 to TE 1995-96*	*TE 1995-96 to TE 1998-99*	*Districts*	*TE 2001-02 to TE 2004-05*
Ambala	0.358184	Ambala	0.085731	-0.5880003	Ambala	-1.24779
					Panchkula	3.534434
		Yamuna Nagar	0.266648	-0.22777	Yamuna Nagar	0.398524
Kurukshetra	-0.15859	Kurukshetra	-0.35835	0.803388	Kurukshetra	0.010827
		Kaithal	1.256449	-0.32014	Kaithal	0.365393
Karnal	1.10539	Karnal	0.176068	-0.63669	Karnal	0.383017
		Panipat	1.041046	-0.10496	Panipat	-0.0071
Sonipat	-0.19651	Sonipat	0.658275	0.598627	Sonipat	1.04319
Rohtak	-0.64475	Rohtak	0.282767	0.707851	Rohtak	-0.10613
					Jhajjar	-0.15618
Faridabad	0.077881	Faridabad	0.187811	0.359876	Faridabad	1.229577
Gurgaon	-0.69194	Gurgaon	-0.53174	-0.48503	Gurgaon	1.49974
		Rewari	-0.65626	0.688852	Rewari	-0.78291
Mahendragarh	-0.1762	Mahendragarh	0.392523	0.207921	Mahendragarh	-0.51333
Bhiwani	-0.3667	Bhiwani	0.063946	1.056352	Bhiwani	1.76831
Jind	-0.26041	Jind	0.253427	-0.48004	Jind	-0.21661
Hissar	0.794416	Hissar	0.732688	0.657936	Hissar	0.788893
					Fatehabad	-0.14793
Sirssa	1.833004	Sirssa	-0.31068	0.299993	Sirssa	0.209071

Source: Table 4.21

Table 4.23
District-wise Net Area Sown (Triennium Ending)

(thousand hectares)

District-wise	*TE86-87*	*TE89-90*	*Districts*	*TE92-93*	*TE95-96*	*TE98-99*	*Districts*	*TE01-02*	*TE04-05*
Ambala	236.33	239.33	Ambala	145.66	146.66	154.33	Ambala	125.33	133.66
							Panchukla	28.33	23.66
			Yamuna Nagar	124.00	123.33	124.66	Yamuna Nagar	125.00	125.00
Kurukshetra	335.00	343.66	Kurukstra	141.66	147.33	148.00	Kurukstra	148.33	150.00
			Kaithal	210.33	196.33	197.00	Kaithal	197.00	197.00
Karnal	331.33	264.33	Karnal	182.66	194.66	207.66	Karnal	200.33	194.33
			Panipat	115.66	94.00	98.33	Panipat	94.33	91.00
Sonipat	173.33	205.00	Sonipat	150.66	172.33	178.00	Sonipat	168.33	153.00
Rohtak	326.66	332.33	Rohtak	325.66	300.33	303.00	Rohtak	142.00	141.33
							Jhajjar	152.00	155.66
Faridabad	164.66	165.66	Faridbad	156.33	157.33	158.00	Faridbad	156.66	144.33
Gurgaon	187.33	188.00	Gurgoan	178.00	183.66	192.33	Gurgoan	189.00	164.33
			Rewari	127.33	127.33	124.33	Rewari	123.33	126.66
Mahendr-agarh	263.00	252.66	Mahendr-agarh	155.66	154.00	157.00	Mahendr-agarh	153.33	142.00
Bhiwani	394.66	381.66	Bhiwani	363.00	354.66	400.66	Bhiwani	399.66	400.00
Jind	252.00	237.66	Jind	224.66	234.66	246.66	Jind	246.00	243.00
Hissar	561.00	520.00	Hissar	575.66	588.33	550.66	Hissar	318.33	308.33
							Fatehabad	221.33	222.00

Table 4.23 Continued

Table 4.23 Continued

District-wise	*TE86-87*	*TE89-90*	*Districts*	*TE92-93*	*TE95-96*	*TE98-99*	*Districts*	*TE01-02*	*TE04-05*
Sirssa	391.66	335.00	Sirssa	348.66	377.66	388.66	Sirssa	370.00	391.33
Total	3617.00	3465.33		3525.67	3552.67	3629.33		3558.67	3506.67
For above 12 districts			For above 16 districts				For above 19 districts		
Average	301.42	288.78		220.35	222.04	226.83		187.30	184.56
Standard Deviation	114.081	99.28302		124.1743	127.229	124.05518		92.350172	94.990776
C.V.	37.8483	34.38042		56.35214	57.2996	54.690015		49.30648	51.468386

Source: Various issues of statistical abstract, Haryana 1983-2007
Directorate of Land Records, Haryana 1984-2007.

TE period 1992-93 to 1995-96 and 11 districts for TE period 2001-02 to 2004-05. Other hand, there are 6 districts for TE period 1986-87 to 1989-90 and 5 districts for TE period 2001-02 to 2004-05 have their negative growth rates.

Data given in table 4.25 shows the gross cropped area among the districts during the study period. Gross cropped area is the highest in Hisar 868 thousand hectares, 841 thousand hectare, 966 thousand hectare, 1019 thousand hectare and 1030.33 thousand hectares during the all TE period 1986-87 to 1998-99 and Bhiwani district 763 thousand hectare during TE period 2004-05. It is lowest in Faridabad 234 thousand hectare, 240 thousand hectare for TE period in 1986-87 to 1989-90 and Yamunanagar 193 thousand hectares for TE period 1992-93, Rewari 187 thousand hectare, 189.66 thousand hectare for TE period 1995-96 to 1998-99 and Panchkula 43.33 thousand hectares, 46.66 thousand hectare for TE period 2001-02 to 2004-05. The level of disparities among the district in term of gross cropped area measured by co-efficient of variance has increased from 38.044 for TE period 86-87 to 55.88 04-05 which shows the overall disparities increased in the fluctuation during the study period. The picture regarding the situation of districts exists in above and below the state average and standard deviation during the study period shown also in the aforesaid table.

The compound growth rate of gross cropped area (table 4.26) is positive in 5 districts for TE period 1986-87, 11 districts for TE period 1992-93 to 1995-96, 14 district for 1995-96 to 1998-99 and 9 districts for TE period 2001-02 to 2004-05. Other hand there are 7 districts for TE period 1986-87 to 1989-90 and 10 districts for TE period 2001-02 to 2004-05 and 5 districts for TE period 1992-93 to 1995-96 have their negative growth rate.

Data presented in table 4.27 reveal the sown area as a percentage of reporting area. The sown area as a percentage of reporting area is highest in Kurukshetra 93.30 percentage, 93.07 percentage for TE period 1986-87, 1989-90 and Sirsa 91.65

Table 4.24
District-wise Growth Rates of Net Area Sown (Triennium Ending)

Districts	*TE 1986-87 to TE 1989-90*	*Districts*	*TE 1992-93 to TE 1995-96*	*TE 1995-96 to TE 1998-99*	*Districts*	*TE 2001-02 to TE 2004-05*
Ambala	0.163728	Ambala	0.088768	0.662714	Ambala	0.06487
					Panchkula	-0.18122
		Yamuna Nagar	-0.06989	0.139559	Yamuna Nagar	0
Kurukshetra	0.331805	Kurukshetra	0.509951	0.058572	Kurukshetra	0
		Kaithal	-0.88934	0.043975	Kaithal	0
Karnal	-2.88742	Karnal	0.828587	0.841924	Karnal	0.292892
		Panipat	-2.65418	0.58621	Panipat	0.584686
Sonipat	2.199998	Sonipat	1.757815	0.420476	Sonipat	-0.97449
Rohtak	0.223293	Rohtak	-1.04477	0.114713	Rohtak	0.216131
					Jhajjar	-0.2744
Faridabad	0.078553	Faridabad	0.082729	0.054856	Faridabad	0.211597
Gurgaon	0.046085	Gurgaon	0.40727	0.599763	Gurgaon	0.845829
		Rewari	0	-0.30874	Rewari	0.171931
Mahendragarh	-0.51849	Mahendragarh	-0.13951	0.25053	Mahendragarh	2.097233
Bhiwani	-0.43345	Bhiwani	-0.30075	1.594185	Bhiwani	-0.09686
Jind	-0.7566	Jind	0.566383	0.648893	Jind	0.490661
Hissar	-0.97943	Hissar	0.28267	-0.85458	Hissar	0.39944
					Fatehabad	-0.17393
Sirssa	-2.00643	Sirssa	1.041568	0.373041	Sirssa	0.178125

Source : Table 4.23

Table 4.25
District-wise Gross Cropped Area (Triennium Ending)

(thousand hectares)

District-wise	*TE86-87*	*TE89-90*	*Districts*	*TE92-93*	*TE95-96*	*TE98-99*	*Districts*	*TE01-02*	*TE04-05*
Ambala	376.33	392.66	Ambala	237.33	240.33	241.66	Ambala	201.66	200.66
			Yamuna Nagar	193.00	196.00	194.66	Panchukla	13.33	44.66
Kurukshetra	559.00	567.00	Kurukstra	260.00	263.00	281.00	Y. Nagar	192.66	198.66
			Kaithal	366.00	376.33	368.33	Kurukstra	267.00	269.66
Karnal	536.33	455.33	Karnal	349.33	377.00	383.00	Kaithal	373.66	384.33
			Panipat	197.00	176.00	180.00	Karnal	380.66	384.66
Sonipat	255.66	307.00	Sonipat	229.33	276.33	300.00	Panipat	189.33	182.66
Rohtak	456.66	443.00	Rohtak	436.33	410.00	436.66	Sonipat	283.00	272.33
Faridabad	234.00	240.66	Faridbad	240.33	245.33	253.33	Rohtak	220.66	218.33
Gurgaon	281.00	326.66	Gurgoan	276.33	273.33	276.00	Jhajjar	226.33	233.66
			Rewari	194.00	187.00	189.66	Faridbad	265.33	261.66
Mahendragarh	409.00	325.00	Mahendragarh	256.33	261.66	270.66	Gurgoan	299.00	289.33
Bhiwani	607.66	577.00	Bhiwani	581.33	570.00	697.66	Rewari	194.00	188.66
Jind	461.33	434.66	Jind	414.00	442.33	447.33	Mahendragarh	272.33	243.00
Hissar	868.66	841.00	Hissar	966.66	1019.66	1030.33	Bhiwani	667.00	763.66
Sirssa	539.33	530.33	Sirssa	581.66	617.33	650.33	Jind	462.66	451.00
							Hissar	571.00	604.33
							Fatehabad	409.00	407.66
							Sirssa	635.33	683.66
Total	5585.00	5440.33		5779.00	5931.67	6200.67		6154.00	6282.67

Table 4.25 Continued

Table 4.25 Continued

District-wise	*TE86-87*	*TE89-90*	*Districts*	*TE92-93*	*TE95-96*	*TE98-99*	*Districts*	*TE01-02*	*TE04-05*
For above 12 districts			For above 16 districts				For above 19 districts		
Average	465.42	453.36		361.19	370.73	387.54		323.89	330.67
Standard Deviation	177.0635	161.7299		205.141	216.8275	229.293		164.253	184.79585
C.V.	38.04409	35.67352		56.7962	58.48677	59.1661		50.7119	55.885842

Source: Various issues of statistical abstract, Haryana 1983-2007
Directorate of Land Records, Haryana 1984-2007.

Table 4.26
District-wise Growth Rates of Gross Cropped Area (Triennium Ending)

Districts	*TE 1986-87 to TE 1989-90*	*Districts*	*TE 1992-93 to TE 1995-96*	*TE 1995-96 to TE 1998-99*	*Districts*	*TE 2001-02 to TE 2004-05*
Ambala	0.552529	Ambala	0.163042	0.071422	Ambala	-0.06445
					Panchkula	0.393811
		Yamuna Nagar	0.200243	-0.33458	Yamuna Nagar	0.793376
Kurukshetra	0.18446	Kurukshetra	0.148898	0.862265	Kurukshetra	0.128972
		Kaithal	0.361739	-0.27828	Kaithal	0.365697
Karnal	-2.10101	Karnal	0.993396	0.204991	Karnal	0.13566
		Panipat	-1.45125	0.29188	Panipat	-0.46381
Sonipat	2.401392	Sonipat	2.44733	1.071439	Sonipat	-0.49704
Rohtak	-0.39328	Rohtak	-0.80407	0.820376	Rohtak	-0.13778
					Jhajjar	0.414405
Faridabad	0.364993	Faridabad	0.267405	0.417027	Faridabad	-0.18031
Gurgaon	1.97217	Gurgaon	-0.14147	0.125996	Gurgaon	-0.42532
		Rewari	-0.47548	0.183809	Rewari	-0.36088
Mahendragarh	-2.93748	Mahendragarh	0.267432	0.439537	Mahendragarh	-1.46717
Bhiwani	-0.66935	Bhiwani	-0.25501	2.655793	Bhiwani	1.770763
Jind	-0.76923	Jind	0.862226	0.145884	Jind	-0.33068
Hissar	-0.4189	Hissar	0.694666	0.13501	Hissar	0.738542
					Fatehabad	-0.04234
Sirssa	-0.21801	Sirssa	0.774802	0.677668	Sirssa	0.955446

Source : Table 4.25

for TE period 2004-05. However, the sown area as a percentage of reporting area is lowest Jind 66.83 percentage for TE period 86-87, Mahendragarh 76.03 percentage for TE period 1989-90, Gurgaon 64.73 percentage, 67.60 percentage and 71.23 percentage for TE period 1992-93, 1995-96 and 1998-99 and Panchakala 41.52 percentage during TE period 2004-05. As a result, inter-district variations in this indicator there are oscillatory trends. This is also evident from the C. V figures which were 10.16 in TE period 1986-87, declined to 4.97 in TE period 1989-90, 7.51 in TE period 1992-93 which increased to 11.68 during TE period 2004-05. The district which exist in above and below to mean and standard deviation during the study period depicts in table 4.27. There are 6 districts, 12 districts, 9 districts 11 districts in above and 6 districts, 4 districts, 8 districts are below the state average.

Data presented in table 4.28 depicts the growth pattern among the districts in the term of sown area as a percentage of reporting area. The growth rate of sown area as a percentage of reporting area is positive in 4 districts for TE period 1986-87 to 1989-90, 8 districts for TE period 1992-93 to 1995-96, 12 districts for TE period 1995-96 to 1998-99 and 7 districts for TE period 2001-02 to 2004-05. On the other hand, there are 8 districts, 7 districts, 4 districts; 12 districts have their negative growth rates during the study period. The highest increase in growth rate of sown area occurs in Jind district which is 2.07 percent during the study period.

District-wise Irrigation Facilities

It is well know fact that irrigation plays a key role to improving the cropping pattern and cropping intensity and resulting high productivity and returns from farming. Irrigation covering two indicators, gross irrigated area as a percentage of gross cropped area and number of electric and diesel pumpset. Table 4.29 depicts the picture regarding gross irrigated area as a percentage of gross cropped area is highest in Karnal 96.87 percentage for TE period 1989-90 , again Karnal

Table 4.27

District-wise Sown Area as a percentage of total reporting area (Triennium Ending)

(percentage)

Districts	*TE 1986-87*	*TE 1989-90*	*Districts*	*TE 1992-93*	*TE 1995-96*	*TE 1998-99*	*Districts*	*TE 2001-02*	*TE 2004-05*
Ambala	71.57	63.27	Ambala	69.97	67.50	63.38	Ambala	81.17	86.80
							Panchkula	39.77	41.52
			YamunaNagar	70.70	71.63	72.47	Yamuna Nagar	72.70	72.69
Kurukshetra	93.30	93.07	Kurukshetra	88.10	87.67	87.37	Kurukshctra	88.50	89.29
			Kaithal	89.47	86.23	86.40	Kaithal	86.40	86.40
Karnal	86.90	82.87	Karnal	80.20	79.20	83.83	Karnal	80.50	78.99
			Panipat	80.13	74.00	76.23	Panipat	73.13	69.98
Sonipat	78.53	81.33	Sonipat	80.03	80.63	85.67	Sonipat	80.63	71.84
Rohtak	85.43	82.43	Rohtak	84.77	85.10	85.27	Rohtak	84.80	84.61
							Jhajjar	78.00	81.47
Faridbad	78.40	78.67	Faridbad	75.17	75.63	78.67	Faridbad	75.97	71.45
Gurgoan	68.67	69.90	Gurgoan	64.73	67.60	71.23	Gurgoan	70.40	60.84
			Rewari	82.37	82.00	81.66	Rewari	81.23	83.88
Mahendragarh	77.17	76.03	Mahendragarh	80.23	79.37	80.93	Mahendragarh	79.07	73.22
Bhiwani	85.77	82.87	Bhiwani	85.93	85.93	86.10	Bhiwani	85.73	85.85
Jind	66.83	78.27	Jind	81.30	84.50	88.73	Jind	88.37	87.41
Hisar	84.97	78.93	Hisar	80.67	82.87	80.58	Hisar	76.60	76.12
							Fatehabad	88.63	89.18

Table 4.27 Continued

Table 4.27 Continued

Districts	*TE 1986-87*	*TE 1989-90*	*Districts*	*TE 1992-93*	*TE 1995-96*	*TE 1998-99*	*Districts*	*TE 2001-02*	*TE 2004-05*
Sirsa	91.73	78.47	Sirsa	81.47	88.43	91.03	Sirsa	86.53	91.66
For above 12 districts			For above 16 districts				For above 19 districts		
Average	80.77	78.84		79.70	79.89	81.22		78.85	78.06
Standard Deviation	8.20796	3.91894		5.99249	5.99882	5.66072		5.63001	9.121619
C.V.	10.1619	4.97064		7.51861	7.5085	6.96938		7.14024	11.685001

Source: Various issues of statistical abstract, Haryana 1983-2007
Directorate of Land Records, Haryana 1984-2007.

Table 4.28
District-wise Growth Rates of Sown Area as a Percentage of total Reporting Area (Triennium Ending)

Districts	*TE 1986-87 to TE 1989-90*	*Districts*	*TE 1992-93 to TE 1995-96*	*TE 1995-96 to TE 1998-99*	*Districts*	*TE 2001-02 to TE 2004-05*
Ambala	-1.58593	Ambala	-0.46501	-0.81346	Ambala	0.873518
					Panchkula	0.560047
		Yamuna Nagar	0.16963	0.151318	Yamuna Nagar	-0.00178
Kurukshetra	-0.03201	Kurukshetra	-0.06344	-0.04445	Kurukshetra	0.115323
		Kaithal	-0.47723	0.025546	Kaithal	0
Karnal	-0.61395	Karnal	-0.16259	0.739561	Karnal	-0.24528
		Panipat	-1.02685	0.385797	Panipat	-0.5694
Sonipat	0.455399	Sonipat	0.096917	0.789447	Sonipat	-1.48588
Rohtak	-0.46255	Rohtak	0.050402	0.025885	Rohtak	-0.02909
					Jhajjar	0.566094
Faridabad	0.044598	Faridabad	0.079154	0.512409	Faridabad	-0.79238
Gurgaon	0.23051	Gurgaon	0.564231	0.680674	Gurgaon	-1.875
		Rewari	-0.05837	-0.05387	Rewari	0.417212
Mahendragarh	-0.19283	Mahendragarh	-0.13967	0.252753	Mahendragarh	-0.99192
Bhiwani	-0.4451	Bhiwani	0	0.025636	Bhiwani	0.018142
Jind	2.070433	Jind	0.501938	0.63551	Jind	-0.14156
Hissar	-0.95175	Hissar	0.349563	-0.36277	Hissar	-0.08149
					Fatehabad	0.080265
Sirssa	-2.00456	Sirssa	1.068839	0.376526	Sirssa	0.749756

Source: Table 4.27

98.25 percentage for TE period 1992-93, Kurukshetra 99.52 percentage for TE period 1998-99and again Kurukshetra 100.13 percentage for TE period 2004-05.

On the other hand there is lowest in Mahendragarh district, Bhiwani district during the study period over time, irrigation improved in almost all the districts, but no significant change in the degree of inter-district variations was witnessed. This is also evident form the coefficient of variations figures which varied between the range of 34.78 to 19.45 during the period 1984-2005.

The district which exist in above and below to state average and standard deviation during the study period depicts in table 4.29 .There are 7 districts for TE period 1986-87, 6 districts for TE period 1989-90, 9 districts for TE period 1992-93, 1995-96, 1998-99 and 12 districts for TE period 2004-05 above and 5 districts for TE period 1986-87, 6 districts for TE period 1989-90, 2001-02 and 7 districts for TE period 1992-93, 1995-96 and 2004-05 are below in the state average.

The compound growth rate of percentage of irrigated area to cropped area shows table 4.30. The compound growth rate of positive in 12 districts for TE period 1986-87 to 1989-90, 14 districts for TE period 1992-93 to 1995-96 and 12 districts for TE period 2001-02 to 2004-05. The highest increase in growth rate of irrigation occurs in Sirsa district 1.83 % in TE 1986-87 to 1989-90. In case of number of pumpsets (table 4.31) is the highest Kurukshetra 82310 for TE period 1986-87 again Kurukshetra 85300 for TE period 1998-99 and Karnal 66685 for TE period 2004-05. Other hand there is lowest in Bhiwani district during all the TE time period. Number of pumpsets expanded in all the districts rapidly during the study and as a result inter-district disparities declined significantly in this indicator. This is also evident from the coefficient of variation figures. Coefficient of variation was 68.58 in TE period 1986-87, declined to 29.76 in TE period 1992-93, and 41.76 in 2001-02, which shows the overall disparities among districts decrease with fluctuation during the study period.

Table 4.29

District-wise Percentage of Gross Irrigated Area to Total Cropped Area (Triennium Ending)

(percentage)

Districts	*TE 1986-87*	*TE 1989-90*	*Districts*	*TE 1992-93*	*TE 1995-96*	*TE 1998-99*	*Districts*	*TE 2001-02*	*TE 2004-05*
Ambala	58.10	64.60	Ambala	65.86	71.33	75.01	Ambala	88.09	88.86
							Panchkula	43.93	44.16
			Yamuna Nagar	77.77	81.15	85.25	Yamuna Nagar	86.60	91.26
Kurukshetra	93.84	96.33	Kurukshetra	97.29	99.36	99.52	Kurukshetra	100.00	100.13
			Kaithal	96.74	98.74	99.18	Kaithal	99.65	99.82
Karnal	93.01	96.87	Karnal	98.25	98.33	99.21	Karnal	99.47	99.65
			Panipat	96.97	99.24	99.44	Panipat	99.83	100.00
Sonipat	71.73	92.78	Sonipat	95.90	94.63	95.77	Sonipat	97.40	97.68
Rohtak	54.03	71.01	Rohtak	70.65	78.97	75.29	Rohtak	84.76	83.16
							Jhajjar	79.47	76.75
Faridbad	64.10	73.93	Faridbad	75.21	76.40	78.29	Faridbad	84.67	87.88
Gurgoan	42.65	56.22	Gurgoan	44.41	51.84	54.93	Gurgoan	61.98	69.49
			Rewari	56.01	59.60	62.21	Rewari	71.51	81.26
Mahendragarh	27.47	44.63	Mahendragarh	39.58	42.74	44.75	Mahendragarh	52.67	60.57
Bhiwani	31.12	40.93	Bhiwani	39.49	41.80	41.51	Bhiwani	56.05	54.79
Jind	83.97	86.47	Jind	87.70	88.20	90.46	Jind	93.58	92.60
Hisar	78.20	84.95	Hisar	82.17	81.06	85.69	Hisar	89.88	86.57
							Fatehabad	97.22	97.21

Table 4.29 Continued

Table 4.29 Continued

Districts	***TE 1986-87***	***TE 1989-90***	***Districts***	***TE 1992-93***	***TE 1995-96***	***TE 1998-99***	***Districts***	***TE 2001-02***	***TE 2004-05***
Sirsa	66.33	79.86	Sirsa	82.26	84.87	86.92	Sirsa	93.21	90.39
For above 12 districts			For above 16 districts				For above 19 districts		
Average	63.71	74.05		75.39	78.08	79.59		83.16	84.33
Standard Deviation	22.1605	19.1962		20.9985	19.7148	19.4561		17.63	16.405957
C.V.	34.7818	25.9241		27.8524	25.2498	24.4454		21.2005	19.45504

Source: Various issues of statistical abstract, Haryana 1983-2007
Directorate of Land Records, Haryana 1984-2007.

Table 4.30

District-wise Growth Rate of Percentage of Gross Irrigated Area to Total Cropped Area (Triennium Ending)

Districts	*TE 1986-87 to TE 1989-90*	*Districts*	*TE 1992-93 to TE 1995-96*	*TE 1995-96 to TE 1998-99*	*Districts*	*TE 2001-02 to TE 2004-05*
Ambala	1.381868	Ambala	1.040128	0.654541	Ambala	0.112936
					Panchkula	0.067747
		Yamuna Nagar	0.55328	0.641283	Yamun Nagar	0682066
Kurukshetra	0.340222	Kurukshetra	0.273419	0.02087	Kurukshetra	0.01685
		Kaithal	0.265743	0.057681	Kaithal	0.022109
Karnal	0.528757	Karnal	0.010556	0.115618	Karnal	0.02345
		Panipat	0.300551	0.026114	Panipat	0.022069
Sonipat	3.393569	Sonipat	-0.17275	0.155426	Sonipat	0.037237
Rohtak	3.607793	Rohtak	1.454333	-0.61699	Rohtak	-0.24685
					Jhajjar	-0.45065
Faridbad	1.867596	Faridbad	0.203804	0.317433	Faridbad	0.483762
Gurgoan	3.647628	Gurgoan	2.026561	.753711	Gurgoan	1.494356
		Rewari	0.80897	0.55741	Rewari	1.671493
M.Gragh	6.4964	M.Gragh	1.001159	0.597794	M.Gragh	1.829017
Bhiwani	3.61762	Bhiwani	0.740008	-0.09025	Bhiwani	-029444
Jind	0.381214	Jind	0.073758	0.32867	Jind	-0.13644
Hisar	1.079546	Hisar	-017623	0.722994	Hisar	-048545
					Fatehabad	-0.00133
Sirsa	2.436721	Sirsa	0.405923	0.310021	Sirsa	-0.39764

Source: Table 4.29

The district which exist in above and below to the state average and standard deviation during the study period depicts in Table 4.31. There are 7 districts for TE period 1986-87, 1989-90, 1992-93, 1998-99 and 2004-05, 6 districts for TE period 1995-96, 1998-99 the above and 5 districts for TE period 1986-87 and 1989-90, 10 districts for TE period 1995-96, 1998-99 and 12 districts are below in state average during TE period 2004-05. Similarly, 9 districts, 16 districts are above and 3 districts are below of the standard deviation during the study period.

Table 4.32 presents data regarding the compound growth rate of pumpsets. The growth rate of pumpset is positive in districts namely Ambala for TE period 86-87 to 89-90, Panchkula, Yamuna Nagar, Karnal, Jhajjar, Rewari Fatehabad, Sirsa during the all the TE period. The highest increase in growth rate of pumpsets occurs in Hisar district 3.09% in TE period 86-87 to 1989-90.

However, with the increase in area under irrigation, the production and productivity levels in all the districts improved significantly.

District-wise Adaptation of New Farm Technology

New farm technology covering four indicators area under (major crops) H.Y.V. (high yield varieties), Number of tractors, consumption of fertilizer (Tonnes) and consumption of pesticides. Area under H.Y. V. seed is repotted separately for the four foodgrains crops for which this seed has been adopted. It provided with required inputs like irrigation and fertilizers the H.Y.V. possess the potential of giving high yields resulting in high return. It is clear from the table 4.33 that the area under H. Y. V. is quite high in all districts and the increase shows the same trend in all the periods under study. Table 4.33 shows that, the area under H.Y.V. is highest Kurukshetra 413 thousand hectares, 404.33 thousand hectares for TE period 1986-87, 1989-90, Hisar 351 thousand hectares, 404 thousand hectares and 436 thousand hectares for TE

Table 4.31
District-wise Number of Pump Sets (Triennium Ending)

Districts	*TE86-87*	*TE89-90*	*Districts*	*TE92-93*	*TE95-96*	*TE98-99*	*Districts*	*TE2001-02*	*TE04-05*
Ambala	33602.00	37162.33	Ambala	21835.66	19495.33	22519.66	Ambala	19941.00	21347.00
							Panchukla	4386.00	4413.33
			Yamuna Nagar	25548.33	25778.00	26066.00	Yamuna Nagar	26066.00	27044.00
Kurukstra	82310.66	85300.00	Kurukstra	34971.66	35378.66	37004.66	Kurukstra	36169.33	35813.33
			Kaithal	42942.66	36212.00	43602.00	Kaithal	51801.00	53000.00
Karnal	79749.33	83774.33	Karnal	56553.33	58921.33	63319.00	Karnal	65155.00	66685.33
			Panipat	29320.33	26149.33	27721.00	Panipat	29212.33	31079.00
Sonipat	23940.00	26867.33	Sonipat	33698.00	38037.33	40617.00	Sonipat	41487.66	38127.33
Rohtak	23822.66	22346.66	Rohtak	38444.33	50879.00	35932.33	Rohtak	19568.33	17825.33
							Jhajjar	35261.33	35360.00
Faridbad	22181.00	23757.66	Faridbad	26593.33	27533.00	27086.66	Faridbad	24641.00	29302.00
Gurgoan	33499.66	37269.33	Gurgoan	35187.33	33781.33	33277.00	Gurgoan	31833.00	31705.00
			Riwari	24392.00	25795.66	25827.33	Rewari	27844.33	29641.00
Mahendr-agarh	36596.33	41623.33	Mahendr-agarh	23579.66	24297.33	21602.66	Mahendr-agarh	20958.33	22591.33
Bhiwani	12289.33	14742.66	Bhiwani	21975.00	27436.66	26723.00	Bhiwani	28297.00	29467.00
Jind	20240.00	24978.33	Jind	29749.00	34581.33	37388.33	Jind	39773.66	39486.33
Hissar	23862.66	30195.00	Hissar	41581.33	50082.00	52226.33	Hissar	25650.66	24025.33
							Fatehabad	27711.66	29538.00

Table 4.31 Continued

Table 4.31 Continued

Districts	*TE86-87*	*TE89-90*	*Districts*	*TE92-93*	*TE95-96*	*TE98-99*	*Districts*	*TE2001-02*	*TE04-05*
Sirssa	14221.33	17125.33	Sirssa	24233.00	26602.33	30306.00	Sirssa	33596.66	39807.33
Total	406315.00	445142.33		510605.00	540970.67	551219.00		589567.33	606896.67
Average	33859.58	37095.19		31912.81	33810.67	34451.19		31029.86	31941.93
Standard Deviation	23224.12	23579.77		9499.89	11039.45	11308.83		12959.87	13116.63
C.V.	68.589504	63.56558		29.768266	32.650802	32.825687		41.765833	41.064

Source: Various issues of statistical abstract, Haryana 1983-2007
Directorate of Land Records, Haryana 1984-2007.

Table 4.32
District-wise Growth Rates of Use of Pump Sets (Triennium Ending)

Districts	*TE 1986-87 to TE 1989-90*	*Districts*	*TE 1992-93 to TE 1995-96*	*TE 1995-96 to TE 1998-99*	*Districts*	*TE 2001-02 to TE 2004-05*
Ambala	1.314694	Ambala	-1.45956	1.887936	Ambala	0.887549
					Panchkula	0.080604
		Yamuna Nagar	0.121171	0.139159	Yamuna Nagar	0.677153
Kurukshetra	0.463731	Kurukshetra	0.150176	0.584472	Kurukshetra	-0.1282
		Kaithal	-2.18667	2.437779	Kaithal	0.297208
Karnal	0.640624	Karnal	0.533402	0.937923	Karnal	0.301546
		Panipat	-1.47346	0.759841	Panipat	0.806566
Sonipat	1.507378	Sonipat	1.583356	0.854652	Sonipat	-1.08946
Rohtak	-0.82608	Rohtak	3.701327	-4.41062	Rohtak	-1.20263
					Jhajjar	0.036247
Faridabad	0.894563	Faridabad	0.451369	-0.21174	Faridabad	2.272266
Gurgaon	1.392579	Gurgaon	-0.52746	-0.19489	Gurgaon	-0.05224
		Rewari	0.728284	0.015909	Rewari	0.81425
Mahendragarh	1.683312	Mahendragarh	0.389594	-1.51296	Mahendragarh	0.977828
Bhiwani	2.388664	Bhiwani	2.920674	-0.34123	Bhiwani	0.526832
Jind	2.765592	Jind	1.97128	1.017316	Jind	-0.09399
Hissar	3.099506	Hissar	2.441738	0.545216	Hissar	-0.84538
					Fatehabad	0.83118
Sirssa	2.439151	Sirssa	1.217159	1.704863	Sirssa	2.224263

Source : Table 4.31

period 1992-93, 1995-96 and 1998-99 and Jind 298 thousand hectares, 299 thousand hectares for TE period 2001-02 and 2004-05. There are lowest in Sonipat 154.66 thousand hectares for TE period 1986-87 and Panchkula 25.73 thousand hectares, 27.50 thousand hectares for TE period 2001-02, 2004-05. Coefficient of variation figures revealed that falling tendency of area under high yielding varieties did not affect the extent of regional disparities amongst the districts. C.V. was 44.57 in TE period 1886-87 rightly increased to 45.40 in TE period 2004-05. The districts which exist in above and below in the state average and standard deviation explained as there are 8 districts in above and 4 districts in below in the state average during TE period 1986-87. The more details have been shows in the table 4.33.

Table 4.34 presents district wise compound growth rate of area under HYV during the study period. The growth rate of Area under HYV is positive in all districts except Kurukshetra, Rohtak, Karnal, Bhiwani Jind for TE period 1986-87 to 1989-90, 7 districts for TE period 1992-93 to 1995-96, 14 districts for TE period 1995-96 to 1998-99 and 9 districts for TE period 2001-02 to 2004-05 and 9 districts for TE period 1992-93 to 1995-96, 2 districts for TE period 1995-96 to 1998-99 and 8 districts for TE period 2001-02 to 2004-05 have their negative growth rates.

Use of chemical fertilizers which is one of the major important input required for increasing agricultural production also plays a crucial role. The use (consumption) fertilizer was almost known in the area now performing Haryana. The farmers were made councilors about the latest technology in agriculture especially on the use of adequate of quantities of fertilizers for higher production of crops. Many studies have shown that the potential yield of crop can be obtained through the balanced use of fertilizers. H.Y.V. which is more responsive to high dozes of chemical fertilizers have increased the consumption of fertilizers tremendously. Table 4.35 provides the data consumption of fertilizers (Tonnes). Use of fertilizers is the highest in Kurukshetra 72694 thousand

Table 4.33
District-wise (Major Crops) H.Y.V. Area (Triennium Ending)

(thousand hectares)

Districts	*TE86-87*	*TE89-90*	*Districts*	*TE92-93*	*TE95-96*	*TE98-99*	*Districts*	*TE2001-02*	*TE04-05*
Ambala	197.33	212.66	Ambala	141.33	141.33	152.66	Ambala	135.00	141.83
							Panchukla	25.73	27.50
			Yamuna Nagar	98.00	95.33	97.33	Yamuna Nagar	108.26	115.06
Kurukshetra	413.00	404.33	Kurukstra	176.33	161.00	169.66	Kurukstra	179.63	183.36
			Kaithal	253.66	244.66	235.00	Kaithal	275.66	302.66
Karnal	372.33	263.33	Karnal	237.00	250.66	246.00	Karnal	263.26	271.33
			Panipat	122.33	98.00	101.33	Panipat	113.33	119.36
Sonipat	154.66	219.33	Sonipat	129.00	150.66	168.66	Sonipat	171.06	169.03
Rohtak	181.66	140.00	Rohtak	180.66	167.66	204.66	Rohtak	111.76	107.33
							Jhajjar	125.66	119.00
Faridabad	124.33	131.66	Faridbad	130.66	143.00	149.00	Faridbad	163.20	151.36
Gurgaon	118.00	119.00	Gurgoan	119.33	132.00	148.66	Gurgoan	172.66	160.00
			Rewari	70.33	64.66	76.33	Rewari	99.23	92.33
Mahendragarh	146.00	152.33	Mahendragarh	89.66	88.00	105.00	Mahendragarh	130.36	119.00
Bhiwani	190.66	181.00	Bhiwani	150.00	130.33	197.33	Bhiwani	281.06	273.33
Jind	236.00	217.00	Jind	211.00	238.66	262.33	Jind	298.66	299.66
Hissar	292.66	309.00	Hissar	351.66	404.00	436.66	Hissar	272.00	276.70
							Fatehabad	224.00	234.93
Sirssa	159.66	163.33	Sirssa	187.00	218.33	245.33	Sirssa	268.96	269.60
Total	2586.33	2513.00		2648.00	2728.33	2996.00		3419.57	3433.43

Table 4.33 Continued

Table 4.33 Continued

Districts	***TE86-87***	***TE89-90***	***Districts***	***TE92-93***	***TE95-96***	***TE98-99***	***Districts***	***TE2001-02***	***TE04-05***
Average	215.53	209.42		165.50	170.52	187.25		179.98	180.71
Standard Deviation	96.0754	83.2364		71.71786	84.65293	88.2017		78.57079	82.047539
C.V.	44.5768	39.7468		43.33406	49.64374	47.1037		43.65597	45.403627

Source: Various issues of statistical abstract, Haryana 1983-2007
Directorate of Land Records, Haryana 1984-2007.

Table 4.34
District-wise Growth Rate of (Major Crops) H.Y.V. Area (Triennium Ending)

Districts	*TE 1986-87 to TE 1989-90*	*Districts*	*TE 1992-93 to TE 1995-96*	*TE 1995-96 to TE 1998-99*	*Districts*	*TE 2001-02 to TE 2004-05*
Ambala	0.975235	Ambala	-0.65663	1.67245	Ambala	0.642443
				1.746876	Panchkula	0.864859
		Yamuna Nagar	-0.35715	0.269629	Yamuna Nagar	0.793138
Kurukshetra	-0.27467	Kurukshetra	-1.17289	0.682312	Kurukshetra	0.267138
		Kaithal	-0.46741	-0.52144	Kaithal	1.219209
Karnal	-4.39272	Karnal	0.729755	-0.24343	Karnal	0.392182
		Panipat	-2.83536	0.43473	Panipat	0.674943
Sonipat	4.634587	Sonipat	2.033975	1.474394	Sonipat	-0.15496
Rohtak	-3.32243	Rohtak	-0.96381	2.619412	Rohtak	-0.52355
					Jhajjar	-0.70445
Faridabad	0.746005	Faridabad	1.176622	0.534479	Faridabad	-0.97146
Gurgaon	0.109505	Gurgaon	1.316948	1.554053	Gurgaon	-0.98325
		Rewari	-1.0835	2.174421	Rewari	-0.93032
Mahendragarh	0.552246	Mahendragarh	-0.24304	2.317101	Mahendragarh	-1.17618
Bhiwani	-0.67251	Bhiwani	-1.80618	5.526939	Bhiwani	-0.36119
Jind	-1.08266	Jind	1.610767	1.233757	Jind	0.04336
Hissar	0.706802	Hissar	1.815512	1.013324	Hissar	0.222433
					Fatehabad	0.619968
Sirssa	0.294891	Sirssa	2.029429	1.523632	Sirssa	0.030506

Source : Table 4.33

tonnes for TE period 1986-87, Kurukshetra 81472 thousand tonnes for TE period 1989-90, Hisar 94321.33 thousand tonnes for TE period 1998-99 and Sirsa 100433 thousand tonnes for TE period 2004-05. It is lowest in Bhiwani for TE period 1986-87, 1989-90 and Panchula for TE period 2001-02 and 2004-05. This led to slight declining trend in regional disparities in this indicator. Coefficient of variation 73.55 in TE period 1986-87 marginally reduced to 46.94 in TE period 1998-99 but increased to 55.06 during 2002-05 which shows the overall disparities have been decreased with fluctuations during the study period.

Table 4.35 depicts the situation of districts which exist in above and below the state average and standard deviation during the study period. In the TE period 2004-05 the districts in reference to use of fertilizers, there are 5 districts and 6 districts are above and 7 districts and 6 districts are below the mean and standard deviation.

Table 4.36 shows district wise compound growth rate of use of fertilizers during the study period. The growth rate of use of fertilizers is positive in all of districts except Kaithal, Mahendragarh, Panipat for TE period 1992-93 to 1995-96, Sirsa for TE period 1995-96 to 1998-99 and Mahendragarh for TE period 2001-02 to 2004-05. The highest increase in growth rate of fertilizers is in Mahendragarh district which is 7.56 percent in TE period 1986-87 to 1986-90.

In the term of consumption of pesticides (table 4.37) is highest in Ambala district 522 thousand tonnes for TE period 1986-87, Kurukshetra 738.51 thousand tonnes for TE period 1989-90, Sirsa 668.66 thousand tonnes for TE period 1992-93, Sirsa 601.46 thousand tonnes for TE period 1998-99 and Sirsa 734 thousand tonnes for TE period 2004-05. There are lowest in Mahendragarh, 64.99 thousand tonnes, 86.51 thousand tonnes for TE period 1986-87, 1989-90 and Panchkula 57.83 thousand tonnes for TE period 2004-05. Consumption of pesticides expanded in all the districts during the period 1984-2005 and as a result inter-district disparities increased with fluctuation in this indicator. This is also evident from the

Table 4.35
District-wise Use of Fertilizers (Triennium Ending)

(thousand tonnes)

Districts	*TE86-87*	*TE89-90*	*Districts*	*TE92-93*	*TE95-96*	*TE98-99*	*Districts*	*TE2001-02*	*TE04-05*
Ambala	37483.00	43135.33	Ambala	29400.33	30561.66	35994.66	Ambala	33757.33	39495.33
							Panchukla	5232.00	6964.00
			Yamuna Nagar	28341.00	31759.33	41756.66	Yamuna Nagar	45247.33	53658.00
Kurukstra	72694.00	81472.66	Kurukstra	49165.33	53835.33	62648.33	Kurukstra	65889.33	68521.00
			Kaithal	55743.33	55266.33	64579.33	Kaithal	74608.00	77160.66
Karnal	68193.66	77607.66	Karnal	57135.66	71621.33	80161.33	Karnal	113396.00	127233.67
			Panipat	40882.66	31065.00	42820.33	Panipat	45308.33	57544.66
Sonipat	20439.00	26964.33	Sonipat	23035.33	40842.33	47948.00	Sonipat	65344.00	75951.66
Rohtak	19292.33	25967.33	Rohtak	29223.66	40090.33	43918.33	Rohtak	34961.33	35388.66
							Jhajjar	21665.33	23162.00
Faridbad	12370.00	16111.00	Faridbad	22096.00	26758.33	41714.33	Faridbad	37760.00	43958.00
Gurgoan	8599.00	9874.66	Gurgoan	13313.33	21433.66	26788.33	Gurgoan	26901.66	27933.66
			Rewari	14806.66	16452.33	26121.00	Rewari	22087.00	23406.33
Mahendr-agarh	11331.66	19879.66	Mahendr-agarh	19504.00	19478.00	26185.66	Mahendr-agarh	26071.33	24260.33
Bhiwani	5306.33	9294.33	Bhiwani	15117.33	23283.33	30459.00	Bhiwani	35823.00	38147.33
Jind	26406.33	36385.00	Jind	44298.66	45956.66	57448.33	Jind	61344.00	75251.00
Hissar	47832.33	71861.00	Hissar	94321.33	112483.33	113702.67	Hissar	66507.66	73236.00
							Fatehabad	62259.00	67426.00

Table 4.35 Continued

Table 4.35 Continued

Districts	*TE86-87*	*TE89-90*	*Districts*	*TE92-93*	*TE95-96*	*TE98-99*	*Districts*	*TE2001-02*	*TE04-05*
Sirssa	44570.66	60966.66	Sirssa	73656.66	81872.00	79547.00	Sirssa	94591.66	100433.00
Total	374518.33	479519.67		610041.33	702759.33	821793.33		938754.33	1039131.33
For above 12 districts			For above 16 districts				For above 19 districts		
Average	31209.86	39959.97		38127.58	43922.46	51362.08		49408.12	54691.12
Standard Deviation	22955.184	26636.702		23138.872	26119.572	24114.383		27104.137	30116.436
C.V.	73.551061	66.658459		60.688011	59.467463	46.949776		54.857653	55.066406

Source: Various issues of statistical abstract, Haryana 1983-2007
Directorate of Land Records, Haryana 1984-2007.

Table 4.36
District-wise Growth Rate of Use of Fertilizers (Triennium Ending)

Districts	*TE 1986-87 to TE 1989-90*	*Districts*	*TE 1992-93 to TE 1995-96*	*TE 1995-96 to TE 1998-99*	*Districts*	*TE 2001-02 to TE 2004-05*
Ambala	1.838278	Ambala	0.5037	2.144746	Ambala	2.056833
					Panchkula	3.778304
		Yamuna Nagar	1.487852	3.613052	Yamuna Nagar	2.235702
Kurukshetra	1.489587	Kurukshetra	1.183792	1.985678	Kurukshetra	0.509214
		Kaithal	-0.11139	2.040232	Kaithal	0.437264
Karnal	1.691247	Karnal	2.973938	1.471681	Karnal	1.50447
		Panipat	-3.49898	4.250052	Panipat	3.149119
Sonipat	3.658715	Sonipat	7.710106	2.10202	Sonipat	1.970131
Rohtak	3.928768	Rohtak	4.185511	1.189768	Rohtak	0.157688
					Jhajjar	0.870102
Faridabad	3.486216	Faridabad	2.514023	5.927324	Faridabad	1.990667
Gurgaon	1.810173	Gurgaon	6.370587	2.934401	Gurgaon	0.489411
		Rewari	1.376198	6.178663	Rewari	0.755275
Mahendragarh	7.562222	Mahendragarh	-0.0173	3.912529	Mahendragarh	-0.92935
Bhiwani	7.540012	Bhiwani	5.761184	3.545498	Bhiwani	0.818649
Jind	4.244936	Jind	0.477682	2.936853	Jind	2.685443
Hissar	5.42069	Hissar	2.31012	0.139932	Hissar	1.257681
					Fatehabad	1.039366
Sirssa	4.146268	Sirssa	1.380839	-0.37293	Sirssa	0.78016

Source : Table 4.37

Table 4.37
District-wise Use of Pesticides (Triennium Ending)

(thousand tonnes)

Districts	*TE86-87*	*TE89-90*	*Districts*	*TE92-93*	*TE95-96*	*TE98-99*	*Districts*	*TE2001-02*	*TE04-05*
Ambala	522.00	465.53	Ambala	342.12	322.56	311.05	Ambala	234.66	174.83
							Panchukla	75.06	57.83
			Yamuna Nagar	351.12	344.93	267.16	Yamuna Nagar	266.90	249.33
Kurukstra	508.66	738.51	Kurukstra	405.50	354.73	303.50	Kurukstra	305.56	274.00
			Kaithal	434.50	454.16	426.90	Kaithal	425.26	260.00
Karnal	520.10	698.10	Karnal	566.83	416.95	397.70	Karnal	396.30	329.33
			Panipat	226.78	330.90	338.93	Panipat	337.93	301.33
Sonipat	311.33	296.61	Sonipat	354.39	367.65	335.73	Sonipat	334.13	296.33
Rohtak	141.66	260.98	Rohtak	134.03	146.00	158.00	Rohtak	85.33	115.00
							Jhajjar	72.23	79.33
Faridbad	143.16	204.12	Faridbad	186.87	196.70	317.63	Faridbad	316.30	257.00
Gurgoan	240.16	192.49	Gurgoan	92.01	107.56	116.46	Gurgoan	115.90	124.00
			Rewari	91.133	165.03	177.73	Rewari	176.56	145.66
Mahendragarh	64.92	86.513	Mahendragarh	143.71	134.33	127.16	Mahendragarh	126.40	104.66
Bhiwani	101.32	128.24	Bhiwani	142.50	187.85	285.03	Bhiwani	283.96	206.00
Jind	227.53	305.53	Jind	339.61	332.16	288.40	Jind	287.16	229.00
Hissar	365.06	311.23	Hissar	687.72	654.33	596.93	Hissar	271.10	261.00
							Fatehabad	323.76	554.00
Sirssa	426.00	577.60	Sirssa	668.66	627.45	601.46	Sirssa	599.50	734.00

Table 4.37 Continued

Table 4.37 Continued

Districts	*TE86-87*	*TE89-90*	*Districts*	*TE92-93*	*TE95-96*	*TE98-99*	*Districts*	*TE2001-02*	*TE04-05*
Total	3571.92	4265.48		5167.51	5133.32	5049.82		5033.33	4752.67
For above 12 districts			For above 16 districts				For above 19 districts		
Average	297.66	355.46		322.97	320.83	315.61		264.91	250.14
Standard Deviation	169.13672	216.55319		194.75665	164.15912	142.39463		135.24248	163.09236
C.V.	56.822065	60.922482		60.301895	51.166646	45.116769		51.051798	65.200341

Source: Various issues of statistical abstract, Haryana 1983-2007
Directorate of Land Records, Haryana 1984-2007.

coefficient of variation figures coefficient of variation was 56.82 in TE period 1986-87 declined to 45.11 in TE period 1998-99 but increased 65.20 in TE period 2004-05. The districts which exist above and below the standard deviation during the study period show in aforesaid table.

Table 4.38 shows the compound growth rate of consumption of pesticides during the study period. The growth rate of pesticides is negative in 4 districts for TE period 1986-87 to 1989-90, 8 districts for TE period 1992-93 to 1995-96, 10 districts for TE period 1995-96 to 1998-99 and 14 districts for TE period 2001-02 to 2004-05 and 8 districts for TE period 1986-87 to 1989-90, 8 districts for TE period 1992-93 to 1995-96, 6 districts for TE period 1995-96 to 1998-99 and 5 districts for TE period 2001-02 to 2004-05 have their positive growth rates.

Table 4.39 provides the data of tractors . The number of tractor is highest Karnal district 11958 for TE period 1986-87, Hisar 15468 for TE period 1989-90, again Hisar 20445 for TE period 1992-93 and Sirsa 22108 for TE period 2004-05. There are lowest in Mahendragarh district 2445 for TE period 1986-87, again Mahendragarh 2815 for TE period 1989-90 and Panchkula 1289 during the TE period 2004-05. C.V. was 49.05 in TE period 1986-87 slightly increased 54.14 in TE period 1992-93 but declined to 40.04 in TE period 2004-05, which shows the overall disparities with fluctuation during the study period.

The district which exist in above and below to the state average and standard deviation during the study period depicts in aforesaid table.

Table 4.40 shows the compound growth rate of tractor during the study period. The growth rate of tractor is positive in all districts during all the TE time period. The highest increase in growth rate of tractors in Hisar district 5.10 percent.

Table 4.38
District-wise Growth Rate of Use of Pesticides (Triennium Ending)

Districts	*TE 1986-87 to TE 1989-90*	*Districts*	*TE 1992-93 to TE 1995-96*	*TE 1995-96 to TE 1998-99*	*Districts*	*TE 2001-02 to TE 2004-05*
Ambala	-1.4738	Ambala	-0.76036	-0.4704	Ambala	-3.74532
					Panchkula	-3.32594
		Yamuna Nagar	-0.61088	-2.88861	Yamuna Nagar	-0.84372
Kurukshetra	4.954271	Kurukshetra	-1.71973	-2.00267	Kurukshetra	-1.4042
		Kaithal	0.575773	-0.79976	Kaithal	-6.18195
Karnal	3.891164	Karnal	-3.90448	-0.61116	Karnal	-2.37203
		Panipat	5.021874	0.311578	Panipat	-1.47568
Sonipat	-0.62619	Sonipat	0.477539	-1.17088	Sonipat	-1.54496
Rohtak	8.246493	Rohtak	1.114954	1.029681	Rohtak	3.945421
					Jhajjar	1.223372
Faridabad	4.708672	Faridabad	0.66687	6.412265	Faridabad	-2.65667
Gurgaon	-2.8288	Gurgaon	2.046616	1.03631	Gurgaon	0.879967
		Rewari	8.005731	0.966132	Rewari	-2.46411
Mahendragarh	3.794218	Mahendragarh	-0.87155	-0.70853	Mahendragarh	-2.41722
Bhiwani	3.103653	Bhiwani	3.648387	5.556547	Bhiwani	-4.0774
Jind	3.896886	Jind	-0.287	-1.81571	Jind	-2.89279
Hissar	-2.04781	Hissar	-0.64333	-1.18373	Hissar	-0.4912
					Fatehabad	7.214673
Sirssa	4.027353	Sirssa	-0.82173	-0.547	Sirssa	2.659893

Source : Table 4.39

Table 4.39
District-wise Number of Tractors (Triennium Ending)

Districts	*TE86-87*	*TE89-90*	*Districts*	*TE92-93*	*TE95-96*	*TE98-99*	*Districts*	*TE2001-02*	*TE04-05*
Ambala	6706.66	8769.00	Ambala	5585.00	6039.33	8750.33	Ambala	7811.33	7749.66
							Panchukla	1131.66	1289.66
			Yamuna Nagar	6688.66	7616.66	8885.66	Yamuna Nagar	10872.3	11818.33
Kurukshetra	10604.67	13620.33	Kurukstra	8742.66	10684.33	11505.33	Kurukstra	12249.66	13035.00
			Kaithal	7877.00	9556.66	9824.00	Kaithal	12724.00	11917.33
Karnal	11958.33	14246.00	Karnal	10505.3	12428.00	14007.66	Karnal	14895.66	16345.00
			Panipat	7645.33	6161.33	6697.33	Panipat	8913.66	10107.66
Sonipat	5602.00	6596.66	Sonipat	8088.66	10582.33	11911.33	Sonipat	12309.66	15205.66
Rohtak	8304.00	11220.33	Rohtak	14519.33	16549.00	19007.00	Rohtak	10462.00	10981.66
							Jhajjar	11355.00	14212.3
Faridabad	3965.00	4743.66	Faridbad	5770.00	6188.33	10220.66	Faridbad	11704.00	12721.00
Gurgaon	3226.00	4210.00	Gurgoan	5454.66	6124.33	7113.00	Gurgoan	9432.00	10950.33
			Rewari	3242.33	4112.00	5019.00	Rewari	5414.00	6441.33
Mahendr-agarh	2445.00	2815.66	Mahendr-agarh	1884.00	1783.33	3194.33	Mahendr-agarh	3983.33	4424.66
Bhiwani	3179.00	4003.66	Bhiwani	6437.66	9032.00	12698.33	Bhiwani	16034.66	17304.00
Jind	6140.66	6841.66	Jind	8224.33	9536.33	11612.33	Jind	13543.66	14153.3
Hissar	10534.67	15468.33	Hissar	20445.00	22253.00	26820.00	Hissar	15691.00	17398.00
							Fatehabad	12032.66	12857.3.

Table 4.39 Continued

Table 4.39 Continued

Districts	*TE86-87*	*TE89-90*	*Districts*	*TE92-93*	*TE95-96*	*TE98-99*	*Districts*	*TE2001-02*	*TE04-05*
Sirssa	10860.67	11517.66	Sirssa	13075.66	16488.00	13208.33	Sirssa	17472.00	22108.66
Total	83526.67	104053.00		134185.67	155135.00	180474.67		208032.33	231021.00
For above 12 districts			For above 16 districts				For above 19 districts		
Average	6960.56	8671.08		8386.60	9695.94.00	11279.67		10949.07	12159.00
Standard Deviation	3414.412	4425.4964		4540.6552	5225.1043	5616.9105		4175.8577	4869.4563
C.V.	49.05373	51.03741		54.141762	53.889624	49.796777		38.138926	40.048164

Source: Various issues of statistical abstract, Haryana 1983-2007
Directorate of Land Records, Haryana 1984-2007.

Table 4.40
District-wise Growth Rates of Number of Tractors (Triennium Ending)

Districts	*TE 1986-87 to TE 1989-90*	*Districts*	*TE 1992-93 to TE 1995-96*	*TE 1995-96 to TE 1998-99*	*Districts*	*TE 2001-02 to TE 2004-05*
Ambala	3.538472	Ambala	1.019471	4.926453	Ambala	-0.10274
					Panchkula	1.709419
		Yamuna Nagar	1.699289	2.018665	Yamuna Nagar	1.087903
Kurukshetra	3.299037	Kurukshetra	2.635263	0.964762	Kurukshetra	0.809149
		Kaithal	2.538524	0.358452	Kaithal	-0.84584
Karnal	2.296197	Karnal	2.203651	1.563906	Karnal	1.211488
		Panipat	-2.75998	1.087714	Panipat	1.643704
Sonipat	2.14232	Sonipat	3.546543	1.546143	Sonipat	2.77806
Rohtak	3.980787	Rohtak	1.711431	1.81222	Rohtak	0.630699
					Jhajjar	2.953739
Faridabad	2.352684	Faridabad	0.911894	6.723632	Faridabad	1.086498
Gurgaon	3.512949	Gurgaon	1.513143	1.959852	Gurgaon	1.954658
		Rewari	3.129667	2.618736	Rewari	2.278941
Mahendragarh	1.847513	Mahendragarh	-0.70965	7.852746	Mahendragarh	1.37208
Bhiwani	3.036453	Bhiwani	4.489318	4.517631	Bhiwani	0.992948
Jind	1.411817	Jind	1.938136	2.587295	Jind	0.572675
Hissar	5.107939	Hissar	1.10505	2.450515	Hissar	1.34831
					Fatehabad	0.863416
Sirssa	0.764646	Sirssa	3.052966	-2.8354	Sirssa	3.099629

Source : Table 4.41

District-wise Land Holdings and Workers

Table 4.41and 4.42 are presenting the data for land holdings and workers. In case of average size of holdings (table 4.41) are highest in Sirsa 6.07 average size for year 1980-81, 4.35 average size for year 1985-86 and Sirsa 3.15 average size for year 1995-96, and Fatehabad 3.38 average size for year 2000-01. These are lowest in Faridabad 2.14 average size for year 1980-81, 1.83 average size for year 1995-96 and 1.59 average size for year 2000-01. This kind of changes in size of holdings occur became of increasing population pressure in the district. To examine the disparities level among districts in average size of holdings the coefficient of variation was 35.25 in year 1980-81 increased to 48.30 in year 1985-86, decreased to 24.63 in year 1990-91, again increase to 53.98 in year 1995-96 and again decrease to 27.09 in year 2000-01 which shows overall disparities among districts with fluctuation decreased during the study period but there is high fluctuation in the trend. Table 4.42 presented the data for agricultural labour and cultivator of agricultural sector. In case of agricultural labor four districts namely Ambala, Kurukshetra and Hisar were above the state average during the year 1980-81 and Yamuna Nagar, Karnal, Kaithal, Kurushetra, Sonipat, Faridabad, Jind, Hisar, Sirsa, Fatehabad were above the mean during 1990-91.

Coefficient of variation figures revealed the fallings tendency of agricultural labour. The C.V. was 48.26 in 1980-81 decreased 39.80 in the year 2000-01 which shows the disparities among districts decreased, but the tendency as cultivator did not affect the extent of regional disparities among districts. C.V. was 27.79 in the year 1980-81 increased and 49.22 in the year 2000-01 which shown the overall disparities level among districts increased during the study period.

Spatial Pattern of Agricultural Development in Haryana

In an earlier section, districts were classified as above and below in term of state average and standard deviation for

Table 4.41
District-wise Average Size of Holding

District	*1980-81*	*1985-86*	*Districts*	*1990-91*	*1995-96*	*Districts*	*2000-01*
Ambala	2.86	2.09	Ambala	1.88	1.67	Ambala	1.74
			Panchkula		1.14	Panchkula	1.70
			Yamuna Nagar	2.17	1.99	Yamuna Nagar	2.15
Kurukshetra	3.69	2.63	Kurukshetra	2.33	2.12	Kurukshetra	2.36
			Kaithal	2.69	2.18	Kaithal	3.02
Karnal	3.18	2.36	Karnal	2.45	2.22	Karnal	2.12
			Panipat	1.86	1.79	Panipat	1.47
Sonipat	2.81	2.14	Sonipat	1.87	1.68	Sonipat	1.60
Rohtak	3.04	2.62	Rohtak	2.25	1.81	Rohtak	2.29
			Jhajjar		0.00	Jhajjar	2.07
Faridbad	2.14	1.83	Faridbad	1.63	1.44	Faridbad	1.59
Gurgoan	2.45	1.93	Gurgoan	1.87	1.50	Gurgoan	1.77
		0.00	Rewari	2.26	1.96	Rewari	2.05
Mahendragarh	3.18	2.52	Mahendragarh	2.32	2.16	Mahendragarh	2.01
Bhiwani	4.09	3.28	Bhiwani	2.80	2.89	Bhiwani	3.16
Jind	4.59	3.39	Jind	2.73	2.30	Jind	2.77
Hisar	4.35	3.72	Hisar	2.86	2.44	Hisar	2.96
						Fatehabad	3.38
Sirsa	6.07	4.35		3.55	3.15	Sirsa	2.62

Table 4.41 Continued

Table 4.41 Continued

District	*1980-81*	*1985-86*	*Districts*	*1990-91*	*1995-96*	*Districts*	*2000-01*
For above 12 districts			For above 16 districts			For above 19 districts	
Average	3.54	2.53		2.35	1.81		2.25
Standard Deviation	1.24702	1.22105		0.57776	0.97856		0.61067
C.V.	35.2514	48.3071		24.6379	53.9857		27.0902

Source: Various issues of statistical abstract, Haryana 1983-2007
Directorate of Land Records, Haryana 1984-2007.

Table 4.42
District-wise Number of Agricultural Labour and As Cultivator (Main and Marginal)

	Agricultural Labour			*As Cultivator*		
Districts	*1980-81*	*1990-91*	*2000-01*	*1980-81*	*1990-91*	*2000-01*
Ambala	67415	42817	42270	116195	47759	53016
Panchukla		8693	10879		20822	30159
Yamun Nagar	54163	54470		58016	58701	
Kurukstra	77408	49744	70111	147571	58684	73083
Kethal		58772	83948		112151	149838
Karnal	87522	86587	107946	139926	94552	121027
Panipat		37331	55042		57692	89493
Sonipat	40405	59925	87390	101526	118350	189673
Rohtak	46257	35936	45462	164593	84892	143314
Jhaggar		28326	44844		92024	177377
Faridbad	26461	49316	82175	97040	111626	186400
Gurgnoa	25642	43656	57928	112229	127705	195768
Rewari		18586	44441		63339	148218
Mahendragarh	20208	17874	39000	115234	84755	192519
Bhiwani	24362	41031	70068	156575	173944	319272
Jind	45802	56686	85740	157234	140695	261073
Hissar	80438	75177	100806	228680	175836	289710
Fatehabad		55085	82944		87921	161370

Table 4.42 Continued

Table 4.42 Continued

Districts	Agricultural Labour			As Cultivator		
	1980-81	1990-91	2000-01	1980-81	1990-91	2000-01
Sirssa	48404	77104	113357	100079	118767	178000
Total	590324.00	896809.00	1278821.00	1636882.00	1829530.00	3018011.00
Average	49193.67	47200.47	67306.37	136406.83	96291.05	158842.68
Standard Deviation	23740.19	20477.11	26786.69	37915.99869	41267.85	78193.35945
C.V.	48.25863	43.38328	39.79815	27.79626047	42.8574	49.22691897

Source: Various issues of statistical abstract, Haryana 1983-2007
Directorate of Land Records, Haryana 1984-2007.

each indicator. There also calculated C.V. to measure the disparities levels among districts. These results show the trend of individual variables for the TE periods from 1984 to 2005. Some variables as per their C.V. results have declining trend of disparities among districts and some variables have increasing trends of disparities among districts. Thus, to access the combined trend of the all variables or the collective influence of the all variables among districts in the state during the aforesaid time period, there has been used the principal component analysis, so there can be explained the disparities trend among districts in the state. Now, in present section there also try to prepare the composite index of districts to measure the development level of agricultural sector development and test the level of variation among districts, on the basis of selected ten indicators are ; Productivity of Food grain (A_1) ; Production of Food grain (A_2) ; Percentage of gross irrigated area to total cropped area (A_3) ; Cropping intensity (A_4) ; Area under HYV (A_5) ; Number of tractors (A_6) ; Use of Fertilizers (A_7) ; Number of pumsets (A_8) ; Use of pesticides (A_9) ; Agricultural labour (A_{10}).

Principle components analysis (PCA) commonly called factor analysis is applied in present analysis to identify the inter-district variations in agricultural sector and composite indices of agricultural development of 16 districts of Haryana on three TE period of time, 1992-93,1998-99 and 2004-05. The composite indices have been calculated not only to measure the level of development but also to divide the districts objectively into four categories, high, medium high, medium low and low. Simple analysis of district wise disparities has been carried out on all the seven TE period, 1986-87, 1989-90, 1992-93,1995-96, 1998-99, 2001-02 and 2004-05. However, composite index of development was not construction for TE period 1986-87 and 1989-90 due to the indicator values for the districts are not strictly comparable to those at other points of time. There were 12 districts in the state up to 1989-90 and 16 districts up to 1998-99 and 19 districts up to 2004-05. In the present study to access the general picture agricultural development there are taken the 16 districts from 1990-91 to 2004-05. The three districts Panchula, Fatehabad and Jajjar from 1998-99 to 2004-05, merged in Ambala, Hisar and Rohtak respectively.

Factor Analysis result for the TE period 1992-93 are presented in table 4.43. The table shows that out of ten selected variable, two factor are derive. First 'Factor' explained 62.9 percent varience while second 'factor' explained 13.3 percent of variance respectively. All the two 'factors' taken together explained 76.2 percent of total variations communality values varied between 0.94940 to 0.70311, suggesting that two factor derived from 10 variable are sufficient (because of factor rotation and eigen values) to account for most of the variance. Production of food grain (A_2) area under HYV (A_5), number of tractors (A_6), Use of fertilizer (A_7), agricultural labour (A_{10}) are most important variables having strong association with the first 'factor' which explained 62.9 percent variance. The variable cropping intensity (A_4) was strongly associated with the second 'factor' (factor loading .84879).

Table 4.43
Result of Factor Analysis for TE-92-93

Variables	*Factor 1*	*Factor 2*	*Communality*
Productivity of food grain (A1)	.39066	.77510	.75340
Production of food grain (A2)	.90566	.35942	.94940
% of gross irrigated area total cropped area (A3)	.29182	.82131	.75972
Cropping intensity (A4)	.06721	.84879	.72497
Area under HYV (A5)	.89039	.35032	.91551
Number of tractors (A6)	.95159	.09074	.91376
Use of fertilizers (A7)	.79058	.50892	.88402
Number of pumpsets (A8)	.55643	.38225	.70574
Use of pesticides (A9)	.33187	.50296	.70311
Agriculture labour (A10)	.91587	.25146	.90205
Variance explained (in %)	62.9	13.3	
Cummulative variance explained (in %)	62.9	76.2	

Table 4.44 presents the result of factor analysis for the TE period 1998-99. Two principal components come out from selected 10 variables. First 'factor' explain and 68.5 percent of total variance second explained only 12.3 percent of variance. Two "factor" taken together explained 80.8 percent of observed variance. Communality values of all the variables varied between 0.71322 and 0.95324. This confirmed that two 'factor' are sufficient to account for most of the variance explained agricultural labour (A_{10}) come out most important variable strongly associated with first 'factor. It is clear from the results, that all variables are highly associated with the 'first principal component' (factor). However, the variable cropping intensity (A_4), percentage of gross irrigated area to total cropped area (A_3) and number of pumpsets (A_8) are comparatively less important constituents of the first 'factor'. During TE period 1998-99, the variable cropping intensity (A_4) was strongly associated with two 'factor' derived.

Table 4.44
Result of Factor Analysis for TE-98-99

Variables	*Factor 1*	*Factor 2*	*Communality*
Productivity of food grain (A1)	.81070	.11881	.72036
Production of food grain (A2)	.85721	.40758	.90094
% of gross irrigated area total cropped area (A3)	.19816	.81648	.70591
Cropping intensity (A4)	.12133	.86768	.76760
Area under HYV (A5)	.90639	.28802	.90450
Number of tractors (A6)	.92924	.10411	.87433
Use of fertilizers (A7)	.79372	.58105	.96760
Number of pumpsets (A8)	.55654	.56875	.71322
Use of pesticides (A9)	.62431	.55588	.69876
Agriculture labour (A10)	.91211	.34829	.95324
Variance explained (in %)	68.5	12.3	
Cummulative variance explained (in %)	68.5	80.8	

Table 4.45 gives factor analysis results for the TE period 2004-05. In this case also, two 'factor' came out from the 10 variables explaining 70.9 percent, and 10.4 percent variance

respectively. Taken together, these two principal components explained 81.9 percent of observed variance. Communalities varied between .70066 and .96458 suggesting factors derived from variables are sufficient to account for most of the variations. Production of food grains (A_2), Area under HYV (A_5) and use of pesticides (A_1) are most important variables having strong association with the first 'factor' which explaining 70.9 percent variance. The variable number of pumpsets (A_8) was strongly associated with the second 'factor'. Number of tractor (A_6) come to be a unique variable in TE 04-05 which was almost equally associated with first 'factor' (Factor loading 0.36230) and with second 'factor (factor loading 0.49291).

Table 4.45
Result for Factor Analysis for TE-04-05

Variables	*Factor 1*	*Factor 2*	*Communality*
Productivity of food grain (A1)	.75647	-.05684	.75974
Production of food grain (A2)	.93280	.30634	.96458
% of gross irrigated area total cropped area (A3)	.10439	.10945	.77646
Cropping intensity (A4)	.27644	.79743	.72137
Area under HYV (A5)	.92913	.27287	.95033
Number of tractors (A6)	.36230	.49291	.70566
Use of fertilizers (A7)	.78584	.29475	.82202
Number of pumpsets (A8)	.11346	.85290	.87353
Use of pesticides (A9)	.80491	.24268	.78689
Agriculture labour (A10)	.72055	.59190	.89264
Variance explained (in %)	70.9	10.5	
Cummulative variance explained (in %)	70.9	81.4	

The correlation matrix of the selected variables of agriculture sector development for the TE period 1992-93 is given in table 4.46. The variables production of foodgrain (A_2), area under HYV (A_5), number of tractors (A_6) and productivity of food grain (A_2) are highly correlated.

Table 4.46
Correlation Matrix of Agriculture Sector Development Indicators (TE 92-93)

Var-iables	*A1*	*A2*	*A3*	*A4*	*A5*	*A6*	*A7*	*A8*	*A9*	*A10*
A1	1.0000									
A2	.5891	1.0000								
A3	.9058	.4965	1.0000							
A4	.5047	.4351	.4943	1.0000						
A5	.5014	.9705	.4647	.4351	1.0000					
A6	.5195	.8635	.4348	.0660	.8204	1.0000				
A7	.7563	.9320	.5890	.5273	.8589	.8057	1.0000			
A8	.4016	.6046	.5296	.3729	.6515	.5049	.4774	1.0000		
A9	.3009	.4863	.3594	.4803	.6028	.3254	.4602	.2282	1.0000	
A10	.5898	.8903	.4781	.2817	.8747	.8813	.8441	.5709	.3841	1.0000

Number of cases 16

Table 4.47
Correlation Matrix of Agriculture Sector Development Indicators (TE 98-99)

Var-iables	*A1*	*A2*	*A3*	*A4*	*A5*	*A6*	*A7*	*A8*	*A9*	*A10*
A1	1.0000									
A2	.6378	1.0000								
A3	.4241	.3650	1.0000							
A4	.1587	.5504	.5265	1.0000						
A5	.6654	.9769	.3102	.4475	1.0000					
A6	.7101	.8110	.3049	.2181	.8742	1.0000				
A7	.7225	.9199	.6252	.5884	.8719	.7736	1.0000			
A8	.3689	.6979	.5753	.4790	.6975	.6210	.7515	1.0000		
A9	.6150	.7575	.5731	.5188	.6593	.5603	.8431	.4343	1.0000	
A10	.7705	.8958	.4858	.3626	.8964	.8670	.9252	.7367	.7930	1.0000

Number of cases 16

Table 4.47 presents correlation matrix of the selected variable and composite index of agricultural development for TE period 1998-99. It is seek from the table that all the variables are significantly correlated with the index, but production of foodgrain (A_2), area under HYV (A_5) use of fertilization (A_7) and agricultural labour (A_{10}) are highly correlated.

Table 4.48 presents correlation matrix of the selected variables of agricultural development for TE period 2004-05. The entire variables are positively correlated. Agricultural labour (A_{10}) was highly correlated is evident from the above table, all of the ten variables of agricultural development are positively associated with each other in all the TE period (1992-93, 1998-99 and 2004-05). In respect of TE period 1992-93 the first principal component explains 76.2, percent 1998-99 the first principal component explains 80.8 percent and 2004-05 the first principal component explains 81.9 percent of the total variation.

Table 4.48
Correlation Matrix of Agriculture Sector Development Indicators (TE 04-05)

Variables	*A1*	*A2*	*A3*	*A4*	*A5*	*A6*	*A7*	*A8*	*A9*	*A10*
A1	1.0000									
A1	1.0000									
A2	.6509	1.0000								
A3	.3373	.2082	1.0000							
A4	.0835	.5237	.2428	1.0000						
A5	.6245	.9788	.0881	.5210	1.0000					
A6	.4631	.4760	.2876	.2425	.4102	1.0000				
A7	.6024	.8690	.5417	.5325	.7823	.4176	1.0000			
A8	.2913	.3557	.3161	.5479	.2706	.6281	.4231	1.0000		
A9	.6247	.7904	.3015	.3315	.7047	.5882	.8012	.3798	1.0000	
A10	.6486	.8259	.1663	.5268	.7866	.6893	.6970	.7180	.7824	1.0000

Number of cases 16

Composite Index of Agricultural Development

The estimates of composite indices of agricultural development for different districts separately for the year TE period 1992-96, 1998-99 and 2004-05 are given in table 4.49. The

Table 4.49
Composite Index of Agriculture Sector Development Indicators

Districts	*T.E. 92-93*	*TE 98-99*	*TE-04-05*
Ambala	0.281158	0.291188	-0.931801
Yamuna Nagar	-2.456480	-1.916396	-0.677789
Kurukhetra	0.695067	0.740229	0.946886
Kaithal	1.380752	2.000783	2.364208
Karnal	1.993405	2.023261	2.070029
Panipat	0.468486	0.657720	0.927212
Sonipat	0.628333	0.743622	0.753470
Rohtak	0.169741	1.006231	0.766259
Faridabad	0.221251	0.231355	0.290906
Gurgaon	0.212595	-0.625547	-1.610016
Rewari	-1.969942	-1.460489	-1.383381
Mahendragarh	-2.515550	-2.145593	-1.928442
Bhiwani	-1.228535	-1.091585	0.237615
Jind	0.77083	1.703116	1.986616
Hissar	2.175062	2.449332	2.094222
Sirsa	1.505049	1.833978	1.960305
Average	0.1437	0.4125	0.4931
Std. Dev.	0.522509038	1.7104896	1.974375854
C.V.	407.14282	414.290838	492.731686

classification of districts according to composite index of agricultural development for different categories namely; high, medium high, medium low and low categories for the years TE 1992-93, TE 1998-99 and TE 2004-05 are given in table 4.50. In TE period 1992-93, the four districts Kaithal, Karnal, Hisar and Sirsa are in the category of high level of agricultural development. It is seeking from the table that the four districts; Jind, Kurukshetra, Sonipat and Panipat are into the category of medium high. The districts namely; Ambala, Rohtak, Faridabad and Gurgaon are in the category of medium low and the remained districts, Rewari, Mahendragarh, Bhiwani and Yamuna Nagar are in the category of low in the sense of development of agriculture. The number of districts following in the category of high level of agricultural development increased from 4 in TE period

1992-93 to 6 in TE period 1998-99. The three districts Kurukshetra, Sonipat and Panipat are in the category of medium high and two districts Ambala and Fridabad are in to the category of medium low and remained five districts, Yamuna Nagar, Gurgaon, Rewari, Mahendragarh and Bhiwani are still found to be underdevelopment or low category in the sense of agricultural development. During the TE period 2004-05 seven districts - Kurukshetra, Kaithal, Karnal, Jind, Hisar, Sirsa and Panipat, Rohtak are in to the category of high level of agricultural development. The two districts belonged to the category of medium high level of agricultural development and other two Fridabad and Bhiwani are in to the category of medium low. The remained five districts are in low category.

Table 4.50
Classification of districts according to composite index of Agriculture Development

Category of Development	*TE 92-93*	*TE 98-99*	*TE 04-05*
High (0.7808 above)	Kaithal , Karnal, Hisar,Sirsa (4)	Kaithal, Karnal, Jind, Hisar,Sirsa, Rohtak(6)	Kaithal, Karnal, Jind, Hisar,Sirsa, Kurushetra, Panipat(7)
Medium high (0.7808 >0.3033)	Jind, Kurush-etra, Sonipat, Panipat(4)	Kurushetra, Sonipat, Panipat(3)	Rohtak, Sonipat(2)
Medium low (0.3033 > -0.579)	Ambala,Farid-abad, Gurgaon, Rohtak(4)	Ambala , Faridabad (2)	Faridabad, Bhiwani(2)
Low (-0.578 below)	Rewari, Mahe-ndragarh, Bhi-wani, Yamuna Nagar(4)	Yamuna Nagar, Gurgaon, Rew-ari Mahendra-garh, Bhiwani] (5)	Ambala, Yamuna Nagar, Gurgaon, Rewari, Mahendra-garh(5)

The mean value of composite indices increase from 0.14 to 0.49 is the indication of improvement in the agricultural development position among districts in the state and the size of composite indices also increases is indication of improvement in the situation of agricultural development among districts in the state. The coefficient of variation figures for the composite indices increased from 407.1428 to 492.7142 during the time period from 1992-93 to 2004-05, that indicated the disparities among the districts increased in the agricultural development.

Conclusion

In sum, from the analysis, a clear picture of the state emerged for the time period 1984-2005. When observed the pattern of agricultural development of districts by the variables through their C.V. results individually, some variables have declining trends and some of them have their increasing trends of disparities. The variables such as area under pulses, area under oilseeds, production of cereals, production of pulses, production of oilseeds, productivity of cereals, percentage of irrigated area, number of pumpsets, use of fertilizers, use of labour and number of tractors showed their declining trends with oscillations during the whole time period. The other variables like, the area under cereals, productivity of pulses, oilseeds, cropping intensity, net area sown, gross cropped area, Use of HYV and use of pesticides have their increasing trends with oscillations in the whole time period. Hence, the variables individually have shown a mix picture of disparities in case of some variables decline and in case of some variables increase. Therefore, to access a combined picture of agricultural development pattern among districts in the state there used the factor analysis method, which showed the overall trend of agricultural development pattern have increasing disparities trends among districts during the aforesaid time period in the state. The another things the level of development of districts improved shown through composite index increases but the level of disparities among districts exist and increases and the development advantage goes in favour to more develop districts. The next important result is the category of agricultural development of districts (low, medium low, medium high and high) changed in case of some districts they have reshuffle their position from low to high but, the overall situation of the districts category of agricultural development situation changed in the whole time period. Last but not least, it may be possible the less development category of districts of Haryana may be better as compared to other districts of nation from per capita income point of view, but, with in state there exist the disparities among districts. These kinds of changes in the results according to composite index occur due to change in the irrigation facility in the districts and the changing pattern of crops in some districts also.

5

Conclusions and Suggestions

Summary of Findings

Development being at the center stage in the policy agenda of almost all countries in the world has not only led to fast depletion of natural resources but also thrown up new challenges to the agrarian sector endangering the viability and sustainability of farm enterprises. There is a lurking fear that the fast changing global economic environment particularly after WTO might give a big jolt to the agricultural sector in the developing countries .The problem of these countries are further compounded by their inherent deficiencies in infrastructure both social and physical.

Globalization is a fact of life and India is taking serious measures to get ready to operate in a new liberalized framework where foreign direct investment and capital inflows are expected to play a major role in accelerating investment and in promoting growth through the application of improved technology. In this context, it is impossible to keep insulated from global developments. The clear lesson is that India should learn to walk on two legs. While liberalization the economy, policy makers should remember that it is only agricultural growth which is going to determine the fortunes of a vast majority of working people in India and that it is only agricultural growth that makes a dent in their poverty. There need of effective research and development to evolve cost saving technology, improved infrastructure, efficient markets and several other bold initiatives to improve competitive edge of Indian agriculture.

The liberalization policy of 1991 has allowed the states to play a larger role in determining their development paths and attracting investment. India's success in fostering economic growth has created new challenges. The question now is how India can sustain that success and expand the opportunities for all to participate in it and benefit from it. Increased growth since the mid 1980s has helped to substantially reduce the national poverty rate to 22% of the population in 2004, with the speed of poverty reduction appearing to increase between 1999 and 2004. To meet one of its Millennium Development Goals, of halving poverty by 2015, the government is aiming to achieve an even higher medium term economic annual growth rate of 10%. In addition growth needs to become more inclusive by increasing the prosperity of poorer states, whose economies have expanded at a slower pace than those of richer states in the past decade, and so reducing their difficulties in lowering poverty.

No doubt, after independence, India has pursued a deliberate policy to modernize and revitalize its agriculture with the objective of improving the leaving conditions of the large proportion of population dependent on agriculture. The policy has consisted of a combination of institutional reforms, including land reforms, and large investment in irrigation, power, roads and other rural infrastructure with a view to accelerating agricultural growth. The agriculture in India is very much characterized by inter-personal and inter-regional inequalities. Inter-personal inequalities have primarily arisen because of skewed distribution of land ownership due to the failure of land reforms in general, and legislation pertaining to ceilings on land holdings, in particular. Wide inter-regional disparities exist because of differences in agro-climatic conditions and in resource endowment mainly in terms of availability of irrigation and other rural infrastructure. A moot question is, therefore, to find out if the introduction of new technology would further accentuate the existing inter-personal and inter-regional inequalities. There was a widespread feeling that the new technology would lead to an increase in inter-personal inequality. Moreover, being highly irrigation intensive, the new technology was also expected to bypass the rainfed regions, thereby further accentuating regional disparities.

The chapter third of the book focus on present scenario of agriculture development of India and the points of the better strategy lines of national policy can help to nation to compete the forthcoming challenges of globalization. The major finding occurs form the lesson the growth rate analysis shows that the initial years of reforms were somewhat favourable for agricultural growth, but the post-world trade organization period witnessed a sharp decline in the growth rate of almost all sub-sectors and commodity groups in the agricultural sector. At the state level, the growth rate has turned negative in four out of 20 major states while six states show a growth rate ranging between 0.10 and 0.95 per cent, further, the growth rate of agriculture in most of the low productivity states was much higher than the national average during 1984-85 to 1995-96. However, after 1995-96, their growth rates not only declined, but also turned out to be much lower than the national average. The main reasons for deceleration and stagnation in agricultural output after 1995-96 are a slowdown in growth of fertilizer use, irrigation, and energy (electric power) in some cases, stagnation or even a decline in other cases. Crop intensity and area under cultivation have also shown either a poor growth or a decline. Diversification towards high-value crops has also slowed down and in some cases farmers have been diversifying away from the high-value crops towards low-value, less risky and less input-demanding crops. Low level of input use and low productivity in most of the states offer some ray of hope to revive agricultural growth, but this would require simultaneous efforts on several fronts include ; stepping up invest-ments and putting in place suitable institutional mechanisms to exploit irrigation potential that exists in most of the states; increasing power supply to the sector; promoting fertilizer use by expanding the distribution network and improving credit facilities for farmers; establishing competitive seed markets and ensuring attractive prices for seeds; improvement in terms of trade for agriculture; and measures to mitigate risk in farming. Thus, the present scenario and growth rate of agricultural is witness to stress more on agricultural development in 11th plan.

The present study has made an attempt to analyse the regional disparities in agricultural development among districts in Haryana with an aim to identify ways for increasing the pace of agriculturally advance economy of Haryana, in which agriculture determines the rate of overall economy growth. In any regional scheme of Haryana agricultural development need to be the starting points. The present study is undertaken on the assumption that the overall agricultural development in Haryana conceals considerable regional differences because of farming practices, techniques, availability of irrigational facilities, attitude of farmers, etc. in different districts of the State. The presence of regional disparities in agricultural development was taken to indicate that there is scope to boost up the pace of agricultural development and thereby that of economic development in State.

No doubt, a number of studies conducted by several economists at international, national or regional levels, in present work there references and work results mentioned in review of literature and some other parts of the work. These all propounded lot of results, characteristic and reasons they are responsible for disparities. More or less the general features such as social, political, geographical, climatic etc. are more or less remained similar in all parts of country so these things were mentioned in the present work at different places, hence at here no need to repeat them again. In the present study an attempt is made to measure empirically the extent and time pattern of the change of inter-district disparities in agricultural development in Haryana during the period 1984-85 to 2004-05 on the basis of published data of Trienniums 1986-87, 1989-90, 1992-93, 1995-96, 1998-99, 2001-

02 and 2004-05. The agricultural development pattern among districts on the points of TE period 1986-87, 89-90, 92-93 1995-96, 98-99, 2001-02 and 04-05 have been examined through co-efficient variance and growth rates analysis. However, to show a combined influence of development pattern among districts in the state has been examined mainly on three points of TE period, 1992-93, 1998-99 and 2003-05 by applying the method of factor Analysis.

The main objective is to capture the changes in agricultural development pattern among districts that have been brought about primarily as a conscious of adaptation of new seed fertilizer technology, agricultural mechanization and extension of irrigated facilities over this period. Thus, this kind of study efforts is mainly to show and analyse the physical pattern of agricultural development in Haryana over this period around 20 years. This study is unique particularly in reference to Haryana in which there has been try to examine and analyse the overall pattern of agricultural development among districts. The statistical methods that have been applied in the present study explained in detailed in first chapter and at some other places in the study. On the basis of these methods the results occurs explain below.

When observed the pattern of agricultural development of districts by the variables through their C.V. results individually, some variables have declining trends and some of them have their increasing trends of disparities. The variables such as area under pulses, area under oilseeds, production of cereals, production of pulses, production of oilseeds, productivity of cereals, percentage of irrigated area, number of pumpsets, use of fertilizers, use of labour and number of tractors showed their declining trends with oscillations during the whole time period. The other variables like, the area under cereals, productivity of pulses, oilseeds, cropping intensity, net area sown, gross cropped area, Use of HYV and use of pesticides have their increasing trends with oscillations in the whole time period. Hence, the variables individually have shown a mix picture of disparities in case of some variables decline and in case of some variables increase. Therefore, to access a combined picture of agricultural development pattern among districts in the state there used the factor analysis method, which showed the overall trend of agricultural development pattern have increasing disparities trends among districts during the aforesaid time period in the state.

It can be concluded that a disparities in the trends and variability in area, production and productivity of cereals, pulses and oil seeds exists over districts in the state. In term of area under cereals, Kurukshetra retained the top position followed by Karnal during the TE period 1986-87. The disparities among districts in area under cereals during the analyzed time period, estimated by coefficient of variance, the results for the cereals in the TE year 1986-87 was 35.353 which increased to 43.786 during TE period 2004-05. Thus, the disparity among districts in area under cereals has increased. This is also evident from the coefficient of variation indicated that inter-district disparities in area under cereals only declined from 35.35 for TE period 1986-87 to 32.444 for TE period 1989-90, but increased later on continuously. On the other hand, the disparities among the districts in reference to area under pulses and oil seeds have been increases the CV increased from 95.10 to 201.76 during the study period.

In term of production of cereals, four districts Kurukshetra, Karnal, Jind and Hisar are above the state average during the TE period 1986-87. The coefficient of variance of production of cereals has been increased with fluctuations from 10.48, 26.45, 19.15, 26.57 and 11.59 during the study period. However, in term of production of pulses and oil seeds the Bhiwani and Hisar district have highest their proportions during the TE-1986-87. Co-efficient of variation figures indicated that inter-district disparities in the area widened during TE period 2001-02 but declined marginally during the TE period 2004-05. In case of area under pluses, C. V. was 95.106 for TE period 1986-87 to increased 201.77 for the TE period 2001-02 which shows the disparities among districts have been increased but declined 164.41 during TE period 2004-05, which is again the indication of decrease the disparities among districts. To examine the disparities level among districts in area under oilseeds the C.V. was 79.08 for TE period 1986-87, 79.82 for TE period 1989-90 and 99.25 for TE period 1998-99 and 133.34 for TE period 2001-02 and 129.66 for TE 2004-05. Thus, Coefficient of variation figures indicated that inter district disparities in area widened during up TE period 2001-02 but declined during the period TE 2004-05, but the trend is increasing with oscillations. The coefficient of variance of production of cereals has declined from 62.57 in the TE period 1986-87 to 48.96 in the TE period 2001-02, but C. V. has increased in TE 2004-05. To explain the disparities level among districts in production of pulses the C. V. indicates that the inter-district disparities in the production of pluses widened during TE 2001-02 but declined for TE period 2004-05. The C. V. was 89.69 for TE period 1986-87 increased to 187.67 for TE period 2001-02 which shows the disparities have been increased. The disparities among districts in the production of oilseeds has increased from 80.97 for TE period 1986-87 to 130.60 for TE period 2001-02 but declined 129.26 for TE 2004-05 which shows the disparities in the production of oilseeds has increased among districts in the state during 1986 to 2002 and decrease from 2001-02 to 2004-05. To measure the disparities level among districts in productivity of cereals the C.V. figures indicated that the inter-district disparities continuously declined during the study period. Thus, the variations among districts during the study period decrease from productivity point of view. The C.V. results for whole time period increased from 15.58 TE period 1986-87 to 31.85 TE period with a oscillatory trend for different TE periods, but the trends shows there increase in variation during the whole TE time period. To measure the disparities among districts in the productivity of oilseeds with help of C.V. indicated a very fluctuational position among districts during the all TE time period. The C.V. is 10.48, 26.45, 16.14, 13.38, 23, 27 and 12 for different TE time period. There is overall a increasing trend in the results. To measure the disparities level among districts in the forest area the C.V. has increased from 106.17 in TE period 1986-87 to 157.32 in TE period 2004-05, but declined 86.16 during TE period 1998-99, which shows the overall disparities in the forest area has increased, except to the TE period 1995-96 to 1998-99.

The C.V. has increased from 37.84 for TE period 86-87 to 51.46 for TE period 2004-05 which shows the overall disparities in net area sown has increased. On the other hand the irrigation facilities improved in almost all the districts, and there is significant change in the degree of inter-district variations irrigation facilities this is evident form the coefficient of variations figures which varied from 34.78 to 19.45 during the period 1984-2005. Consumption of pesticides expanded in all the districts during the period 1984-2005 and as a result inter-district disparities increased with fluctuation in this indicator. This is also evident from the coefficient of variation figures 56.82 in TE period 1986-87 declined to 45.11 in TE period 1998-99 but increased 65.20 in TE period 2004-05. To examine the disparities level among districts in average size of holdings the coefficient of variation was 35.25 in year 1980-81 increased to 48.30 in year 1985-86, decreased to 24.63 in year 1990-91, again increase to 53.98 in year 1995-96 and again decrease to 27.09 in year 2000-01 which shows overall disparities among districts with fluctuation decreased during the study period but there is high fluctuation in the trend. Coefficient of variation figures revealed the fallings tendency of agricultural labour. The C.V. was 46.25 in 1980-81 decreased 39.79 in the year 2000-01 which shows the disparities among districts decreased, but the tendency as cultivator falling did not affect the extent of regional disparities among districts. C.V. was 27.79 in the year 1980-81 increased and 49.22 in the year 2000-01 which shown the overall disparities level among districts decreased during the study period. The aforesaid changes of increase and decrease in disparities in an individual variable are in favour to overall improvement in the agricultural situation in the state and the direction of development move towards prosperity.

The classification of districts according to composite index of agricultural development for different categories namely; high, medium high, medium low and low categories for the years TE 1992-93, TE 1998-99 and TE 2004-05 positions show the changes in the process of development. In TE period 1992-93, the four districts Kaithal, Karnal, Hisar and Sirsa are in the category of high level of agricultural development. The four districts; Jind, Kurukshetra, Sonipat and Panipat are into the category of medium high. The districts namely; Ambala, Rohtak, Faridabad and Gurgaon are in the category of medium low and the remained districts, Rewari, Mahendragarh, Bhiwani and Yamuna Nagar are in the category of low in the sense of development of agriculture. The number of districts following in the category of high level of agricultural development increased from 4 in TE period 1992-93 to 6 in TE period 1998-99. The three districts Kurukshetra, Sonipat and Panipat are in the category of medium high and two districts Ambala and Fridabad are in to the category of medium low and remained five districts Yamuna Nagar, Gurgaon, Rewari, Mahendragarh and Bhiwani are still found to be underdevelopment or low category in the sense of agricultural development. During the TE period 2004-05 seven districts - Kurukshetra, Kaithal, Karnal, Jind, Hisar, Sirsa and Panipat, Rohtak are in to the category of high level of agricultural development. The two districts belonged to the category of medium high level of agricultural development and other two Fridabad and Bhiwani are in to the category of medium low. The remained five districts are in low category.

The mean value of composite indices increase from 0.14 to 0.49 is the indication of improvement in the agricultural development position among districts in the state and the size of composite indices also increases is indication of improvement in the situation of agricultural development among districts in the state. The coefficient of variation figures for the composite indices increased from 407.1428 to 492.7142 during the time period from 1992-93 to 2004-05, that indicated the disparities among the districts increased in the agricultural development.

Another thing is the level of development of districts improved shown through composite index increases but the level of disparities among districts exists. The next important result is the category of agricultural development of districts (low, medium low, medium high and high) changed in case of some districts they have reshuffle their position from low to high but, the overall situation of the districts category of agricultural development situation changed in the whole time period. Last but not least, it may be possible the less development category districts of Haryana may be better as compared to other districts of nation from per capita income point of view, but, with in state there exist the disparities among districts. These kinds of changes in the results according to composite index occur due to change in the irrigation facility in the districts and the changing pattern of crops in some districts also.

The major conclusions find in the present study are; the regional disparities among districts continuously increases through out the time period (1984-85 to 2004-05), but there are the fluctuations in the different Triennium Ending (TE) period, it is clear from co-efficient variance and factor analysis in tables in chapter 4, and to measure the spatial pattern of agricultural development among district, there are three interesting findings noticeable from the foregoing analysis are (1) An upward movement of certain districts in level of agricultural development (2) An increase in value of composite indices in sizeable number of districts and (3) An Increase in inter-district disparities among districts in level of agricultural development. These findings in turn, provide substantial support to further conclude that there has been definate improvement in agricultural development during 2004-05 as compared to 1984-85, but the level of disparities among districts continuously going to increase and the pattern of agricultural development is uneven among districts in the state.

Suggestions

Changes in agricultural sector have strong repercussions in the Indian economy, through the channels of poverty, food security, inflation etc. The crucial role played by the agricultural sector has been identified as central to inclusive growth and its recent economic slow down calls for a special attention for its revival. Although it provides employment to more than 60 per cent people, it contributes only about 20 per cent of Gross Domestic Product (GDP). The output growth of agricultural sector would definitely reduce poverty to a greater extent than growth in any other sector by providing employment, by stabilizing prices, by providing food security and by a multitude of other spill-over effects.

Important challenges persist for agriculture. The need to accelerate growth in India's agricultural sector prompts special consideration due to the slow down on agricultural production, employment and wages. Where growth in nonagricultural sector has accelerated, the reallocation of labour out of agriculture is lagging, concentrating poverty in rural areas and widening rural-urban income disparities. More divergence of agricultural income in low income states implies the need for strategies for these regions. There should be new strategy which should rely much more on policies to liberalise agricultural inputs and outputs by reforming land administration and tenancy requirements and by supporting research and development that is tailored by specific needs. A workable strategy to accelerate productivity in agriculture has to promote four directions for agriculture in the overall rural economy. Intensification: Increase the productivity of traditional crops through greater use of irrigation, high yield verities, agrochemical inputs and mechanization. Diversification: Shift to new more profitable crops (fruits, vegetables, higher value cereals, medicinal plants) and livestock. Non farm linkage: Emphasize related activities that add value to agricultural products such as trading, agro processing and supplying inputs. Exit: Switch from agriculture to other more productive activities. The government of India's justifiable concern with the inclusiveness of economic growth can be addressed by focusing on expanding the regional scope of economic growth, expanding access to assets and thriving markets and expanding equity in the opportunities for the next generation of Indian citizens.

The balanced agricultural development does not imply equality in the agricultural income in different regions of the state. By balanced regional development of agriculture we simply mean raising the rate of agricultural growth to the maximum possible extent by making optimum use of the resources and potentialities of region

1. A suitable balanced agricultural strategy is needed for making optimal use of agricultural resources and potentialities and balancing the rate of agricultural growth over regions. The strategy for agricultural development combines policies and programmes that influence the pattern of agricultural development as well as the rate of increase in farm output. It is one of the components of agricultural planning, evolv-ing a strategy for agricultural development in harmony with the objectives of overall economic development of the state. Agricultural develop-ment involving production technique suitable to the factor endowments and being able to stimulate overall economic progress makes the most rational use of scarce resource.

2. The persistence of regional disparities in agricultural development in Haryana may be attributed to lack of suitable plan efforts towards balanced regional development. As disparities are more pronounced at lower spatial level, reduction in regional disparities lies in implementation of area specific development

plans. Area-based planning is required to take full account of the potentials, needs and priorities of different areas. Such an exercise would help farmers get optimal benefits of their efforts. Area planning should involve activities like improving fertility of soils encouraging farmers for improved input use, innovative farm practices and for making production for exchange value and not for use value only, supervision of farming operations and tackling the problems of farmers.

3. The land leveling activity is used in a small area and there has been partiality in case of different categories of the farmers. This study suggested that sand dunes should cover the large area. So, expenditure on land leveling activity should be increased. Funding for this activity should be increased for small and marginal farmers to avoid partiality. Afforestation activity including plantation should be increased in private as well as common land. So that soil conversation and sand dunes can be stabilize.

4. There exist significant disparities in gross income from agriculture between different agro climatic conditions. Observed variations in agriculture income are the direct out come of the growth of necessary infrastructure and input supply in agriculture like irrigation, fertilizer, high-yielding variety seeds, etc. The adoption of improved production technology like use of fertilizers, HYV seeds, cropping intensity differs considerably between different districts. Karnal, Kairthal, Kurukshetra, Sirsa district having more area under rice, wheat, and sugarcane have much more income from agriculture than the Mahendragarh, Bhiwani, Rewari district where low income crops like bajra, jowar and pulses are grown. The study also reveals that the gap in agricultural income between different districts of the state widened due to uneven

availability of irrigation facilities and inadequate and untimely availability of fertilizers etc.

5. After the formation of Haryana as a separate state, the increase in productivity in the state has been due to tremendous growth of physical inputs in agriculture. The net area irrigated increased from 1532 thousand hectares in 1970-71 to 2954 thousand hectares in 2004-05. At the district level Kurukshetra, Kairthal, Karnal, Jind have above state average percentage of irrigated area to cropped area while Bhiwani, Mahendragarh, Gurgaon, Rewari, Faridabad have below state average. This is one of the region that Kurukshetra, Kairthal have higher growth rates in area, production and productivity of almost all the crops, in comparisons the other districts. Increase productivity of the entire district and the state as a whole, has to be achieved through intensive cultivation with greater use of better and adequate inputs, mechanized farming, timely availability of credit facilities, marketing and research facilities etc.

6. There is a wide scope in reducing regional disparities in agriculture by extending the infrastructure and the known new agriculture technology to such areas where the development has not been faster. The major policy thrust therefore, should be an increasing irrigation facility in the south western region of the state, comprising the districts of Mahendergarh, Gurgaon and Faridabad. The unexploited vast potential of these districts should be tapped by providing necessary infrastructure and institutional support. Rainfall has deficient and erratic nature in the major parts of Haryana; the state must therefore exploit and develop other sources of water for setting aside socio-economic regional imbalances.

7. Though the level of economic development attained by Haryana is slightly above that of the national level,

there are wide variations from district to district both in structure of the economy and extent of its development. A few important selected indicators for measuring the level of the agricultural development in various district show that some district are better off according to one indicator while other appears more developed, when judged by another indicators. However, taking all the factors into consideration, it is clear that Karnal, Kairthal, Sirsa the most prosperous district and south western part is the most backward in the state.

8. The interdependence of agriculture and industry would lead to the modernisation of agriculture accelerating the rate of agricultural growth. However, it must be borne, here, in mind that farm sector has to remain a surplus population supporting sector for several decades to come. As such, agricultural strategy should be so designed as to support a large section of the rural population by providing them with productive work.

9. The agricultural strategy should also aim at the full and rational use of the physical inputs and infrastructural facilities as resources are quite limited. In order to achieve maximum efficiency in agricultural development, agricultural strategy should ensure an efficient sequence of different investments and a co-ordination between timings of different policies and programmes. While evolving a strategy for agricultural development of a region, it is essential to take into account the stage of agricultural development of that region, the accompanying peculiarities of the demographic and social make-up and the state of its technological progress. It would make the strategy adoptive.

10. The organisational changes would be impossible without the implementation of land-reform measures

offering incentive and ensuring security to the cultivators. Radical land reforms demand a strong politi-cal will and commitment on the part of the Government and unfortunately the same have been lacking in Haryana. This along with elitist composition of political leadership and bureaucracy and structural inequalities in the ownership of land and other assets and consequent control of the ex-feudal elements on the social economic and political institutions had led to the failure of land reform measures and the persistence of exploitative agrarian set up. The structural impediments to production remain to be there, they have rather increased. The social, political and economic power of the rural elite has increased. The land reform measures instead of bringing economic solace to the rural poor have aggravated their problems. The eviction galore and the preference of the landlords to cultivate their lands by hired labour have resulted in a rapid increase of agricultural labour force.

11. The Government can influence agricultural growth in an indirect way by providing physical and service infrastructural facilities. Physical and service infrastructural facilities affect the cost structure through the creation of external economies which induce efficient input-use. There are gross inadequacies of physical infrastructural facilities like irrigation, flood control, transport and power in Haryana attempt to fill these infrastructural gaps will pay very high dividends in agricultural economy.

12. Marketing and storage services ensure higher income to the farmers, adequate and timely supply of inputs and reflect correctly the price signals in order to help the peasant in formulating his production plan. However, these services are very inadequate in the rural areas of the State to the detriment to agricultural

development. On an average, there is only one wholesale market for a rural population of one lakh and the rural markets for wholesale market. Most of the markets lack basic infrastructure facilities. Marketing and storage facilities should be spread over wide base. Attempts may be made to widen the base of co-operative marketing structure and revitalize it in order to fill the gap of marketing structure in Haryana.

13. Because of widespread illiteracy and low exposure to mass media farmers require knowledge and training in the use of modern farm inputs. They are required to learn the nature of soil and proportion and frequency of inputs suitable to the soil in order to achieve the optimal yield rate. Extension education is also to be supplemented by the facilities relating to adaptive research. As every type of inputs or techniques is not uniformly suitable to all areas, there is need for selective adoption of inputs and techniques for healthy agricultural progress. For the purpose an agency with experts of various fields relating to agriculture may be created at the block-level. This agency will be responsible for providing extension and adoptive education to the farmers through the help of the village Development Board/Gram Sabha. This is the area where voluntary agencies can play a vital role. An increasing help of mass-media is also needed to educate the farmers. A fast modernisation of agriculture is not possible in absence of a comprehensive programme of extension education and adaptive research.

14. Development of Agro-industries not only makes cheap and easy availability of farm inputs possible but also provides additional avenues for farmers to earn income and invest their surplus. It also absorbs surplus labour force in agriculture increasing agricultural productivity. Prospero agriculture by

making cheap raw materials available and expanding the markets for industrial products induces industrial growth agriculture and industry get benefit of their mutual development and there is cumulative process of development and prosperity. As such, attempt should be made to develop agro-industries in order to supplement agriculture and thereby promote agricultural development. Industries to be developed should be ones which lead to better processing and transforming of farm products, increase the production of agricultural inputs and provide employ-ment for rural labour. Care must be taken to see that labour- intensive technology is used to mechanise and modernise agriculture. The rural labours would thus find higher employment opportunities as well as higher wages. It could put a check on the large scale out migration of agricultural labours which is hampering agricultural operations in the State.

15. To motivate the farmers towards the commercial crops, demonstration plots are very useful. So it is suggested that farmers can be stimulate is change the cropping pattern through the Demonstration plots which is valuable for them.

16. It has been found that the rain occurs mostly in the rainy season of monsoon in the month of July to September which is approximately 90 percents. Most of the rainy water goes waste and there is no provision of harvesting the rainy water. Hence, the study suggests that every drop of rainy water should be utilised for the purpose of irrigation, drinking water, plantation and pasture development etc. Ponds should be used for the micro irrigation as well as for drinking water to human and animals. Hand pumps should be installed near the ponds.

17. Mostly, the policies are made at the centre level. It has been found that these policies become less useful

to local specific areas because the policy makers are not aware of their local problems. So, it is suggested the there should be local people participation in policy making and implementation of the policies. Technical and institutional arrangements can be easy and affordable for the policies. It is very much close to the concept of inclusive growth.

18. To increase the output of food grain coarse grains and pulses, it is necessary to raise their productivity by evolving high-yielding varieties with stable yields. This may be followed by appropriate extension education programme to the farmers to acquaint them with better and efficient methods of crops husbandry. To encourage the production of cotton and surgarcane (commercial crops), crop insurance scheme may be started and popularised among the farmers to cover loss / risk, as there crops are highly sensitive to the weather conditions. Special attention should be given to increase the production of pulses and cash crops in the state to meet the increasing demand for money for further investments.

19. The increase in area under cultivation and total cropped area in all the district has been achieved through land reclamation and change in cropping pattern induced by all round improvement in irrigation facilities.

20. The high priority given to agricultural production makes it necessary that special attention be paid to irrigation in the state. Many farmers would like to irrigate their land but they have extremely scanty or unusable water resources which can not be economically developed on their own farms. The increase in agricultural production over the past years has mainly depended upon the provision and expansion of irrigation supplies. This will remain the principle base for future economic development of

Haryana agriculture. Fixation of higher procurement prices for oilseeds and pulses (main crops of the rainfed area) and proper arrangements for procurement of the produce of these crops should be given top priority. It will improve the income of the farmers on one hand, and on the other, help in solving the national problem of scarcity of oilseeds and pulses. There is a need for the availability of cheap and timely supply of credit facilities to the farmers in order to boost the agricultural production in the state.

21. To remove disparities in agricultural development among districts, it is necessary to accelerate the rate of investment in most potential sector in the agricultural backward districts. This is not a problem of the state of Haryana alone, it is rather a problem for the entire nation.
22. On the basis of analysis of the trends in institutional finance for less agricultural districts in the state, it seems that All Haryana institutions need to pay more attention to project assistance for units in backward districts. The development finance institutions can, therefore, no longer act as purveyors of finance. They have to assume additional responsibilities.
23. The institutions should concentrate more on labour intensive projects for backward districts. The past experience has shown that the spread effects of high technology projects are low and the surrounding districts continue to remain poor and under developed. It is also necessary that a much greater share of assistance from these institutions should be earmarked for less developed districts.
24. In the agricultural districts where we have already created substantial production capacities, focus has to be on fuller capacity utilisation as to reap the full benefits of the investments they have already been made. An important pre-requisite for such

development is infrastructural facilities, particularly in the realm of power, transport and communications. The development finance institutions may have to evolve strategies to ensure that infrastructural development is brought about facilitating better capacity utilisation by existing industrial units.

25. The things new farm technology and promotion and contract farming etc. can be apply as experiment purpose in agricultural backward districts .
26. In the interest of the quick development of agricultural backward districts, it is essential that National Bank for Agriculture and Rural Development (NABARD) should play a catalytic role in promoting and encouraging sound agricultural projects. They should not only limited their role to identification of project ideas and commissioning of preliminary feasibility studies, but should undertake detailed investigation into the viability of the projects, implement the projects and managed them.
27. The state government has the primary responsibility of bringing about balanced regional development and accelerating the process of industrialization of backward districts. Most of the states are now in a position, through the district surveys and other studies made in the recent past, to assess the resource potential of these districts and their development potential. Thus, the district economic planning becomes an inseparably part of the overall planning of the state. This can best be done by the state planning department with such assistance as necessary from the planning commission and other institutions.
28. The shortage of power is the acute problem in the state. Due to the slow pace of creation of new capacity and the poor rate of utilisation of existing capacity, the gap between supply and demand is expected to widen further. State's agricultural tempo received the

worse set back during the last few years due to continuing power shortage. This position should be improved. The state has now put forward its claim for the gas based power stations.

29. Last but not least, in brief the Agriculture Policy document must articulate a clear vision on following few basic parameters of the agricultural sector around which a policy framework must be developed under the changed scenario of globalization and liberalization; Organization of agriculture: A clear long-term vision where inter-sectoral linkages are explicit; Sustainability and natural resource management: Prescription must lie in the domain of political economy. Otherwise, allocating funds for watershed development, agroforestry, soil conservation, and so on will not produce desired results; Institutional change: Policy document must spell out new approaches and new institutions free from the shackles of bureaucratic and self-help framework.; Investment priorities: There is a need to develop a consensus on investment themes, priorities and policies. Policy document must lend strength to the claim for greater investment in rural areas, and also re-examine its programmes in the light of complementarities; Incentives: Document must articulate a clear vision on the incentive framework and there is need to stress on Risk management also.

Thus, the aforesaid suggestions can help to run the nation/state on balanced development path. As Nobel laureate Arthur Lewis pointed out long ago, the development is bound to be inegalitarian, because it does not start in every part of the economy at the same time. However, the structure of agriculture growth and variation across states in India is a key outcome of this unfolding development process. It is clear from the development experience and the simmering unrest in several less developed states and particularly less developed districts of Haryana. The regional disparities in development may accentuate further to crisis proportions threatening social harmony and state peace, apart from depriving the state of the opportunities for higher and sustainable development. Hence, the states revels need for pulling up the agricultural development from unevenness and setting it on a path of balanced agricultural development and sustained growth with condition of optimal use of natural resources. In this connection, identification and stimulation of real policy variables warrant priority in the agricultural strategy of the state in changed scenario of Globalization, liberalization and Privatization.

At the end that globalization offers both opportunities and challenges. The opportunities consist of contribution the benefits of world trade and growth. The challenges lie in enabling the sharing of these benefits not by a small minority of elite population but by the majority of working people in rural and urban India.

References

Acharya S. (2007), Can India Grow without Bharat?, Academic Foundation, New Delhi.

Agenor, Pierre Richard (2003), 'Does Globalisation Hurt the Poor?' The World Bank.

Ahamad, A. and Singh, D.K. (1980), 'Regional Planning with Particular' Reference to India, Oriental Publishers and Distributors, New Delhi.

Ahluwalia, Montek, S. (2002), 'State Level Performance Under Economic Reforms in India' in Anne 0 Krueger (ed), Economic Policy Reforms and the Indian Economy, Oxford University Press, New Delhi, pp 91-125.

Ahluwalia, Montek, S. (2000), 'Economic Performance of States in Post-reforms period', Economic and Political Weekly, May, 6, pp 1637-48.

Alan Winters L. and Yusuf S. (Ed.) (2007), Dancing with Giants: China, India, and the Global Economy, The World Bank and The Institute of Policy Studies, Singapore.

Alonso, W. (1968), 'Urban and Regional Imbalances in Economic Development', Economic Development and Cultural Change, Vol. 17, No.1, pp. 1-14.

Anuradha and Rao (1995), 'An Analysis of Inter-State Disparities in India, 1970-71 to 1985-86', Indian Journal of Regional Science, Vol. XXVII, Nos. 1 and 2.

Atkinson, A.B. (1983), 'The Economic of Inequalities', Oxford University Press, New Delhi.

Barro, R. J. (1991), 'Economic Growth in a cross-section of Countries', Quarterly Journal of Economics, 106: 407-444.

Barro, R. J. and Sala-i-Martin, X. (1995), Economic Growth, Singapore: McGraw-Hill International Editions.

Barro, R. J. and Sala-i-Martin, X. (1992), 'Convergence', Journal of Political Economy, 100 (May): 223-252.

Baumol, W. J. (1986), 'Productivity Growth, Convergence and Welfare: What the long-run data show', American Economic Review, 76 (5): 1072-1085.

Baumol, W. J. and Wolff, E. N. (1988), 'Productivity Growth, Convergence and Welfare: Reply', American Economic Review, 78 (5): 1155-1159.

Bloom D. E., Canning D., Hu L., Liu Y., Mahal A. and Yip W. (2006), 'Why has Chinas Economy Taken Off Faster than India's?', Princeton University.

Bosworth B. and Collins S. M. and Virmani, A. (2007), 'Sources of Growth in the Indian Economy', NBER Working Paper 12901, Cambridge, MA, February

Bosworth B. and Collins S.M. (2007), 'Accounting for Growth: Comparing China and India', NBER Working Paper No. 12943, Cambridge, MA, February.

Bourguignon, F. (1979), 'Decomposable Income Inequality Measures', Econometrica, 47(4): 901-920.

Bathla, S. (2005), 'Intersectoral Growth Linkages in India: Implication for Policy and Liberalized Reforms', Institute of Economic Growth, New Delhi.

Bhatia, Bela, (1968), 'Luch Field and Parehad Throats' : Political Economy of Ground Water in Gujrat EPW Dec. 19-26.

Bhalla, Surjit S. (2003), 'Recounting the Poor' 1993-99 EPW Jan 25, 2003 pp. 338 49.

Bhalla G.S. and Tyagi, D.S. (1989), 'Patterns in Indian Agriculture Development A District level Study', Institute for Studies in Industrial Development, New Delhi.

Bhalla G.S and Alagh, Y.K. (1979), 'Performance of Indian Agriculture: A Districtwise Study', New Delhi.

Bhalla G.S (1987), 'Some Issues in Agricultural Development in India' in Brahmananda and Panchmukhi (ed.) 'The Development Process of the Indian Economy, Bombay.

Bhalla G.S. and Singh G.(2001), 'Indian Agriculture : Four decades of Development' Sage Publications, New Delhi.

Bharadwaj, K. (1982), 'Regional Differentiation in India', Economic and Political Weekly, Annual Number, Vol. XVII, Nos. 14, 15 and 16, April, pp. 605-14.

Bhattacharya, B.B. and Sakthivel (2005), 'Regional Growth and Disparity in India: A Comparison of Pre and Post reform Decades', Institute of Economic Growth, New Delhi.

Bhattacharya, B.B. and Sakthivel, S. (2004), 'Regional Growth and Disparities in India: Comparison of Pre- and Post- Reforms Decades', Economic and Political Weekly, March, 6, pp, 1071-1077.

Bhowmik, D. (2000), 'A Decade of India's Economic Reforms, Article Published in S. Murty (Ed), Economic Reforms Today : Pros and Cons (RBSA, Jaibur) pp. 28-63.

Birdsall, Nancy (2002), 'A Symmetric Globalisation: Global Markets Require Good Global Politics', Center for Global Development Paper No. 12, October.

Booth, E.J.R. (1964), 'International Income Differences', Southern Economic Journal, July, pp. 44-51.

Booth, J.A., and M.A. Seligson (1984), 'The Political Culture of Authoritarianism in Maxico: A Reexamination,' Latin American Research Review, no. 1: 106-124.

Bright, Joseph (2003), 'Trade Libaralization and Primary Commodity Prices Empirical Evidence from Select Tropical Crops in Kerela India ; GTAP Resource # 1537 7th Annual Conference on Global Economic Analysis http//wwwgtab : ageron produce edu / conference / 2004 / program.asp.

Cashin, P. and Sahay, R. (1996), 'Regional Economic Growth and Convergence in India', Finance and Development, March: 49-52.

Chakarvarty, S. (1984) 'Power Structure and Agricultural Productivity', in Desai (ed.) vol. 'Agrarian Power and Agricultural Productivity in South Asia, New Delhi.

Chakarvarty, S. (1986) 'Development Planning: The Indian Experience' Oxford University Press, Delhi.

Chand, M. & Puri V.K, (1983), 'Regional Planning in India', Allied Publishers Pvt. Ltd., New Delhi, 1983, P. 1

Chand, R. (2005a), 'Explorating possibilities of achieving four percent growth rate in Indian Agricultural', NCAP – Working Paper, New Delhi.

Chhipa and Sagar (1981), 'Banking Development in India: A Study into the Causes of Regional Differentials', Indian Journal of Regional Science, Vol XIII, No.1, pp. 86-89.

Daniel, Bell (1974), 'The Coming of Post Industrial Society. New Delhi. p.9.

Das, T. K. (2000), 'Economic Growth and Convergence across India States', International Symposium on Development Policies for the New Millenium, IGIDR, Mumbai, 12th -14th July: 89-94.

Dasgupta, D. et al. (2000), 'Growth and Inter State Disparities in India', Economic and Political Weekly, July 1st, 35(27): 2413-2422.

De Long, J. B. (1988), 'Productivity Growth, Convergence and Welfare: Comment', American Economic Review, 78 (5): 1138-1154.

Dowrick, S. and Nguyen, D. T. (1988), 'OECD Comparative Economic Growth 1950-1985: Catch up and Convergence', American Economic Review, 79: 1010-1030.

Das and Dalvi, (1981), 'Application of Shift and Share Technique for Forecasting Regional and Sectoral Growth in India for the Sixth Plan Period" Indian Journal of Regional Science, Vol. XIII, No.2.

Das, Sandwip and Barua, (1996), 'Regional Inequalities, Economic Growth and Liberalisation': A Study of the Indian Economy', The Journal of Development Studies, Vol. 32, No.3, Feb., pp. 364-90.

Desai, Rohit, (1986), 'The Changing Pattern of Regional Industrial Diversification: A Comparison Over Time', Indian Journal of Regional Science, Vol. XVII, No.1, pp. 11-16.

Dev, Mahendra S. (1985), 'Direction of Change in Performance of all crops in Indian Agriculture in the late 1970', EPW,21-28,Dec., pp.A130-A136.

Dev, Mahendra S. (1986), 'Growth of Labour Productivity in Indian Agriculture: Regional Dimentions',EPW,21-28,June, pp.A65-A74.

Dev, Mahendra S. (1988), 'Prospective of Enhancing Labour Productivity in Indian Agriculture', EPW, 24 Sep., pp.A106-A113.

Dev, S.M. and C. Ravi (2003), 'Macroeconomic Scene: Performance and Policies', in C.H.H. Rao and S. Mahendra Dev (ed.), Andhra Pradesh Development. Economic Reforms and Challenges Ahead, Hyderabad: Centre for Economic and Social Studies.

Dholakia, R. (1994), 'Regional Dimension of Acceleration of Economic Growth in India', Economic and Political Weekly, Vol. 26, No. 35, August 21.

Dholakia, R.H. (1985), 'Regional Disparities in Economic Growth in India', Bombay.

Dholakia, R.H. and Dholakia B.H. (1993), 'Growth of Total Factors Productivity in Indian Agricultural', Indian Economic Review, 33(1), p-25.

Dutta B., (1972) 'Regional Balance in Economic Development in T.B. Lahiri, ed. Balance Regional Development Concept Strategy and Case Studies (Calcutta: Oxford and IBH Publishing Co.,) p.20.

Economic Times, (ET). (2006), dated 28.2.06.

Ernst & Young (2006), Doing Business in India, Ernst & Young Private Limited, New Delhi.

Feder, G., Just R.E. and Zilberman D. (1985), 'Adoption of Agricultural Innovation in Developing Countries', A Survey', Economic Development and Cultural Change, 33(2).

Fisher, J. L. (1969), 'Regional Planning, Determining the Public Interest in M.M. Hufschmidt (ed.), Regional Planning', Challenge and Prospects, Frederich, Praeges A., 1969, P.P. 7-8.

Funke, M. and Strulik, H. (1999), 'Regional Growth in West Germany: Convergence Divergence', Economic Modeling, 16: 489-502.

Government of India (2006), 'Towards Fast or and more inclusive Growth' : An Approach to the 11th Five Year Plan. Planning Commission, New Delhi.

Goyari, P. (2005), 'Flood Damages and Sustainability of Agriculture in Assam', Economic and Political Weekly, Vol. XL (26), June 25, pp. 2723-2729.

Goyari, P. (2007), 'Adoption of Modem Agricultural Technology: A Micro Level Study in Assam', Ph.D. Thesis Submitted to University of Hyderabad, July 2007.

Gulati, Ashok and Anil Sharma (1995), 'Subsidy Syndrome in Indian Agriculture', Economic and Political Weekly, Vol. 30, No. 39, September 30. pp. A-93-A-I01.

Gupta S.P and Sdasuk. S. (1961), 'Economic Regionalisation of India' Problems and Approaches, Census of Indian, 1961, Monograph Series, Vol. 1, No.8, Government of India, P. 102.

Gupta, Deepak, (1985), 'Inter-State Industrial Disparities in India: The Changing Scene', Reserve Bank of India Occasional Papers, Vol. 6, No.1, June, pp. 54-68.

Ghosh, B., Marjit, S. and Neogi, C. (1998), 'Economic Growth and Regional Divergence in India, 1960 to 1995', Economic and Political Weekly, June 27: 1623-1630.

Goddar, J. and Wilson, J. (2001) 'Cross Sectional and Panel Estimation of Convergence', Economic letters, 70: 327-333.

Gordon, J. and Gupta, P. (2003), 'Understanding India's Services Revolution', IMF-NCAER Conference, New Delhi, November 14 -16.

Government of India (2006), Towards Faster and More Inclusive Growth An Approach to the 11th Five Year Plan (2007-2012), Planning Commission, Yojana Bhavan, New Delhi, December.

Hanna, F.A. (1957), 'Analysis of Inter-State Income Differentials: Theory and Practice' in National Bureau of Economic Research (ed.), Regional Income; Studies in Income and Wealth, Vol. 21, Princeton University Press, Princeton, pp. 113-61.

Hausmann R., Rodrik D. and Velasco A. (2005), 'Growth Diagnostics', John F. Kennedy School of Government, Harvard University, Cambridge, MA, March.

Henry Villard, H. (1963), 'Economic Development', Holt, Rinehart and Winston Inc., New York

Hirschman, A.O., (1958), 'The Strategy of Economic Development, Yale University Press, New Haven.

Hughes, R.B. (1961), 'International Income Difference Self-prepetuation.' Southern Economic Journal, Vol. XXVIII, July, PP. 41-45.

Hurroll, A. and Woods, N. (2000), 'Globalisation and Inequality in R. Hoggott' (Ed) The New Political Econometrics, Wiley.

Islam, N. (1995), 'Growth Empirics: a panel data approach', Quarterly Journal of Economics, 60: 1127-1170.

Izraeli, O. and Murphy, K. (1997), 'Convergence in State Nominal and Real per capita Income', Public Finance Review, 25 (6): 555-576.

Jagdish N. Bhagwati, (2009), 'Indian Reforms: Past Achievements and Future Challenges' A Series of Prof. Raj Krishana Memorial Lecture, University of Rajasthan, Jaipur, (India), August 12.

Jha, Raghabendra (2000), 'Reducing Poverty and Inequality in India-Has Liberalisation Helped?' WIDER, WP-204, November.

Johnson, B.F. and Millor, F.W. (1961), 'The Role of Agriculture in Economic Development, American Economic Review, 4(4) PP 565-93.

Joshi, W.B.M. (1987), 'Inter-State Disparities and Economic Development', Yojana, Vol. 31, No.4, March I-IS, pp. 4-10

Kaldor, N. (1970), 'The case for regional policies', Scottish Journal of Political Economy, Vol. 17, No.3, pp. 337-48.

Kannanm, R. (1987), 'Banking Development and Regional Disparities', The Indian Economic Journal, Vol. 35, No.2, pp. 58-76.

Kantawala and Rao (1992), 'Sectoral Development in India An Inter-State Analysis', Indian Journal of Regional Science, Vol. XXIV, No. I, pp. 27-35.

Kehdall, MG and Buckland, W.R. (1983), 'Dictionary of Statistical Terms', Prepared for the International Statistical Institute, Edinbourgh, Oliver & Boyd.

Kim, K., and Chavas, J.P. (2003), 'Technology Change and Risk Management: An Application to the Economics of Corn Production', Agricultural Economics, Vol. 29.

Krishnaji N., (1975), 'Inter-Regional Disparities in Per Capita Production and Productivity of Foodgrains:APreliminary Note on Trends', EPW,special number, pp1375-1385.

Kundu, A. and M. Raza (1982), Indian Economy: The Regional Dimension, Centre for the Study of Regional Development, Jawaharlal Nehru University, New Delhi.

Kurian, N.J. (2000), 'Widening Regional Disparities in India: Some Indicators', Economic and Political Weekly, Vo1.35, No.7, February 2000, pp-538-550

Kuznets, S. (1961), 'Economic Growth and Contribution of Agriculture Notes on Measurement,' International Journal of Agricultural Affairs Vol. 3, No.2, PP 56-57.

Kuznets, S. and Easterlin, R.A. (1960), 'Population Redistribution and Economic Growth, United States, 1870-1950, The American Philosophical Society, Philadelphia.

Ladejinsky, W., (1979), 'Agrarian Reforms as Unfinished Business: Selected Papers of Wolf Ladejinsky, (ed. Wilinsky,L.), Oxford.

Leberger, C.P. (1968), 'Economics Development', McGraw Hill Inc. Nogakusha P. 218.

Leipziger D. and Zagha R. (2006), 'Getting Out of the Rut', Finance & Development, Vol. 43, No.1, Pp. 16-18.

Lindert, P.H. and Williamson, J.G. (2001), 'Does Globalization make the World Unequal' University of California, Davis and Harvard University.

Losch, A. (1940), 'The Economics of Location' (English Translation), Yale University Press, New Haven, 1954.

Lucas, R. E. (1990), 'Why Does not Capital Flow from Rich to Poor Countries?,' American Economic Review, 80(May): 92-96.

Mankiew, N. G., Romer, D. and Weil, D. N. (1992), 'A Contribution to the Empirics of Economic Growth', Quarterly Journal of Economics, 107 (May): 407-437.

Mahajan, O.P. (1982), 'Economic Planning and Regional Development in India', Ess Publications, New Delhi.

Mahalanobis. P.C. (1960), 'A foreword Mysore State' Vol. 1, An Atlas of Resources, Edited by A.T.A.s earmonth and Bott. L.S. 1.S., Calcutta, 1960.

Marjit, S. and Mitra, S. (1996), 'Convergence in Regional Growth Rates: Indian Research Agenda', Economic and Political Weekly, August 17: 2239-2242.

Mazumdar, K. (1993), 'Inter-State Disparities in Per Capita State Domestic Product in India: 1960-61 to 1985-86', Indian Journal of Regional Science, Vol. XXV, No. pp. 13-17.

Metha, S. J., Crihfield, J. B and Giertz, F. (1992), 'Economic growth in American States: The end of Convergence', Working Paper no. 20, The Institute of Governments and Public Affair, University of Illinois.

Minhas, B.S. and Vaidyanathan, A. (1965), 'Growth of Crop Output in India: 1951-54 to 1958-61, An Analysis by Component Element' in Journal of Indian Society of Agriculture Statistics, Vol. XVII, No.2.

Mishra, G.P. (ed.), (1985), 'Regional Structure of Development and Growth in India, vols, 1&2,New Delhi.

Mitra, A. (1964), 'Levels of Regional Development of India', Census of India, 1961 , Vol. I, Part IA (1), Govt. of India, New Delhi.

Moser, C. (1973), 'Social Indicators - System, Method and Problems', Review of Income and Wealth p. 133-143.

Myrdal G. (1969), 'Objectivity in Social Research,' Panthern, Middlesex, 1969, P.P. 20-26

Myrdal, G. (1964), 'Economic theory and Underdeveloped Regions' (London: Matheun & Co.), p. 38.

Myrdal, G. (1957), 'Economic Theory and Underdeveloped Region', Gerald Duckworth, London.

Nagaraj, R, A Varoundakis and M Beganzones (1998), 'Long-Run Growth Trends and Convergence Across Indian States', Technical Paper, No. 131, OECD Development Centre, Paris, France.

Nair, K.R.G. (1983), 'Inter-State Income differentials in India: 1970-71 to 1979-80', Man and Development, Vol. V, No.2, pp. 43-54.

North D.C. (1973), 'Agriculture in Regional Economic Growth in C. Echer and Lawrence (ed)' Agriculture in Economic Development, McGrw Hill, New York, P. 69.

Ohlin, B. (1933), 'Interregional and International Trade', Harvard University Press, Cambridge.

O'Mara, Gerald (1980), 'The Microeconomics of Technique Adoption by Report, Small-holding Mexican Farmers', Development Research Centre, World Bank.

Pangaria Arvind (2009), "Late PM Rao was man behind liberalization" HT live Jaipur, July13.

Pal, P.K. (2003), 'Dimension of poverty of India: Measurement and Determinant'. 86th IEA conference volume, Kolhapur pp. 126--142.

Perloff, H.S., Dunn Jr., E.S., Lampard, E.E. and Muth, R.F. (1960), 'Regions, Resources and Economic Growth', Johns Hopkins Press, Baltimore.

Pitambar Pant (1962), 'Urbanisation and Long Range Strategy, Indian's Urban Future', Los Angels, 1962, P. 190-91.

Prakash S. (1977), 'Regional Inequalities and Economic Development with Special Reference to Infrastructural Facilities in India',' Indian Journal of Regional Science, Vol. XI, No.2, pp. 173-95.-

Pritchett, L. (1995), 'Livergence, Big Time,' Policy Research Working Paper No. 1522. (Washington DC., World Bank).

Rana, R.K. (1997), 'A Study of Inter-State Disparities and Pattern of Development India' , Indian Economic Association Conference Volume, Hyderabad, pp. 493-500.

Rangacharyulu, S.V. (1993), 'Composite Development Index of Rural Areas', Journal of Rural Development, Vol. 12(1), pp. 35-56.

Rao and Brahma, Sulabha (1973), 'Regional Planning As Tool of Development Planning', Anvesak, Vol. 3, Nos. 1-2, pp. 57-66.

Rao,V.M. and Despande, R.S. (1987), 'Agriculture Growth in India A Review of Experience and Prospects', in Brahmananda and Panchmukhi (ed.) pp.161-99.

Rao and Nath (1949), 'Regional Planning' Indian Statistical Institute and Asia Publishing House, Calcutta.

Rao Hanumantha C.H. (1995), 'Liberalization of Agriculture in India: Some Major Issues, Indian Journal of Agricultural Economics, Vol. 50, No.3, pp. 450-472.

Rao, C.H.H. (1994), 'Agricultural Growth, Rural Poverty and Environmental Sustainability, Oxford University Press, New Delhi.

Rao, C.H.H. (2005), 'Essay on Development Strategy, Regional Disparities and Centre-State Financial Relations in India', New Delhi: Academic Foundation.

Rao, C.H.H. and S. Mahendra Dev (2003), 'Economic Reforms and Challenges Ahead. An Overview' in C.H.H. Rao and S. Mahedra Dev (eds.), Andhra Pradesh Development: Economic Reforms and Challenges Ahead, Hydrabad: Centre for Economic and Social Studies.

Rao, Hemlata (1989), 'Poverty and Development Characteristics of Less Developed Regions in India', Economic and Political Weekly, Vol. XIV, Nos. 30, 31, and 32, Special Numbers, Al:lg., pp. 1307-14.

Rao, Hemlata (1977), 'Identification of Backward Regions and the Trend in Regional Disparities in India', Artha Vijnana, Vol. XIX No.2, June, pp. 93-112.

Rao, M J, Archana P, Samant and Nina Asher (1999), 'Indian Macroeconomic Data Base in a Consistency Accounting Framework 1960-61 to 1997-98', Economic and Political Weekly. 34 (Nos. 31 & 32).

Rao, M., Govinda, R. T., Shand and K. P. Kalirajan (1999), 'Convergence of Incomes across Indian States', Economic and Political Weekly, March.

Rao, M. G., Shand, R. T. and Kalirajan, K. P. (1999), 'Convergence of Incomes across Indian States', Economic and Political Weekly, March 27: 769-778.

Rao, C.H.H. (2007), 'Growing Regional Disparities Development in India', : Post Reform Experiences and Challenges, The India Economic Journal Vol. 54 Number 1 April-June.

Reddy, Y.G. (1988), 'Regional Disparities in Small Scale. Industries in Andhra Pradesh', Indian Journal of Regional Science, Vol. XX, No.2, pp. 82-89.

Rennis, G. and H. Fei (1961), 'A Theory of Economic Development' The American Economic Review, Vol. IV (LI), No.4.

Richardson, H.W. (1969), 'Regional Economics, Weidenfeld and Nicolson', London.

Richordson (1973), 'Developed a Growth Theory accommodating Spatial Factors after Evaluating Recently Developed Growth Theories.

Romer, P. (1989), 'Capital Accumulation in the Theory of Long-run Growth', in R. J. Barro (ed.) Modern Business Cycle Theory, Cambridge-Mass: Harvard University Press.

Rosenthal, S Sand W C Strange (2004), 'Evidence on the Nature and Sources of Agglomeration Economics' in J V Henderson and J- F Thiess (eds), Handbook of Urban and Regional Economics, Vol 4, Elsevier-North Holland, Amsterdam.

Saha, A. (2001), 'Risk in HYN and Traditional Rice Cultivation: An Enquiry in West Bengal Agriculture', Indian Journal of Agricultural Economics, Vol. 56(1).

Sawant, S.D., (1987), 'Review of Performance in the Agriculture Sector, in Brahmananda and Panchmukhi (ed.) 'The Development Process of the Indian Economy, Bombay, pp.200-27.

Sasmal, J. (1993), 'Consideration of Risk in the Production of High-Yielding Variety Paddy: A Generalized Stochastic Formulation for Production Function Estimation', Indian Journal of Agricultural Economics, Vol. 48(4) October.

Schultz, T.W. (1964), 'Economic Organization of Agriculture', Tata McGraw Hill Publishing Company, New Delhi, P. 7.

Sen, A.K. (1973), 'On Economic Inequality', Oxford University Press, New Delhi.

Seng, H.C. (1948), 'Monograph on Agrarian Region of India and Pakistan', O.H.H. Spete, Indian and Pakistan Methaon & Co. London.

Shand, R T and S Bhide (2000), 'Sources of Economic Growth: Regional Dimensions of Reforms', Economic and Political Weekly, December.

Shapiro, B.I., Brorsen, B.W. and Doster, D.H. (1992), 'Adoption of Double-Cropping Soybeans and Wheat', Southern Journal of Agricultural Economics, Vol. 24.

Sharma, A. (1992), 'Inter-state Disparities in the Nutritional Level of Living in Indian with Special References to Assam. Indian Journal of Regional Science, Vol. XXIV, No.2, pp. 21-29.

Sharma, P. S. (1973), 'Agricultural regionalization of India,' New Height Publishes & Distributor, New Delhi.

Singh, A.K. (1984), 'Trend in Regional Disparities', Productivity, Vol. XXV, No.2, pp. 159-66.

Singh, Ajit Kumar (2005), 'Finance Commissions Devolutions and Regional Imbalances', Paper Presence at the National Seminar on Accelerated Economic Growth and Regional Balance-Recent Experiences and Implications for Inter-State Variations in Development, organised by the Indian Economic Association, Institute for Studies in Industrial Development and Institute for Human Development, New Delhi, September 16-18.

Singh, N, L Bhandari, A Chen and A Khare (2003), 'Regional Inequality in India: A Fresh Look', Economic and Political Weekly, March.

Singh, Sudama (1988), 'Measuring the Levels of Development 'A Taxonomic Approach', Indian Journal of Regional Science, Vol. XVI, No.1, pp. 87-90.

Singh, Sukhpal (2002), 'Contracting out solutions: Political Economy of Contract Farming in Indian Punjab'. World Development, Vol. 30(9), pp. 1621-1638.

Solow, R. M. (1956), 'A Contribution to the Theory of Economic Growth', Quarterly Journal of Economics, 70(February): 65-94.

Somra, S.S. (1999), 'Issues in Economic Development', RBSA Publication, Jaipur.

_______ (1999): Paper Presented on "An Econometric Analysis of Spatial Pattern of Agricultural Development in Rajasthan" in 35th TIES Conference (March, 11-13) Department of Economic. University of Rajasthan, Jaipur.

_______ (1999) 'Sustainable Agricultural and Markets Development in Developing Countries' Indian Journal of Agricultural Marketing, (13)2,p.146.

_______(2000): The Problem of food Security in Developing Countries: Paper Presented in 3rd International Conference of Asian Socity of Agricultural Economists (ASAE), Pub. In Souvenir and edited Value of Conference papers.

_______ (2001): "Agriculture Development of Rajasthan, Political Economics Journal of India Vol. 10 Issue 1 & 2 January-June.

_______ (2003), "Inter-State Imbalances and Economic Reforms in India" in the Journal of Sardar Patel Institute of Economic and Social Research, Ahmedabad '<u>anvesak</u>', July-Dec. 2002, Volume 32, No.2, pp. 77-88.

_______(2008), 'Agricultural Development in Haryana and Analytical View Paper presented in 44th Annual Conference of the Indian Econometric Conference held at University of Hyderabad, 3rd-5th January.

Somra,S.S., Malik Naresh and Kuldeep (2008) "Inequalities in Agricultural Development in Haryana" full paper published in 91st h IEA conference volume.

Stamp, L.D. (1927), 'Natural Regions of India' Geography, Vol 17, 1927.

Stiglitz, J.E. (1998), More instruments and broader goals : moving towards the post Washington consensus.

Subramaniam, M.S. (1995), 'Inter-State Variation in the Development of Family Health in India-A Taxonomic: 'Approach', Indian Journal of Regional Science, Vol. XXVII, Nos. 1 and 2, pp. 57-61.

Swaminathan, M. S. (1996), 'Sustainable Agriculture: Towards an Evergreen Revolution, Konark Publication, Pvt.Ltd. Delhi. Pp. 232.

Sukhpal Singh. (2005), 'Contract Farming system in Thailand' 'Economic and Political Weekly'

Teriba O. & Kayoda M.O. (1968), 'Industrial Location and Development' Policy, 21st International Geographical Congress, National Committee for Geography, Culcutta, India, 22-26 Nov. 1968.

Thorner, D. (1959), 'Delimitation of Agrarian Region of India - some Preliminary notes 'In Rational of Regional variation in Agrarian structure of India, Indian Society of Agricultural Economics, Bombay.

Thunen, V. (1926), 'Isolated State, Hall, P. (ed.) (1966).

Verma and Das (1974), 'Measurement of Regional Development Levels in Bangladesh', Indian Journal of Regional Science, Vol. VI No.1.

Verma and Das. (1995), 'Regional Pattern of Agricultural Development in India (1891-1976) : An Institutional Approach', Indian Journal of Regional & Science, Vol. XXVII, Nos. 1 and 2, pp. 197-206.

Verma, P.C. (1972), 'Regional Disparity in Per Capita Product in Pakistan (1949-50 to 1967-68)', Indian Journal of Regional Science, Vol. IV, No. I, pp. 90-98.

Vaidyanathan, A. (1988) India's Agricultural Development in a Regional Perspective, Delhi.

Vaidyanathan, A. (1994) 'Performance of Indian Agriculture since Independence' in Basu (ed.), p18-74.

Vyas, V.S. (1994) 'Agricultural policies for Ninties- Issues and Approaches, EPW,29(29): A 54-A 64, June 25.

Weber, A. (1909), 'Theory of The Location of Industries (English Translation), The University of Chicago Press, Chicago, 1929.

West, E.G. (1966), 'Regional Planning', Fact and Fallcy, Lloyds Banbs Review, April 1966, No. 80 PP. 34-35.

Wilson D. and Purushothaman R. (2003), Dreaming with BRICs: The Path to 2050, Goldman Sachs Global Economics, Paper No.: 99, New York.

Williamson, J.G. (1965), 'Regional Inequality and the Process of National Development: A Description of the Patterns', Economic Development and Cultural Change, Vol. XIII, No.4, Part II, July.

Williamson, J.G. (1965), 'Regional Inequality and the Process of National Development', Economic Development and Cultural Change, Vol. 13, No.4, Part II, July.

World Bank (2006), Inclusive Growth and Service Delivery: Building on India's Success, Development Policy Review, Washington, DC

Government Publications

Department of Agriculture Haryana, Agricultural Statistics at a Glance - 2001.

Director of Census Operation, Haryana Total Population 2001.

Director, Public Relations, Haryana 'Profile of Districts, Planning Department Chandigarh different years from 1984-85 to 2005-06.

Economic and Statistical Advisor, Planning Department, Haryana, Economic Survey of Haryana 2004-05.

Economic and Statistical Organisation, Planning Department, Haryana 'Statistical Abstract of Haryana', Annual Publication from 1983-84 to 2005-06.

Government of India, 'Census Report'-2001.

Government of India, 'Economic Survey', Annual Publication from 2002-03 to 2006-07.

Websites

www.planningcommission.nic.in/reports/serepOlis. -

www.Haryanaonline.com

www .mospi. nic. in/ mospi_cso_rept_pubn.htm

Index

A

B

C

D

S

T

U

V

W

Y

Z